Preventive Labor Relations

Preventive Labor Relations

JOHN G. KILGOUR

amacom

A DIVISION OF AMERICAN MANAGEMENT ASSOCIATIONS

Library of Congress Cataloging in Publication Data

Kilgour, John G
  Preventive labor relations.

  Includes bibliographical references and index.
  1. Trade-unions—United States—Recognition.
I. Title.
HD6490.R42U544   658.3′153   80-66868
ISBN 0-8144-5637-5

First Printing

To Jack and Laura

Foreword

"Union busting" has become the battle cry of the labor movement. However, most union leaders and too many managers fail to recognize the importance and character of the new wave of employee relations now sweeping the United States, the essence of which is to make union representation unnecessary. This is not an anti-employee, an anti-union, or even an anti-unionism movement. Rather it is positive personnel management that meets the needs of people at work. If the result is employees who see no need for union representation, then it is their gain and a gain for the economic vitality of America.

No one who has studied American history can argue against the need for labor unions in the past, and no one familiar with the United States today will argue that unions have completely outlived their usefulness. However, it does appear that they *have* outlived their usefulness in large numbers of situations in which the employer has learned to become responsive to the needs of the employees as perceived by the employees. This is evidenced by the relative decline of organized labor throughout the private sector of the economy, especially in its old bastions in manufacturing and construction. In fact, if labor leaders were true to their social mission of serving their members, they would withdraw from the employment relationship in whole industries, or would at least end their adversary role.

While the war continues, everyone loses. If free enterprise is to continue to thrive in the United States, it will be based on the efficiencies of the traditional two-party employment relationship. In such a relationship, unionism and other third-party interference is not only not necessary but detracts from the attainment of the important goals of a business organization. These include fair compensation and good working conditions and a reasonably priced product or service, as well as an adequate profit. When conflict between organized parties at interest takes the place of objective decision making by management within the context of the free market, it can only operate to the disadvantage of the employee, the consumer, the company, and ultimately the economy and country.

In this valuable and timely book, Dr. Kilgour has brought together all the information needed by management to remain nonunion without interfering with the employees' legal right to choose. He shows the theoretical and practical ins and outs of preventive labor relations, starting from the plant-location decision and moving through the decertification of a successful union. His recommendations remain within the law and are strictly objective or neutral, as befits his position as a professor. His mission—to teach management how to remain nonunion and how to protect the employees' rights to remain union free—has been accomplished.

Charles L. Hughes

I am indebted to Eric Valentine of the American Management Associations, who first suggested this book, to AMACOM's editorial staff, who greatly improved the quality of the manuscript, and to Linda Caraballo who typed it. I am also indebted to the numerous individuals who provided information and encouragement for this project. Because the list is long and because much of the information was provided in casual conversation and in confidence, they shall remain nameless.

John G. Kilgour

Contents

1

INTRODUCTION

This book will examine what labor relations consultants, lawyers, employee relations professionals, and other managers do to help companies remain nonunion. This is a large subject of critical importance to the overwhelming majority of business organizations in the United States. Yet the subject has received relatively little attention in the management literature. No doubt, one reason is that some of what is done in the course of resisting unionization is either illegal or of questionable legality. Some people may think that such subject matter is better left alone.

A second reason for the relative lack of interest in preventive labor relations may be the sentiment and background of the scholars in the field, many of whom entered the area of industrial relations in search of a cause. While early pro-union leanings often soften with time and the realization that there are professional and monetary advantages to neutrality, there is seldom a complete shift to the management side of the subject.

A third reason is that preventive labor relations has somewhat of a bad name. Much of the information available on the subject comes out of the

PREVENTIVE LABOR RELATIONS

Southern textile industry experience, with all its excesses and inapplicability to other industries. In addition, the pages of administrative and judicial journals are filled with decisions concerning employers who have broken the law and were caught. These companies are then ordered to reinstate the discharged employees, bargain with the unions, or do whatever is determined to be the appropriate remedy to atone for their misdeeds. It is usually this type of information that appears in the press and in the literature that is read by and written by the scholarly observer.

It is in the nature of preventive labor relations that when the work is done right, it is invisible. The company handles itself in such a way that it is not chosen as a target for unionization. Or, if it is chosen, the company conducts itself in such a way that it does not commit unfair labor practices or other illegal acts. If it does get caught, the matter is handled in a quiet and expeditious way that generates little or no attention.

The subject of preventive labor relations is often approached with the premise that unions and unionism are inherently evil or un-American and fighting them is therefore good, regardless of the situation or the economics involved. This is simply not true. There are good unions and bad unions, just as there are good companies and bad companies, and what constitutes "good" and "bad" in this context is at least open to debate.

One purpose of this book is to introduce into the practice of preventive labor relations the commonsense reasoning and objectivity that an effective manager would employ in other business situations. The decision to fight or not to fight union organization may be the same. But the method by which that position is taken will be different, and that will constructively influence everything that follows.

There is nothing inherently right or wrong in a decision to resist unionization, although there are ethical questions involved in some of the practices and techniques that will be discussed in this book. The important consideration is to what extent a technique is effective in furthering the main objectives of the organization. Thus, there is no pat answer to the questions surrounding the adoption of an industrial relations policy and program. Instead, this book will attempt to give the reader an analytical framework within which to evaluate the company's needs and alternatives.

IMPORTANCE OF AN EARLY START

A second purpose of this book is to impress upon the reader the critical fact that effective preventive labor relations start long before there is any

2

sign of union activity, and never end. Most of this effort is very "low key" and an integral part of other employee-related activities of the organization. The union organizing drive, the company counterunion campaign, and the representation election should be only a phase in an ongoing program. They are as armed conflict is to diplomacy, or as an industrial injury is to a safety program, or as a fire is to fire prevention. The war, injury, or fire is something to be prevented if at all possible. If the incident occurs in spite of the best efforts of the people involved, then the program should be able to handle the emergency as expeditiously as possible. It should also have the ability to learn from the experience to minimize the chances of a repeat occurrence.

The analogy to a fire prevention program is particularly apt.[1] The primary purpose of such a program is to prevent fires by identifying and correcting dangerous situations. Inspections are conducted regularly, and trained supervisory personnel are held responsible for implementing the program in their units. A well-designed system has adequate reporting requirements and provides for oversights. Smoke detectors and sprinklers are installed where appropriate. Effective procedures for reporting a fire, isolating it, and fighting it are made known to the people involved. Finally, once the fire is over, the program calls for a thorough investigation to determine how it started, how it spread, how well the parties involved responded, what was done wrong, what was done right, and what should be done to prevent such a situation from occurring in the future. The firetrucks, the hoses, and the axes are only a last resort—to be called upon when all else has failed. In fact, a company that has too many fires would be well advised to examine its fire prevention program. And if it does not have such a program, it would be well advised to start one.

Most people are more familiar with fire and its prevention than with union organization and its prevention. All companies of any size have well-developed fire prevention programs, in recognition of the impact that an industrial accident can have on the success of the business. In many business situations, union organization can be more devastating than a fire of serious proportion. Fire insurance can be purchased. Union insurance cannot. Moreover, the cost of a fire or similar disaster is inherently short run in nature. Unionization usually continues for as long as the company remains in business.

It is strange that many companies do such a fine job in preventing fires and other industrial accidents and such a poor job in preventing unionization. Although there are many exceptions, the usual pattern is to wait until a union drive has started, and is often well under way, before react-

3

ing. And that reaction is typically to call on one's lawyer and let him[2] handle the "problem." Even more strange, many companies that experience a union drive and, for one reason or another, come out of it without a union assume that the matter is behind them and fail to learn from the experience. This is a dangerous way to conduct business. What if management had a similar attitude toward fire prevention?

The importance of an early start in preventive labor relations cannot be overstated. For a company to wait until it has a "union problem" before taking action and then to expect the company's attorney, a labor relations consultant, or an unprepared in-house staff to handle things is short-sighted. At the very least, it gives the union the advantages of surprise and timing. It may also mean that by the time the company gets itself prepared to respond effectively, the battle has been lost, either because the election is at hand and there is no time to communicate the company's position to employees or because an unprepared management and supervisory staff have committed unfair labor practices or other acts that make it impossible for the company to win. In fact, an unprepared manager can respond to the union's demand for recognition in such a way as to recognize the union accidentally.

Many managers (especially personnel managers) state optimistically that they are not worried about unions because their company is small, or because it employs mainly professional people who are presumed to be "safe," or because it pays good wages, or because the firm is new and the employees realize that it would be impossible for it to be more generous at this time. While some of these observations may be valid, it is more likely that they are based on wishful thinking and on the mistaken idea that to admit to a potential union problem is to admit that the manager (or personnel department) is doing something wrong. For reasons that will be developed later, small units are especially vulnerable to union organization, and employees may support unions for many reasons unrelated to the performance of the managers involved.

The prudent firm intent upon remaining nonunion must *assume* that it has at least a potential union problem and act accordingly. If it is wrong, it will never know. For if the work is done right, the company may not face the union drive that would be the only proof of its error. On the other hand, if it is right and a union one day appears, the company will be ready for the encounter, which will greatly increase its chances of winning. Moreover, almost all the things that a company should do to deter unionization either are inexpensive or can be defended as sound employee

4

relations practices that should be adopted anyway. With the exception of a few low-wage firms, most companies will find preventive labor relations a relatively low-cost program. In fact, if the improved personnel practices result in increased productivity, the program could even result in a saving. Since unionization almost always results in significant increases in labor costs in the form of increased wages and benefits and various restrictions that impinge on management's efficiency,[3] most companies would be well advised to adopt measures to deter unionization, regardless of their assessment of their chances of being chosen as a union target. It is as though one were buying a great deal of insurance for a very low premium. In addition, some of the costs involved are in the nature of start-up costs that, once made, go on giving a return indefinitely.

SOURCES OF INFORMATION

As mentioned, there is no well-developed literature on preventive labor relations. There are a few books and serious articles on the subject, as well as a stream of articles and short pieces in various trade publications. In addition, there are various sources that treat those parts of labor law concerned with the representation election process, personnel administration, compensation, organizational behavior, and other matters which, while not directly concerned with preventive labor relations, are related to it. All these sources have been drawn upon liberally in the pages that follow.

One source that will be heavily tapped is *An Outline of Law and Procedure in Representation Cases,* published by the National Labor Relations Board (NLRB).[4] This inexpensive loose-leaf manual may be purchased from the Government Printing Office and is an excellent source of the fundamentals of that part of the law most important in preventive labor relations.

This book is written primarily for the practitioner rather than the lawyer. Legal citations will be relatively sparse and in most cases will be to the last-mentioned source rather than directly to the cases. The reason for this is that often a particular point will be a general rule that is the result of several decisions by the NLRB and the courts over the years, or a rule to which there are numerous exceptions. Rather than clutter the pages with such detail, I will deal mainly with the well-established general rules and refer the reader with a particular interest or need to *An Outline of Law and Procedure.* Only important landmark decisions will be cited—

5

and those mainly because they have become part of the language of industrial relations.

Another major source of information for this book is a number of conversations I have had with men and women involved in the various aspects of employee relations in companies (and unions) over the years. Many of the observations were shared with the understanding that they were "off the record" and that the source would not be identified.

Taken together, the practitioners with whom I have talked have a wealth of information on the subject of preventive labor relations. Individually, however, there seems to be a lack of the larger picture and an integration of the material into a systematic framework within which to examine and respond to the whole problem. Thus, a third purpose of this book is to provide such a framework so that we may approach the problems and opportunities associated with remaining nonunion from a broader and longer-range perspective.

LABOR LAW: AN OVERVIEW

Throughout the following pages we will deal with labor law and with employee-related matters that must be handled in such a way as not to conflict with that law. In effect, the law establishes the groundrules within which we work. It will be helpful to sketch the highlights of that law before proceeding further.

Chapter 2 will deal, in part, with the question of legal jurisdiction. At this time, let us merely note that the activities associated with preventive labor relations can fall under various statutes and their respective administrative and enforcement agencies. The three that are most important for our purposes in the private sector are (1) the National Labor Relations Act (NLRA), administered by the National Labor Relations Board (NLRB); (2) the Railway Labor Act (RLA), administered by the National Mediation Board; and (3) the fifty state laws and codes administered by various state-level departments, divisions, commissions, and boards. Public-sector employers are covered by Executive Order 11491 if they are part of the federal government, or by one of the numerous state laws or local ordinances and their repsective administrative agencies. In addition, various other laws may come into play in an incidental manner. Included in this category are the Fair Labor Standards Act, the Civil Rights Act, the Equal Pay Act, and/or their state-level equivalents. This list is by no means exhaustive.

By far, the most important statute for our purposes is the National

Labor Relations Act (also known as the Labor-Management Relations Act, or Taft-Hartley Act), and the most important administrative body is the National Labor Relations Board. Most references in this book will be to that law. As will be developed in Chapter 2, it is this law which applies to most employers of any size who are interested in maintaining nonunion status. In addition, when Congress passed the NLRA in 1935, it drew heavily upon the provisions of the Railway Labor Act, which had been enacted in 1926.[5] Moreover, many public-sector jurisdictions have drawn on the provisions, concepts, interpretations, and rules of the National Labor Relations Act and the National Labor Relations Board. Although there may be a fundamental difference between the private and public sectors in regard to the legality of work stoppages and certain other matters, there is a similarity (but not an identity) in that part of the law dealing with questions of representation and unfair labor practices throughout much of the United States regardless of jurisdiction. For our purposes, as practitioners acting before the initiation of legal action, it is safe to assume that if something is allowed under the NLRA, it is probably also allowed under other laws. If it is illegal under the NLRA, there is a good chance that it is illegal under other laws as well. Of course, there are exceptions, and no serious action should be taken in employment matters on the basis of comments in this book without advice of counsel.

The highlights of the National Labor Relations Act may be summarized as follows.

1.   A majority of the employees in an appropriate bargaining unit may choose (or refrain from choosing) a bargaining agent (union) to represent all the employees in that unit.
2.   The employer is prohibited from engaging in action that interferes with or restricts that choice.
3.   The NLRB is charged to conduct elections and establish procedures to determine and make effective the employees' choice of a bargaining agent.

Of course, these points are three tips of the same iceberg which will be examined from various perspectives in the pages that follow.

THE HISTORICAL PERSPECTIVE

Before the passage of the National Labor Relations (Wagner) Act of 1935, industrial relations management was with few exceptions a matter of remaining nonunion. This was an easier task at that time, since there were few restrictions on the range of allowable employer activity. Union adherents could simply be fired or neutralized in some way. Moreover, there was little in the way of legal complexity which required a more cautious or more sophisticated approach than leaving most of the matters involving the maintenance of a nonunion shop in the hands of first-line supervision.

Although most of us would not now approve of some of the techniques employed, American managers and supervisors became very good at remaining nonunion during the pre-1935 period. As a result of the so-called open-shop movement, launched after World War I, union membership dropped from about 4.9 million (11.7 percent of the labor force) in 1920 to 3.2 million (6.5 percent) in 1930 and to 3.1 million (5.9 percent) in 1934.[6] Organized labor in the United States had been clobbered during the 1920s, and had it not been for the New Deal legislation, the United States would have remained an essentially nonunion bastion for a long time to come.

Following the passage of the Wagner Act in 1935, with its employer unfair labor practices and NLRB-conducted elections to effectuate the employee's new-found rights, the old methods of deterring unionization became ineffective. All of a sudden most of the things that management had traditionally done to cope with a union threat were illegal. In addition, a major debate arose within the labor movement over whether the new organizing opportunities should be approached in the traditional craft-based form of unionism, which was dominant in the American Federation of Labor (AFL), or whether the industrial form of organization was to be used. The latter was favored by a segment of the AFL leadership most visibly associated with John L. Lewis of the United Mine Workers. As the terms imply, a craft union is one in which employees are grouped by craft or trade, such as in the International Brotherhood of Carpenters. Industrial unionism, on the other hand, organizes workers along industry lines without regard to the type of work performed, such as in the United Steel Workers of America.[7]

The result of this debate was that the more progressive elements within the AFL in 1935 formed the Committee for Industrial Organization, under the leadership of John L. Lewis. In 1938, after its member unions were formally expelled from the AFL, the name was changed to the Congress of Industrial Organizations (CIO).

During the next few years the affiliates of the old AFL and the new

CIO battled intensely to organize the unorganized. Given the new protections and encouragement contained in the law, whole industries fell to unionization in quick succession. By 1941, on the eve of World War II, union membership in the United States had shot up to 10.2 million (17.7 percent).[8]

World War II caused a forced peace in American industrial relations. The timing was important. Management had been caught by surprise by the Wagner Act and by the aggressive organizational activity that followed the creation of the CIO. The groundrules had been changed, and management had not had enough time to adjust to the new situation. Indeed, many management lawyers advised their clients to ignore the new law, since it would probably be declared unconstitutional, as had been its predecessor, the National Industrial Recovery Act.

The war helped to strengthen and make permanent the successes of the labor movement. The strike was unavailable because of a series of statements of principle between labor and management and a realization that the government and the public would not stand for strikes during a time of war. With the expanding wartime economy, consequent tight labor market, and continued organizing efforts, union membership continued to climb. By 1946, it stood at 14.4 million (23.6 percent).[9]

Labor came out of World War II stronger than it had ever been before to face the high inflation and other adjustments caused by shifting from a controlled wartime economy to a peacetime economy. Many managers, no doubt, felt that it was now time to revert to the good old days that existed before 1935. In 1946, strike activity, as measured by estimated working time lost, reached an all-time high of 1.43 percent. The public reaction was strong, and the Republican congressional majority elected that fall felt that it had a mandate to redress the imbalance caused by the Wagner Act. It did so by passing the Taft-Hartley Act of 1947, which expanded on the Wagner Act.

If American management expected a major overhaul of collective bargaining law, it was disappointed. Although decried by organized labor as the "slave labor act" and passed over the veto of President Truman, the Taft-Hartley Act did not change the fundamentals of the law. True, it added a set of union unfair labor practices and made various other technical changes. But the basic law that guaranteed the rights of the employees to select their bargaining agent unhindered by management interference and provided an effective electoral procedure for ensuring these rights remained. The unions were here to stay. They had become a permanent feature of many American industries, and an adjustment in management thinking was necessary.

Even for those industries that had thus far avoided unionization, the rules of the game had become much more restrictive and complicated. Moreover, with each passing year new interpretation and precedent were added to the law itself. In effect, a new management problem had emerged. The response was the birth of a new specialist within American management: the industrial relations manager.

It is difficult to pinpoint a date for this development. Some industries realized early on that things had changed and made the appropriate adjustment quickly. Others took longer. However, between 1947, when the Taft-Hartley Act was passed, and 1955, when the AFL and the CIO merged to form the American Federation of Labor–Congress of Industrial Organizations (AFL–CIO), a fundamental change took place in the industrial relations thinking of management in the United States.

The change is easiest to identify in those large companies and industries which came to realize that unions were there to stay and that the industrial relations problem had changed from one of fighting unions to one of learning to live with them. Clearly, no one in the auto industry could reasonably expect to operate nonunion for any length of time once the essentials of the National Labor Relations Act were reaffirmed by the limits of the Taft-Hartley Act. Even if the United Automobile Workers could be displaced in part of the company, it would be back a year later. Or, even worse, a different union would appear, with the threat of fragmenting the company and the industry among many competing unions. It was better to learn to live with one large union and help it develop into a strong and responsible organization that could offer the industry stability and predictability in the years ahead. To the credit of management of the auto and several other industries, this is exactly what happened. Notwithstanding the media's tendency to report only the breakdowns and problems of labor–management relations, industrial relations in such industries has been highly successful.

In the unorganized part of the economy, the adjustment to the new legal groundrules is less easy to identify, for the simple reason that it generates little of the labor news that is the source of most industrial relations research. The fact that Eastman Kodak, Texas Instruments, Sears-Roebuck, IBM, and other companies have been extraordinarily successful in avoiding and deterring unionization is a nonevent and hence does not attract the attention that a medium-size strike would. At most we occasionally hear of a company winning a union representation election. By definition we are aware of the large number of elections and organizing drives that never take place because the employers are doing something right. However, it must be inferred that those companies that succeed in remaining nonunion, despite the efforts of organized labor and a law that encourages unionization, have made a successful adjustment to the new situation.

INDUSTRIAL RELATIONS MANAGEMENT

There are three basic ways in which a company can respond to a new problem such as that created by the changes in the labor laws of the United States. The problem may be handled by line management and supervision, it may be "farmed out," or the company may develop its own in-house expertise. Of course, all three may be used in combination, and that has certainly been the case in preventive labor relations. The decision is more a matter of emphasis than of going in one direction or the other.

Leaving the job of maintaining nonunion status in the hands of line managers has certain advantages. They are in the best position to enforce and monitor the program. This approach avoids the additional cost of an expanded personnel unit. It may also prove to be the most economical way of responding to the problem. The disadvantages are that the whole area of employee relations has become extremely complex and is undergoing continual change. The people involved in a preventive labor relations program must be knowledgeable about what may or may not be safely done. Just keeping up to date takes a great deal of time. To give this job to line management and supervision is to add a heavy burden on an already overworked group. In addition, line managers are often close to the problems with which the preventive program is concerned. While there are definite advantages to familiarity, there are also drawbacks. One is the emotional involvement in a decision or situation. Another is the "myopia" all of us have in varying degrees in regard to those things with which we are most closely associated. It is easy for a department head to think of union activity as reflecting poorly on his performance. If this kind of thinking results in a failure to recognize or promptly report such activity, the costs can be great. If it results in the department head taking unlawful corrective action on his own, the costs may be even greater.

A second approach to the union problem is to farm it out. There are

11

several ways to do this. One is to ignore the whole thing until an organizing drive begins and then call in a lawyer to straighten matters out. Many companies do just that. In fact, it may be the most popular approach to remaining nonunion. This is a risky way to do business and is not recommended. This comment in no way denigrates the role of attorneys in the counterunion campaign. They are indispensable and should be called upon at the first sign of serious union trouble. Once the campaign has entered the "critical period" (to be discussed), no employee-related action should be taken without advice of counsel. However, to rely solely on one's lawyers to come in at the last minute and work some kind of magic is to expect too much. It is comparable to a fire prevention program whose sole element is calling in the fire department after the fire starts. Even if the firefighters are very good at their work, one of these days they might not get there on time and the plant could burn down. Or there may be so much fire and smoke damage that it would have been better if the plant had been destroyed. A final purpose of this book is to make it easier for the lawyers or whoever is handling the company's counterunion campaign to win.

A second way of farming the problem out is to call in a labor relations consultant. As a practical matter, the line between the consultant and the labor law firm is often blurred. Some labor consultants are attorneys by training, and many work closely with a labor law firm. Some labor law firms, in the course of representing the client, give advice on how to reduce the chances of being organized. The distinction between the two functions is a matter of timing and scope. The consultative function should begin early, preferably long before there are any signs of union activity, and the consultant should be able to offer a broader range of services than the lawyer. The attorney, on the other hand, is usually called in after the fire starts and will usually limit his efforts to the mechanics and legal aspects of the campaign. In addition, the primary objective of the labor consultant should be to reduce the chances that the company will be chosen as a target, rather than to respond to a specific existing union threat. In doing this, he will have to become involved in other employee-related matters such as motivation, communication, and supervisory training.

Another way of farming out an industrial relations problem is to rely on an employers association or some other form of intercompany organization. This approach is used mostly by companies that are already unionized and is most commonly found in industries in which the em-

12

ployer unit is relatively small and the union or unions involved are relatively large or especially difficult to deal with. It almost always involves a multiemployer bargaining unit in which a large number of employers negotiate jointly (either formally or informally) with the union(s). This has the effect of improving the employers' bargaining position in addition to allowing the use of more professional negotiating staff.

In the preventive labor relations area, multiemployer associations usually limit their efforts to providing information and coordination and giving legal support to those companies and individuals who are attacking or defending some principle that is important to the rights of management or employees. The most important modern examples are the efforts of the National Right to Work Committee and the closely associated National Right to Work Legal Defense and Education Foundation, which have since the 1950s been aggressively defending and promoting the so-called state "right to work laws" allowed under Section 14(b) of the National Labor Relations Act.

The third basic way of responding to a new management problem area, such as that under discussion, is to develop an in-house capability. This approach was adopted by most of the larger corporations that were unionized as a result of the Wagner Act and the events that followed. The largest firms have organizational units called industrial relations department, labor relations department, employee relations department, and the like. The titles and organizational relationships vary considerably, but the main function of the units is to negotiate and administer labor agreements, and handle representation cases and other matters concerning unions.

The number of people primarily involved in labor relations (negotiations, the handling of grievances in the final stages of the procedure, and labor arbitration) is relatively small, and they are often located at the company's central office. A six-person staff can handle a large amount of such work. Of course, typically a large number of other people are involved in the process—in the form of handling grievances at the lower levels, generating information to be used in collective bargaining, and the like—as part of their more general personnel work. In addition, the company's negotiations team will often be supplemented with managers from wage and salary administration, benefits administration, industrial engineering, and personnel administration.

When we turn to the nonunionized companies, it is more difficult to generalize. To begin with, many employers do not recognize the labor problem for what it is: an ongoing and important problem area that can be managed in a way that benefits the organization. Rather, it is viewed as an occasional incident that is to be handled by calling in a lawyer or consultant (hired gun) in the same way that we call upon a doctor to take care of a temporary medical problem. It may be thought that there is little need for continuity since there is no ongoing relationship to maintain with the union, and much of the work is interrelated with other personnel functions. Finally, some companies seem to feel that they should not have anyone identifiable as the main person to prevent union organization, presumably because of a fear that this will call attention to the fact that the company is nonunion and prefers to stay that way. Even when there is a person identifiable as having primary responsibility in this area, he is almost never in a separate department or other organizational unit.

It is the strong recommendation of this book that a company intent on remaining nonunion begin by assigning the task to a proven manager with the time and resources to do the job right. This should logically be the head of the personnel unit (by whatever name), who should have direct communication with the top management in the company. The manager should be familiar with and up to date on the topics to be discussed in the pages that follow and should be directly involved in all decisions concerning the location of new properties, organizational change, acquisition of additional operations, and, of course, everything in the areas of personnel administration, compensation, employee communication, and anything else that affects the employer–employee relationship. For the sake of convenience, we will call this person the employee relations manager. In practice, the titles vary considerably.

The employee relations manager should be visible. It should be made known to the employees, other managers, and interested outsiders that this position exists and that the person holding it is responsible for the company's well-known and understood intention of remaining nonunion. It should be explicitly stated in all company handbooks and similar employee communications that this person is the only one authorized to respond to a demand by a union for recognition.

Where does a company find a person with the qualities needed to do this kind of work? The simplest way is to go into the marketplace and hire someone with proven experience. The problems with this approach are that there are not many "proven experts" around and it is difficult to identify the kind of experience needed. Although there are many professional managers available who have had experience with union organizing drives, it is difficult to assess their track record. A tally of the wins and losses will not do. Union representation elections can be won and lost for so many reasons unrelated to the actions of the participants that it becomes very conjectural to assign either credit or blame for the outcome of a particular campaign unless one is knowledgeable about the subject. And the company would be most unlikely to run into an individual who has been involved in so many representation elections that it can assume the law of average is at work.

The ideal candidate for this kind of work should have a broad background in the employee relations area as well as a thorough grounding in labor law (especially that part of it dealing with representation elections). Beware of the attorneys and former NLRB field examiners without in-house personnel experience, and beware of the personnel generalist without a sound and current understanding of the law. After reading this book, the reader will be in a position to ask (and answer) many appropriate questions in this area.

The other way to acquire specialized managerial talent in preventive labor relations is to "grow your own" or develop yourself. This can be done by reading in the area or attending seminars and programs on the subject. There are a number of seminars and programs on preventive labor relations. No doubt, many readers regularly receive advertisements for these programs. The more important organizations offering programs on this subject are the American Management Associations, American Management Research, Inc., and Executive Enterprises, Inc. Many other organizations, including the Associated Industries of Alabama and the Indiana State Chamber of Commerce, have similar programs. American Management Research and many labor consultants will run in-house training programs that cover the same material from a more specific point of view. Some of these organizations are local or regional or industrial in terms of their area of coverage. They often also provide labor relations consulting or are closely related to such consultants and can best be located by referring to the Yellow Pages or to an industry directory.[10]

Finally, the value of information garnered from other professionals in the field should not be underrated. This is one area where the adage "You only get what you pay for" does not hold. There is a wealth of knowledge in the heads of managers and professionals in any community in the United States. Each of us is limited by the relatively narrow range of our personal experience and by the constraints of time on what we can read. By exchanging what we have learned from our experience, we all learn. Try introducing the topic of preventive labor relations during a

luncheon conversation or placing it on the agenda of a trade or professional meeting. It may not be as popular as football, but a lot of information will flow and everyone will come away better for the experience.

TO FIGHT OR NOT TO FIGHT

Some readers may be surprised to learn that there is a decision to be made
in regard to whether or not the company should remain nonunion. For
many managers and companies, it is an article of faith that unionization is
to be avoided at all costs. One of our purposes is to dispel such dogmas
and replace them with a more objective and less impassioned approach. It
is highly probable that the company intent on remaining nonunion will
continue on that path after this new and more reasoned examination.
However, it will be on a more sound footing in its design and implemen-
tation of a preventive labor relations program if it bases that decision on a
reasonable assessment of the importance of remaining nonunion and the
value of that status to the company.

Some companies may discover either that it is not in their long-run
best interest to remain nonunion or that it is worth little. Hence it would
make business sense to take whatever action is necessary to get the right
union in (while staying clear of the prohibition against illegal assistance
contained in Section 8(a) (2) of the NLRA) or not spend much time or
money on preventive labor relations. Under both conditions the guiding
rule is to end up with something that the company can "live with" in the
years ahead.

It is, perhaps, more important for the personnel or industrial relations
professional to develop an objective attitude toward unionization than it is
for the organization to do so. The situation of a given business organization usually remains the same in regard to those factors that should influence the adoption of an industrial relations policy. The main exception
occurs when a company acquires a new operation by merger or acquisition or by moving into a new product market. The context within which
the typical personnel professional operates is less stable. It is a fact of life
in the personnel–industrial-relations profession that the operating unit
within most companies is relatively small. Some large corporations
present important exceptions to this rule, but in general the "personnel
shop" consists of a handful of people at most. Given the several subfunctions found in the typical personnel department, most practitioners in this
area of management face a rather low "ceiling." That is, there is rela-

16

tively little opportunity to advance within the management structure of the company. This is exacerbated by the fact that it is unusual for personnel professionals to move into other areas of management. In some companies, turnover is further heightened by the theory that personnel staff members are interchangeable and that the company may benefit from the regular appearance of new faces and new ideas in this area.

The result is that the career path of most personnel professionals involves several intercompany moves. With the exception of a few large corporations that train their own in-house staff and promote from within, the usual pattern is for a person to remain with a company until he hits a dead end and then make a move either to a position of more responsibility in a comparable or smaller company (personnel generalist to personnel director) or to a more specialized position in a larger company (personnel generalist to compensation manager).

Given the high degree of movement in the typical personnel career, it is not at all uncommon for a person to move from a company in which preventive labor relations is a matter of critical importance to one in which that policy would be inappropriate. For instance, in most parts of the country, someone moving from nongrocery retail to, say, a retail grocery chain would have to make an important adjustment in his thinking about unions. Someone making a move within the same industry from New York to Texas may have to make a similar adjustment.

When Not to Fight Unions

There are many situations in which well-run companies do not avoid unionization, deliberately remove any obstacles to the union's organizing efforts, and even go to great lengths to make sure that the union wins. This preference and cooperation are almost always extended to a particular union with which the employer does business elsewhere in the industry and would like to continue to do business. It is often the case that the certainty of being organized by a known organization with an established record of responsibility and commitment to the industry is preferred to the uncertainty of remaining nonunion and running the risk of being organized by the "wrong" union. This is especially so when the employer is involved in an integrated production process and the unit in question is part of that process.

An example is in order. Suppose one of the large auto producers were going to start up a new production facility to produce transmissions that will go into the vehicles produced in all its assembly plants in the United

States. The company has dealt with the United Automobile Workers of America in its 100 other locations for the past several decades. Should it attempt to operate nonunion in the new location? Of course not. The risk of remaining nonunion under such conditions is that the plant might sooner or later be organized by another, less responsible, less stable, less predictable labor organization. This would almost certainly mean a separate bargaining unit; separate contract expiration dates; a union which, though representing a relatively small number of employees, will be in a position to shut down the whole company; and serious and continuing labor problems. Of course, if this were to happen every time a new plant was opened in a highly integrated industry, such as the automobile industry, it would soon result in an industrial relations disaster and would require the restructuring of the industry in a less integrated and less efficient way. The fact that this has not happened reflects on the good sense of the industrial relations staff of the industry.

As a practical matter, General Motors and any company in a similar production position *must* make sure that it gets the right union in a new plant. The job is usually made easier by the needs of the union leadership involved in the industry. The UAW, for instance, is under strong economic pressure to organize any new plant built in the industry. If it did not do so, it would have to compete with another union, both for the loyalties of its members and at the bargaining table. This would make the jobs of the union leaders much less pleasant.

The result is that General Motors (notwithstanding its so-called Southern strategy) has a natural ally in the UAW in regard to the organization of a new plant. Neither would want to run the risk of allowing the employees (many of whom may be new hires who will not be there a year later) to exercise their rights in a way that disrupts the sensible and predictable pattern that has developed over the years.

A second situation in which an employer would be unwise to fight unionization is when the company gains more from unionization than it loses. There are several situations in which this may take place. In general they fall into two categories: (1) when the union provides the employer with an economic or business service, and (2) when the union is an important political ally. Services rendered to the employer include such things as access to a hiring hall and the pool of skilled and available workers who use it; the elimination of low-wage competition; and the provision of specific industrial engineering and management services by the union. Examples are in order.

18

In the United States maritime industry, the various unions operate hiring halls. While it would be possible for a company running ships on a fixed schedule not to use the hiring halls (some East Coast tanker companies with independent unions do just that), it would be inconvenient. And it would be most inconvenient during periods in which demand for shipping, and hence seagoing labor, is high. This would be especially so for companies that do not operate on a fixed schedule. A typical situation is a ship that calls on a port for 24 hours and must hire a second engineer, a third mate, an electrician, an able-bodied seaman, and a wiper before it sails. Other than during periods of extreme oversupply of merchant seamen, this would be an impossible order to fill if it were not for the union-operated hiring halls. Thus a company entering the industry would in all probability not consider operating nonunion, even if it could.

Hiring halls are also important in longshoring and in parts of the construction industry. A company entering such an industry should carefully consider the value of this service in its decision to fight or live with the unions.

Another service that a union may offer some employers is to limit entry to an industry or market. This service is especially important in those industries in which entry costs are low and the skill levels needed fairly easy to come by. Trucking is the best example.

Ignoring the competition from the independent owners–operators (gypsies) and proprietary trucking, over-the-road common carrier trucking is fairly well organized in the United States. As a result, wage levels are high, often much higher than the skill level and responsibility involved would suggest. Yet, the cost of going into business in the industry is relatively low. All it would take is the downpayment on a truck and two rented buildings to serve as terminals (and, of course, route approval from the ICC). This modest start would allow someone with the appropriate license to compete with the established companies on the basis of lower labor costs. What stops this from happening? The Teamsters, of course. When a new company becomes large enough to present a problem to the established trucking firms that are already organized, it will receive a visit from the local Teamsters organizer. The union will usually do this on its own initiative and for its own reasons. If, however, it should not do so, one of the established carriers will request that the union do its job. This is a legitimate request, since the unionized employers cannot continue to pay union scale and successfully compete with nonunion low-wage companies.

What is the value of this service? It is hard to say. Entry into the trucking industry is also restricted by ICC regulation of rates and allocation of routes. However, the union's activity is no doubt positive and serves to reinforce the other barriers to entry. To the larger trucking firms with substantial economies of scale, high wage rates are no problem, provided the union applies them to the whole market.

Finally, there are a few other situations in which the union provides a service to the employer or to the industry. In the New York garment industry, the unions have a tradition of helping employers in trouble with advice on industrial engineering and business techniques. In other situations, the union (often in conjunction with a hiring hall operation) cooperates with the employers in the operation of apprenticeship and other training programs. This is especially important when the individual company is too small to do its own in-house training and the skill level is relatively high. Parts of the construction and printing trades are good examples.

The second large area of services that may be rendered by labor organizations is political. Labor has a vast and well-run political operation. Its most visible component is the Committee on Political Education (COPE) of the AFL–CIO. The main work of COPE is raising voluntary contributions for political purposes from union members and preparing voting records of legislators on which the Executive Council of the AFL–CIO and the various state AFL–CIO organizations base their political endorsements. However, this is only the tip of the iceberg.

The AFL–CIO maintains one of the most—perhaps *the* most—effective political lobbies in Washington. In addition, the 50 state AFL–CIO organizations operate in a similar capacity in the state capitals. Their influence varies depending on the political coloration of the state and the effectiveness of the political organizations of competing (usually business) interest groups.

Parallel to the AFL–CIO political activities are those of some unions not affiliated with the federation. The International Brotherhood of Teamsters is particularly influential on issues involving trucking at both federal and state levels. The United Automobile Workers, which is now unaffiliated, has been a traditional standard bearer on social and political issues within the labor movement. It is also influential within the state of Michigan. The United Mine Workers (UMW) has had a somewhat similar regional political importance within some of the Eastern coal-producing states.

Some unions are disproportionately influential at the local level or with

20

certain government or quasi-government agencies. The construction unions take a particular interest in local building codes and the commissions or other bodies that administer them. The Amalgamated Transit Union (ATU) is particularly active in matters before the Urban Mass Transportation Administration and the various boards and commissions that run urban mass transit in the United States. And in the public sector, the unions have become a potent force intimately involved in the whole process of government.

Much of this local and administrative influence is due to the fact that the unions are keenly interested in the matters before the particular government body. These matters are often technical and of limited or remote interest to the general public. Because of their presence at the hearings and meetings, the willingness of union leaders to serve on the various boards and commissions, their access to legal and financial resources, and their often considerable political and parliamentary skill, representatives of organized labor have become an important political influence in the United States. A company evaluating its policy in regard to preventive labor relations should not overlook the political advantages and costs of its alternatives.

In summary, there are many situations in which a rational and knowledgeable employer may find that unionization grants the company certain benefits that outweigh the costs associated with having to deal with a union. By far the most important benefit is the reduction of the risk of having to do business with a less desirable labor organization. Another important benefit in some situations is that the union and the employer can operate as a team in facing the government at some level. This is especially important in those industries that are under government regulation or are dependent upon government in some form. When this is the case, the interests of the company and the union tend to become very close, if not identical, on the important issues. The maritime unions and their respective contract companies share many more common interests in their relations with the Federal Maritime Commission and the Maritime Administration than they have issues in conflict at the bargaining table. In fact, the important issues in that industry, which is both regulated and subsidized, are thrashed out in the hearing rooms of Washington to a much greater extent than on the picket lines and bargaining tables. Although the shipping industry may represent the extreme in this regard, the same phenomenon is common when the important decisions that affect the company, and consequently its employees, are made by an outside party. In such cases, what may have started as an antagonistic relationship almost inevitably becomes one of cooperation.

Finally, there are situations in which the employer should not attempt to operate nonunion, for the simple reason that it cannot be done. In some communities and industries in the United States the tradition of unionization is so deeply engrained, or the economic interrelationships with unionized operations are so well established, that it is futile to attempt to remain nonunion. If it is necessary to operate in such localities or industries, such facts of life must be recognized. You don't brew nonunion beer in Pittsburgh and you don't operate a nonunion warehouse in Newark.

When to Adopt a Preventive Labor Relations Strategy

The decision to fight or not to fight unionization is an important business decision and should be made accordingly. There are many situations in which the company has no choice but to resist unionization to the fullest. Indeed, it would often be irresponsible to the owners of the company, to the employees involved, and to one's own career to do otherwise.

In general, a company must resist unionization when it is in a competitive product market and when the competition is not unionized. A competitive product market is one in which there are many providers of the product or service and the product price is determined by the low-cost producer and the customers. If a company has to raise its price above that established by the market, it loses sales to its competitors. In an extreme situation (pure competition) the product demand curve is horizontal at a level equal to the price of the product. Thus any increase in price automatically drops quantity sold to zero and the company theoretically goes out of business.

While there are few business situations in the United States in which pure competition prevails and unions are a threat, there are numerous settings in which the product market is highly competitive (high elasticity of demand). Thus, if an individual firm in such an industry has to raise its prices or lower the quality of its product or service (which amounts to the same thing), it will lose business. Examples include restaurants, especially the fast-food segment; most of the retail industry; the banking industry; and those manufacturing industries that are characterized by a high degree of labor intensity and relatively low transportation costs (such as textiles and electronics assembly). Examples are in order.

There is a high degree of interdependence (cross elasticity) between the price of a meal at Kentucky Fried Chicken, H. Salt Fish and Chips, and Burger King. If one of the chains raised its prices disproportionately, it would soon lose a portion of its highly price-conscious clientele to its competitor. Of course, the relationship between the price of a Whopper, a Barnbuster, and a Big Mac is even more direct.

In addition to the inherent competitive nature of the product served, the economics of the fast-food industry are such as not to allow one of the chains a substantial technological or operational advantage. There are few technical secrets in the industry. To learn anything new that should be developed, one need only go to lunch. The operating unit is necessarily small and must be located where the customers are. Although this does not preclude the possibility of economies of scale on the processing and distribution of the material used or of certain managerial and operational efficiencies, it does suggest that price levels are extremely important.

It may safely be assumed that if a union were to organize a part of a fast-food chain, this would significantly raise labor costs. It would be difficult to ascertain how much labor costs would go up in a given situation. Part of the problem lies in one's definition of "labor costs." Further, the union's impact on cost would vary enormously by industry, section of the country, how far behind (or ahead) of prevailing union rates the employer was to begin with, how effective the employer turns out to be as a negotiator, and all sorts of other things. However, one estimate that claims that labor costs in a unionized shop are between 25 and 35 percent greater than in a nonunion shop does not seem unreasonable.[11]

Given the labor intensity of a typical fast-food operation, an increase of this magnitude in the cost of producing the product would have a profound impact. That part of the additional cost that could not be absorbed by the company or offset by new-found efficiencies would have to be reflected in a price increase. This would result in a loss of business to competing companies that succeeded in remaining nonunion. Thus, the nonunion portion of the market would tend to grow at the expense of the unionized portion.

The only way to prevent this from happening would be to extend unionization to the rest of the industry or, at least, to the rest of the effectively competing market. That is, if a part of a highly competitive product market (such as the fast-food industry) becomes unionized, and as a result has to accept higher costs of production, those companies in the unionized sector are at an inherent cost disadvantage relative to the nonunionized sector. The only way to restore the preexisting equilibrium is to either get rid of the union involved or extend unionization to the whole industry or market. The latter solution will raise the cost curve of the industry and thus allow the additional cost to be passed forward to the consuming public. The reason for this is that the industry product demand curve is less elastic than that of the individual company in the industry. There is a high degree of substitutability between the products of one company and another but relatively little between fast-food and other types of restaurants (or eating at home).

The result of all this is that the management of a company in the fast-food industry, or any other industry with a similar cost and market structure, has no choice but to maintain an effective preventive labor relations program. To do otherwise would be irresponsible.

Please note that this is independent of how the manager feels about unions and collective bargaining. A manager in such an industry could conceivably have strong pro-union sentiments and yet find himself in a situation that requires the fighting of unions as a matter of business survival.

A second example of a situation in which management must adopt a preventive labor relations posture may be found in parts of the electronics industry. Electronics assembly can be done almost anywhere. The product is of high value and low weight. Thus transportation costs are relatively low. While there may be some advantages to doing the work in close proximity to the company's R&D facilities or to complementary industries (such as in the so-called Silicon Valley around Santa Clara, California), there are limits to the value of such convenience, which tend to be closely associated with costs of production. The companies in this industry are in direct competition with each other as well as with similar companies and facilities outside the country. They are also in competition with *potential* facilities that may be started should the costs of production in the United States increase. Indeed, it is extremely easy for this type of work to move "south of the border" to a free-trade zone in Mexico that allows the shipment of components into and out of Mexico for processing without the payment of import and export duties.

The management of an electronics assembly plant operates under the constant threat of the work being lost to a foreign plant. This could occur indirectly if a foreign producer wins contracts or directly if the parent organization decides that it is more economical to do the work overseas. This, of course, places plant management under extreme pressure to keep costs down. There are many components in the costs of production in addition to labor costs, and labor costs are themselves a collection of various elements. However, it is all but certain that unionization will appreciably increase labor costs and, thus, the costs of production. Given the precariousness of the industry, this could have enormous implications.

As in the fast-food example, a management in the electronics industry (or any other industry subject to such foreign competition) may have no choice but to adopt a preventive labor relations policy. To do otherwise may mean sacrificing the jobs of the very employees who may be interested in joining a union, as well as being rather hard on one's own career.

Again, it should be noted that the decision is based on business and economic necessity. How one feels about unions is irrelevant.

When in Doubt

The examples cited deal with the extremes. When the San Francisco Bay Area Rapid Transit District (BART) was put together, there was no question about resisting unionization. To attempt to operate nonunion would have meant the loss of important political support at the state and federal level, without which the project would not have got off the ground. In addition, it would have been unreasonable to expect to operate such a highly visible target in such a heavily unionized community as the Bay Area nonunion for any length of time. On the other hand, when McDonald's moves into a new territory, there is no question that the company will do all in its power to ensure that its properties (or the properties of its franchises) will operate without unions. The more difficult situations fall in between the extremes.

What does a company do when the signals are less clear than those given in the examples? The answer is that, in the absence of clear evidence either that the company would be better off with a union or that it has no reasonable hope of remaining nonunion, the company should assume that it would be better off without a union. In other words, when in doubt, fight.

The reasoning behind this recommendation is simple. If the company makes a mistake, it is better to err on the side of remaining nonunion. If it gets organized when it could have avoided the union, the costs of that mistake may be high. Furthermore, the costs are in all probability going to be long run (assuming they do not put the company out of business). It is easier to remain nonunion than to get rid of a union once it has become established. If, on the other hand, the company errs and remains unorganized when an objective assessment of the facts suggests otherwise, the costs are relatively slight. In fact, it would be most unlikely that the benefits of unionization would outweigh the costs in a given situation and that this fact would not be obvious to the managers involved.

The more difficult situation is when the company cannot remain non-union because of the effectiveness or influence of a particular union. A situation could arise in which the facts say that the company should endeavor to remain nonunion but the union is holding a "kicker" that the company does not know about. For example, other companies (suppliers, customers, competitors, or just friends) or local politicians may be of the opinion that the company should not "rock the boat." Under such conditions a determination of whether it is possible (as opposed to desirable) to remain nonunion is more difficult to make. Again, the guiding rule should be: when in doubt, fight. If there are hidden facts, they will soon surface and can be taken into account at that time. Of course, this question should always be thoroughly researched before a company enters a new area or industry.

A Matter of Degree

In most situations managers will decide to resist unionization, regardless of whether that decision is arrived at after a careful analysis of the facts or from a gut reaction. However, careful examination of the problem has the advantage of preventing the company from falling into the trap of resisting unionization out of habit when it would be better off directing its attention toward structuring a situation that it can live with after it is unionized. The examination of the problem also raises the question of degree.

How much is it worth to stay nonunion? The answer will vary with the company involved. However, the answer should bear some relationship to the consequences of unionization. If the probable outcome is that the plant will shut down and the work be sent to Taiwan, then fighting the union is obviously worth quite a bit. But if it is only a matter of losing a slight competitive advantage over one's already unionized competitors, then the company should take a hard look at what it will cost to fight off the union. What does it cost in lost sales for Coors to remain on the AFL–CIO's "We Don't Patronize" list year after year? (And what does it gain in free advertising, too?) And what does it cost the company in legal fees, management time, employee morale, and all the other things that go into an extended counterunion campaign?

26

Undoubtedly some companies spend more on remaining nonunion than it is worth. A careful assessment of the appropriate industrial relations policy for the company should provide information, not only on the desirability of remaining nonunion, but also on the extent to which the company should be willing to press the campaign. It may turn out that it makes sense to resist unionization only up to a point. Beyond that, it may be more appropriate to reassess the situation.

Preventive labor relations has a certain resemblance to war. But it should never be forgotten that the war is fought for commercial and economic reasons. It is not a holy crusade. The important difference is that the commercial war is fought for limited objectives and the decision makers retain a sense of perspective. There are limits beyond which they do not go and depths below which they do not sink. In a holy crusade, by contrast, the participants are motivated by a higher principle that has historically allowed some of the worst barbarism on record. Preventive labor relations is a legitimate and honorable area of management activity. But it is not a holy war that allows anything and everything in the name of principle. There are limits and rules to the game.

CONCLUSION

Before discussing the technical and legal aspects of preventive labor relations, it may be helpful to recapitulate the objectives of this book. The reader should keep them in mind as we delve into more substantive details.

It will be remembered that our first purpose is to introduce to the subject of preventive labor relations the same commonsense reasoning and objectivity that American managers employ elsewhere. The fact that preventive labor relations is an important business activity for a great many firms needs no emphasis. The problem is that such programs too often are thought of as a crusade that transcends the usual need for objective analysis and pragmatic response. The result is that otherwise objective managers often say and do things that are better left unsaid and undone.

A second purpose of this book is to present a framework within which individual preventive labor relations problems may be addressed and analyzed. No book of any length could fully treat a subject as extensive and untapped as this. There are an infinite number of situations that could be studied with profit. For instance, preventive labor relations in the banking, or retail, or health care, or any number of other industries would be appropriate and challenging topics in their own right. It is hoped that the obviously widespread interest in the subject will be translated into such studies in the future. In the meantime, this more general analysis may help managers in various industrial settings cope with the union problem in a more effective way. Many of the principles that will be developed appear to have universal application. They should serve as a framework for a wide range of situations.

Third, I hope that the reader will come away from this study with an appreciation of the importance of an early start. The name of the game is *prevention,* not reaction. As will be developed, there are so many things a knowledgeable employer can do to avoid and deter the serious attentions of unions that, in the great majority of cases, a union campaign should be a remote possibility. And even in those situations in which the employer is especially vulnerable, for one reason or another, there are so many things the company can do to improve its chances of winning that a union victory should be a very unlikely outcome. However, almost all the things that can be and should be done require substantial lead time to be fully effective. This strongly suggests that the company should establish a preventive labor relations program along the lines recommended here long before any sign of union trouble. This message will be repeated at every opportunity.

Fourth, I attempted to introduce objectivity into the management decision on whether or not to fight unionization. Although it will be assumed for the remainder of this book that the company has decided to stay nonunion and that this is one of the principal objectives of the firm, that does not reduce the importance of making this basic decision early and explicitly. All companies must make this decision at one time or another. The decision should be made in the same way as any other important decision and at the earliest practicable date. The recommendation "When in doubt, fight" is not intended to relieve the reader from addressing this central business decision in the proper way.

The fifth and final purpose of this book is to improve the employer's chances of remaining nonunion. Ideally this will be done by avoiding, deterring, and making unnecessary union representation through the adoption of an effective and comprehensive preventive labor relations program. Should, however, an active union problem occur, the adoption of such a program will have the important effect of increasing the chances that the company will come through the ordeal unscathed. This is by no means unimportant.

28

It must be emphasized that these objectives are pro-management as opposed to antiunion. This book is not a religious tract, an ideological manifesto, or a call to arms. It is certainly not an attack on organized labor in any general sense. I have no philosophical disagreement with unionism. I have been a member of three labor organizations and worked in industrial relations management with unions under the most cordial circumstances. Nor do I have any fundamental disagreement with union officials and staffers, the overwhelming majority of whom are honest and dedicated professionals. Rather, the overriding objective is to examine and recommend those things management should do to respond effectively to economic reality.

NOTES

1. This reference and various others discussed throughout this book were first developed in two articles by the author in *Personnel Journal:* "Preventive Labor Relations, Part I: Before the Union Knocks" (April 1978), and "Preventive Labor Relations, Part II: Responding to the Union Campaign" (May 1978).

2. The masculine gender will be used throughout this book for the sake of brevity and style. This is in no way meant to detract from the importance of the large number of women managers—and especially personnel managers—active in preventive labor relations.

3. This is not always the case. Some companies have found that a union has forced them to become more efficient, and some unions have found themselves in a position of being unable to increase wages and benefits above those prevailing in the industry or area.

4. Office of the General Counsel, National Labor Relations Board, *An Outline of Law and Procedure in Representation Cases,* Washington, D.C.: U.S. Government Printing Office, 1974.

5. This is an oversimplification. Actually, the Wagner Act reenacted the provisions of Section 7(a) of the National Industrial Recovery Act of 1933, which had been held unconstitutional by the Supreme Court in 1935. And the RLA, as passed in 1926, was the culmination of a legislative evolution that began in the 1880s.

6. U.S. Department of Labor, Bureau of Labor Statistics, *Handbook of Labor Statistics, 1968,* Table 129, p. 300.

7. The types of union organization were never that pure and simple and have since the 1930s broken down even further. Many unions with the term "amalgamated" in their name (Amalgamated Transit Union) are an amalgamation of once separate craft unions in an industry. In addition, the ensuing contest between the craft and industrial unions did much to blur the distinction as they scrambled for the same members. Thus some traditional craft unions (International Brotherhood of Electrical Workers) now organize along both craft and industrial lines as the

occasion demands. Moreover, some unions (most notably the International Brotherhood of Teamsters) claim a general jurisdiction and will organize any employee group regardless of craft or industry.

8.   *Handbook of Labor Statistics, 1968,* loc. cit.

9.   Ibid.

10.   For an interesting discussion of this subject from a pro-union point of view, see Phillis Payne, "Consultants Who Coach the Violators," *American Federationist,* September 1977, pp. 22–29.

11.   Thomas M. Rohan, "Would a Union Look Good to Your Workers?" *Industrial World,* January 26, 1976, p. 36.

AVOIDING AND DETERRING UNIONIZATION

One of the primary goals of a preventive labor relations program is to "stay out of harm's way." There are many things that an alert company can do to reduce its chances of being chosen as an organizing target.

While unions are sometimes unpredictable, it is usually safe to assume that they choose organizing targets on a rational least-cost basis. Whether the union's leaders are aware of this or not is as irrelevant as whether managers are aware of the role of economic theory in their production and pricing decisions. The markets within which the union decision maker and the manager operate enforce rational choice. Those unions that fail to employ their organizing resources wisely do not grow and are eventually overcome by attrition as their contract companies go out of business, introduce labor-saving technology, or in some way divest themselves of the union. Similarly, those companies that do not make the correct business decisions on a regular basis do not grow and eventually disappear. Of course, this does not mean that labor organizations and companies do not make mistakes or knowingly take chances that sometimes do not pay off. Nor does it mean that unions and companies do not sometimes encounter "windfalls" and gain members or profits that they had no right to expect. However, if we assume that such chance-caused outcomes are random in their distribution, it follows that labor and business organizations must make more right decisions than wrong decisions in order to survive and prosper.

In preventive labor relations we are especially concerned with the efficient, well-run union that makes the right organizing decisions. The less efficient and less well-run labor organizations either do not enter or are forced out of most "markets." There are relatively few unions actively seeking new members in any given industry or area, and the organizing process is much more orderly than may appear at first glance.

It is also safe to assume that the relative vigor with which a union responds to an invitation or expression of interest from the employees is based on rational decision making. As will be developed, union drives in established firms are almost always initiated by employees already on the payroll. But even though some union officials claim that they never turn anyone away, their response can vary from a disinterested willingness to accept the employees' dues to an aggressive, well-planned, and well-financed organizing drive. The difference to the employer intent upon remaining nonunion is enormous.

The assumption of rationality is important to a dicussion of union avoidance and deterrence. The responsible union official will allocate his scarce resources (time, effort, budget) in a way that maximizes whatever it is that union decision makers maximize (members, dues revenue, their careers in the labor movement). This means that the company can improve its chances of not being selected as a serious organizing target by increasing the cost to the union of organizing (and eventually servicing) the employees in question.

It is unimportant whether the additional cost is imposed in the form of raising the time or dollar costs required to organize the unit or in the form of increasing the risk of failure of the organizing effort. The rational union decision maker will be responsive to both.

This chapter will examine a number of ways in which an employer can greatly reduce the chances of serious union attention. The following chapter will treat bargaining units and the employer's opportunity to influence the bagaining unit decision. This, too, is a way in which the knowledgeable employer can increase the cost (risk) of the organizing drive to the union. However, because of its technical nature and complexity, this subject will be covered separately. In addition, various other topics that are discussed elsewhere serve to raise the cost (risk) of organizing to the union. The mere fact that a company has an established policy in favor of continued nonunion operation and a trained staff who know how to detect and respond to a union drive greatly reduces the chances of an easy (cheap) union victory.

Keep in mind that we are dealing with an essentially rational process that is similar to many other business decisions. It is this rationality that gives a high degree of predictability and control to preventive labor relations, in the same way that the understanding of the process of combustion makes a fire prevention program possible. If unionization and fires struck and spread without reason or cause, there would be no way of dealing with them other than to propitiate the gods. And while a little prayer never hurts, the Lord helps those who help themselves.

ACQUISITIONS

One of the simplest and most inexcusable ways of acquiring a union is to go out and buy one. It happens all the time. Of course, it is seldom done intentionally, but that does not matter. Regardless of intent or knowledge of the presence of the union, the "successor" inherits the duty to bargain and other obligations of the former owner along with the plant. It is common in the United States for a business or a part of a business to change hands. This may take the form of an individual buying an existing company, part of its assets, or a franchise; one company purchasing or in some other way acquiring a plant or other facility from another company; or two existing corporations merging. Whether the case involves an individual buying a restaurant or a conglomerate acquiring a large corporation, there are preventive labor relations considerations that should not be taken lightly.

The simplest cases involve the acquisition of a plant in which one or more unions already exist. This type of problem is easy to identify. Just ask the existing owner or management. It is fairly easy to assess the importance of the union presence to the continued operation of that plant. An analysis similar to that discussed in Chapter 1 in the context of adopting a realistic industrial relations policy should be applied to the new property. If the present owner is selling because of financial problems, it is reasonable to ask about the cause of those problems. And if the cause is the presence of a union in a situation that logically calls for a policy of preventive labor relations, then it must be recognized that new owners will inherit that problem along with the plant. If that is the case, the acquisition should be reviewed very carefully and perhaps called off.

If the situation is not that clear-cut, the decision may hinge on the relative success of the labor–management relationship that is being acquired. Information on past strikes, grievances, and arbitrations (both past and pending) should be available from management and partially verifiable from outside sources (newspapers, arbitration reports, attorneys, and business acquaintances).

It may be that the presence of the union(s) does not offset the other features of the deal and the acquisition should be made anyway. However, the decision should be made only after it is carefully researched and "thought through." Assuming that the past relationship with the union(s) appears to have been acceptable, it would be wise to ask the following questions:

1. How satisfied are the employees with the union?

2. How stable is the union leadership? Is there an opposition faction within the local? If so, what are its chances of coming into power, and will it be more or less militant than the existing leadership?

3. What is the relationship between the national or international union and the local? Who has the final say within the union on such questions as the settlement of grievances, the conduct of negotiations, and the handling of strike funds? In other words, are you dealing with the stable and professional staff of the international union or with a local leadership that may not be there next year? Which is preferable will depend on the attitude and past performance of each. However, in most cases there are advantages to doing business with "professionals" who understand the process and have the technical knowledge to make a success of it. An important exception to this observation occurs when the local union is in a weak position and the members accept that fact.

4. Has collective bargaining taken place locally, or have the important decisions been made, either formally or informally, on an industrywide or areawide basis? That is, is there a history of negotiating in a multiemployer bargaining unit, or is there an established industry or area pattern that you will be required to follow in order to maintain the existing harmonious relationship? If so, what is happening at the industrywide or areawide level that you should know about? If not, are there any plans

to create such an arrangement by the union(s) and/or some of the employers in the industry or area?

5. How will the acquisition affect the existing labor–management relationship? Will the union view the new owner as more able to afford higher wages and benefits? Will it consider the new situation as an opportunity to go after those "improvements" that it was never able to get from the former management? And will the management personnel responsible for creating and maintaining the stable relationship with the union be retained? Will they stay? If not, do you have personnel ready to step in?

6. What has been negotiated or promised (perhaps not in writing) that you should know about? Are the employees coming off a three-year labor agreement expecting to catch up with inflation or make up for all the things they did not get last time? Or are you at the beginning of a three-year contract with a lot of "back loading"? That is, did the company buy an easy settlement in the first year by "giving away the store" in the third year of the agreement? In this regard, particular attention should be paid to the pension plan if one exists. Is it fully funded? Although the Pension Reform Act of 1974 (ERISA) established minimum standards in this area, it gave companies with underfunded plans up to 40 years to become fully funded. If there is no pension plan (or other common benefit), how long can you expect to get along without one? If there is a collectively bargained plan, will this prevent covering the newly acquired employees with the company's other pension and benefit plans? Will problems arise in regard to the transfer and promotion of employees? Is the plan about to be acquired in danger of losing its IRS "qualification" as a tax-exempt fund?

7. What impact will the acquisition have on your efforts to keep the rest of the company nonunion? Will your present employees compare their wages, benefits, and conditions with those of the unionized plant? And how well will they compare? How will wages and benefits compare at the end of the present contract or after the negotiation of the next one? Will the union on the newly acquired property consider it necessary to organize the rest of the company to protect what it has already won? Do you intend to integrate the production of the new plant with that of the rest of the company? If so, what happens when (not *if*) the unionized plant goes on strike? How long will it be possible or practical to operate the new facility separately from the rest of the company?

This list of questions is not exhaustive. No doubt many others are relevant to a particular industry, area, or company. The important thing from a preventive labor relations point of view is to start asking such questions. After that, one question leads to another and the company considering an acquisition at least goes into the deal with its eyes open. After asking the right questions and fully considering the answers, the company may decide to go ahead with the acquisition. However, it is inexcusable for a company intent upon remaining nonunion to acquire a new property without thoroughly researching the preventive labor relations aspects of the matter.

A more likely labor relations problem for a nonunion company is the acquisition of a presumably nonunion plant or other property. In such a case the danger is that there may be a union drive in progress or the company may be ripe for one. This may even be part of the reason the present owner wants to sell!

Should an organizing drive be under way, the acquiring company will almost certainly inherit the sins and liabilities of the former management. For instance, if the company has discharged a number of employees because of their union activities or sympathies, the new owner may find itself responsible for the NLRB-determined remedy. Imagine discovering that you have to reinstate 50 workers with full back pay a year after their discharge. Or you may discover that the former management has inadvertently recognized the union by incorrectly responding to a demand for union recognition (to be discussed in Chapter 10). In this case you may be faced with a legal duty to bargain with the union. There is no end to such intriguing possibilities.

What steps can the acquiring company take to protect itself from such jeopardy? One step is to visit the appropriate regional office of the National Labor Relations Board, which makes information on petitions for representation elections and unfair labor practice charges available to the public. A second step is to ask the owner whether he has received a demand for recognition or knows of any union activity in progress. If the answer is no, insist that this be put in writing and appended to the documents on the acquisition or merger. While such written statements may have little legal value unless the demand for recognition was explicit, they may have a wonderful effect on the memory of the seller.

A third step is to "ask around." Attorneys are excellent sources of information on labor matters. If your counselor does not know, he probably knows whom to ask. This may involve a discreet inquiry to attorneys who represent labor organizations. Such an inquiry may be difficult for management to make directly. A good employee relations manager with local contacts may also be able to provide valuable information. Finally, it may prove helpful to talk with plant-level personnel managers of the proposed acquisition. The managers will have little incentive to conceal such information, since they will probably be acquired with the plant.

How to discover whether the plant is ripe for unionization is more difficult. Information on past union drives and representation elections will throw some light on the subject. The results of any elections held within the past few years should be reviewed with care and evaluated in light of turnover experienced in the unit since the election. Particular attention should be paid to those employees who were active in the past campaign and are still on the payroll. Attention should also be directed at the issues in the campaign and what has been done since then to improve the situation.

Other less direct indicators of a potential organizing drive may be gleaned from personnel records. Have labor turnover and absenteeism increased in the recent past? If so, where and why, and what has been done about it? Have there been disciplinary actions or other signs of employee dissatisfaction? What were the issues? What has been done about them? Inquiries of this sort are well within the rights of the acquiring firm.

Another source of information on potential union interest is the *NLRB Election Report* (discussed more fully in Chapter 9). This monthly report provides accurate and timely information on which unions are organizing where (in terms of industry, part of the country, and company size) and with what success. While such information will not usually be specific to your needs, it can throw light on the acquisition's general vulnerability. If there is little or no organizing activity in the industry or area, then you are probably safe (other things being equal). And if everyone else is having trouble, then it is probably only a matter of time before you have trouble too.

Acquisitions and mergers are dangerous from a preventive labor relations point of view. This does not mean that they should be avoided. But it does mean that they should be handled with care. There is much that an alert employer can do to minimize the chances of accidentally acquiring a union along with a plant.

PLANT LOCATION

One of the most important business decisions is the location of a plant or other facility. Location decisions are usually based on the proximity to customers (product markets) and/or the availability of raw materials and labor (factor markets). In manufacturing, food processing, and other industries, the decision will also be influenced by the differential rates of the railroad and trucking industries on raw materials and semifinished goods relative to the finished product. In some industries there may be overriding constraints such as the need of retail establishments to locate where the customers are and the need for mining operations to take place where the ore is found. A primary paper mill must have ready access to a long-run supply of timber (or other fiber); an aluminum plant must have a relatively cheap source of electricity and access to a dependable source of bauxite; and an auto assembly plant must have access to a large and dependable source of labor. However, within these constraints there may be a great deal of latitude. Indeed, it is often the case that a company faced with a location decision has a large number of suitable sites from which to choose.

For the company intent upon remaining nonunion, the plant location decision is an integral part of a preventive labor relations program. Just as it it inexcusable for a nonunion company to acquire an existing facility without first determining its impact on the company's ability to remain nonunion, it is foolhardy to build a new facility where the probability of encountering serious union attention is higher than necessary.

Organized labor is more effective at unionizing in some areas than in others. This is usually credited to the culture and attitudes toward individualism in the region, its industry mix, and its political characteristics. The general "rule" is that the South and Southwest are safer than the industrial North and the West Coast. However, the matter is by no means that simple. Industrial patterns and social attitudes are changing rapidly, and generalizations often conceal more than they tell.

Table 2-1 presents data on the extent to which each state was unionized as of 1974 (the most recent year for which data were available when this book was written). Note that there are substantial differences among the states. The table suggests that, other things being equal, it is easier to remain nonunion in South Carolina, which is only 6.9 percent unionized, than in Michigan, which is 38.4 percent unionized. No doubt this is true. However, it must be remembered that the current extent of unionization is the result of past efforts by the unions and past losses by employers. Union membership data are, by definition, historical. They reflect what has happened rather than what is happening.

This is not to say that the extent of union organization is unimportant. It can have a significant impact on the employees' receptiveness to the union call and the community's support of a union organizing campaign (in the form of honoring picket lines, supporting boycotts, and the like). The extent of existing unionization will also influence the cooperation extended the organizing union by the rest of the labor movement and the company's ability to hire nonunion replacements in the event of a strike. However, the data remain a snapshot of what has taken place and may hide facts that the employer should take into account in a location decision. For instance, a relatively safe state may be the scene of intensive current organizing activity that has not yet been reflected in union membership. Or the labor movement of a particular state may be relatively inactive and living off its past victories. This, too, takes time to be reflected in state membership figures.

Given the long-range nature of most location decisions, it is important that the company have information on what is taking place now and at least a suggestion of what will be happening five years from now. In Table 2-2 NLRB election data have been used to estimate the current level of organizing effort and the relative degree of risk to the employer by state.[1]

The degree of risk to the employer is not merely a matter of the number of elections held in a state. The unions in some states are more active in petitioning for elections than in others. This is reflected in the column showing the number of elections per 100,000 nonagricultural employees. Note, for instance, that the incidence of election in Massachusetts is considerably higher than it is in neighboring Rhode Island (11.0 compared with 6.1). The risk to the employer is further modified by the success that the unions experience in their organizing efforts. This is shown in Table 2.2 in the column reporting the percentage of representation elections won by the unions. Again, note the important differences among the states. For some reason the unions in South Dakota had a much higher success rate than those in North Dakota (62.5 compared with 37.5).

The Union Risk Index (URI) shown in the table was developed by multiplying the number of representation elections per 100,000 nonagricultural employees by the percentage won by the unions. The higher the

TABLE 2-1. EXTENT OF UNIONIZATION BY STATE.

State	Total Union Membership (in thousands)	Membership as a Percentage of Employees in Nonagricultural Establishments	Rank Order
Alabama	223	19.1	26
Alaska	32	26.4	17
Arizona	118	16.0	34
Arkansas	108	16.8	31
California	2,212	28.2	12
Colorado	181	18.9	27
Connecticut	317	25.1	20
Delaware	47	20.1	25
Florida	354	12.5	46
Georgia	264	14.5	41
Hawaii	121	36.2	6
Idaho	40	15.5	35
Illinois	1,584	34.9	7
Indiana	670	33.2	8
Iowa	212	21.2	24
Kansas	110	14.1	43
Kentucky	269	25.1	21
Louisiana	194	16.3	32
Maine	59	16.2	33
Maryland (incl. D.C.)	462	21.6	23
Massachusetts	579	24.4	22
Michigan	1,255	38.4	1
Minnesota	375	25.3	19
Mississippi	84	12.0	47
Missouri	575	32.3	10

URI number, the higher the risk of unionization, other things being equal. Thus it may be inferred that it is much more dangerous for a nonunion firm to locate a new plant in the state of Washington, where the URI is 1,125, than in Idaho, where it is only 265. The last column in the table reports the rank order of the URIs by state. The highest-risk state (Alaska) is number 1 and the safest state (Virginia) is number 50.

Table 2-3 compares the rank order of the states by degree of unionization (Table 2-1) with the rank order of the URIs (Table 2-2). No significance should be attributed to minor differences. The Union Risk Index was computed for only one year (1976), and there will be variations from

(Continued)

State	Total Union Membership (in thousands)	Membership as a Percentage of Employees in Nonagricultural Establishments	Rank Order
Montana	60	25.7	18
Nebraska	83	15.1	38
Nevada	71	27.4	14
New Hampshire	46	15.1	37
New Jersey	786	28.2	13
New Mexico	51	14.1	42
New York	2,693	38.0	3
North Carolina	140	6.9	50
North Dakota	29	15.1	36
Ohio	1,389	33.2	9
Oklahoma	132	15.0	39
Oregon	222	26.5	16
Pennsylvania	1,695	37.5	4
Rhode Island	101	27.3	15
South Carolina	82	8.0	49
South Dakota	23	11.0	48
Tennessee	295	18.7	28
Texas	567	13.0	45
Utah	65	14.9	40
Vermont	28	17.7	30
Virginia	247	13.8	44
Washington	438	36.7	5
West Virginia	218	38.2	2
Wisconsin	490	28.7	11
Wyoming	25	18.2	29
Total	20,566	26.2	

Source: U.S. Department of Labor, Bureau of Labor Statistics, *Directory of National Unions and Employee Associations, 1975,* Bulletin 1937, Washington, D.C.: U.S. Government Printing Office, 1977, p. 74, Table 18.

year to year. This is especially so in the smaller states where the numbers are too small to be statistically stable. However, some generalizations may be made. West Virginia, for instance, with its very high degree of unionization (38.2 percent), appears to be relatively safe. This probably means that much of the state's union membership is concentrated in the coal industry. Illinois is another state that appears to be safer than its

TABLE 2-2. UNION RISK INDEX BY STATE (1976).

State	Number of Elections	Elections per 100,000 Employees	Percentage Won by Union	Union Risk Index	Rank Order by Index *
Alabama	140	12.2	50.0	610	14
Alaska	45	27.8	62.5	1,738	1
Arizona	78	10.8	47.4	512	26
Arkansas	75	12.1	41.3	500	27
California	1,228	15.7	49.1	771	6
Colorado	126	13.3	57.9	770	7
Connecticut	102	8.4	49.0	412	33
Delaware	18	7.9	38.9	307	42
Florida	162	5.9	42.0	248	46
Georgia	131	7.6	44.3	337	40
Hawaii	88	26.0	53.4	1,388	2
Idaho	28	10.6	25.0	265	44
Illinois	410	9.3	43.2	402	34
Indiana	283	14.7	42.4	623	13
Iowa	127	12.8	57.5	736	9
Kansas	76	9.5	46.1	438	30
Kentucky	118	11.3	34.7	392	35
Louisiana	100	8.3	42.0	349	37
Maine	59	16.6	45.8	760	8
Maryland	110	7.7	39.1	301	43
Massachusetts	256	11.0	49.2	541	24
Michigan	534	17.1	48.7	833	5
Minnesota	177	12.0	50.3	604	17
Mississippi	62	9.3	38.7	360	36
Missouri	210	12.2	53.8	656	11

degree of unionization would suggest. California and Oregon, on the other hand, seem to be even more hazardous than one would expect. Additional observations and conclusions will be left to the reader.

A strong caution is in order. It is convenient to use union membership and organizing activity by states, because the Bureau of Labor Statistics and the National Labor Relations Board report the data on that basis. Yet there are enormous differences within states and important labor markets and union jurisdictional interests that transcend state lines. There is much more similarity between New York City and the industrial centers of northern New Jersey than between New York City and many upstate communities. Chicago, Milwaukee, and the cities that lie between them

(Continued)

State	Number of Elections	Elections per 100,000 Employees	Percentage Won by Union	Union Risk Index	Rank Order by Index*
Montana	42	17.5	35.7	625	12
Nebraska	46	8.3	50.0	415	32
Nevada	32	12.1	50.0	605	16
New Hampshire	28	9.6	35.7	343	39
New Jersey	281	10.0	54.8	548	23
New Mexico	52	14.2	42.3	601	19
New York	537	8.4	52.0	437	31
North Carolina	82	4.1	42.7	176	49
North Dakota	32	15.8	37.5	593	21
Ohio	594	14.8	48.8	722	10
Oklahoma	95	10.7	48.4	518	25
Oregon	154	18.5	47.4	877	4
Pennsylvania	520	11.8	50.6	597	20
Rhode Island	21	6.1	57.1	348	38
South Carolina	40	4.1	50.0	205	47
South Dakota	16	7.7	62.5	481	29
Tennessee	197	13.2	46.2	610	15
Texas	284	6.4	49.3	316	41
Utah	23	5.2	39.1	203	48
Vermont	20	12.5	20.0	250	45
Virginia	59	3.4	44.1	150	50
Washington	267	22.1	50.9	1,125	3
West Virginia	67	11.9	46.3	551	22
Wisconsin	211	12.6	47.9	604	18
Wyoming	12	8.4	58.3	490	28

*Alphabetical order in case of tie.
Source: Election data from 41 NLRB Annual Report 244 (Table 15A) (1976). Employment data (not shown) from Statistical Abstracts of the United States (1976), p. 367 (Table 596).

have more in common in this regard than they have with their respective hinterlands. Thus, while the state data available and the above analysis may throw some light on the subject, they may also be misleading. Use them with caution.

There may also be important differences in the probability of being unionized within a local area. Locating on one or the other side of a

43

TABLE 2-3. COMPARISON OF RANK ORDERS OF THE DEGREE OF UNIONIZATION AND THE UNION RISK INDEX BY STATE (1976).

State	Unionization	Union Risk	State	Unionization	Union Risk	State	Unionization	Union Risk
Alabama	26	14	Louisiana	32	37	Ohio	9	10
Alaska	17	1	Maine	33	8	Oklahoma	39	25
Arizona	34	26	Maryland*	23	43	Oregon	16	4
Arkansas	31	27	Massachusetts	22	24	Pennsylvania	4	20
California	12	6	Michigan	1	5	Rhode Island	15	38
Colorado	27	7	Minnesota	19	17	South Carolina	49	47
Connecticut	20	33	Mississippi	47	36	South Dakota	48	29
Delaware	25	42	Missouri	10	11	Tennessee	28	15
Florida	46	46	Montana	18	12	Texas	45	41
Georgia	41	40	Nebraska	38	32	Utah	40	48
Hawaii	6	2	Nevada	14	16	Vermont	30	45
Idaho	35	44	New Hampshire	37	39	Virginia	44	50
Illinois	7	34	New Jersey	13	23	Washington	5	3
Indiana	8	13	New Mexico	42	19	West Virginia	2	22
Iowa	24	9	New York	3	31	Wisconsin	11	18
Kansas	43	30	North Carolina	50	49	Wyoming	29	28
Kentucky	21	35	North Dakota	36	21			

*Indices for the state of Maryland are not comparable. The District of Columbia is included in the data for the state by the BLS but not by the NLRB.

bridge, tunnel, or other restriction to traffic may have an important effect on the chances of remaining nonunion. While it is difficult to pinpoint them, there are socioeconomic and cultural differences that play a part in the propensity of employees to vote for or join unions voluntarily. In addition, the ability to attract nonunion replacements for strikers and the effectiveness of a union's picket line will be partially determined by local considerations. These factors may be especially important in the retail industry.

An example is in order. In the San Francisco Bay Area, the Caldecott Tunnel links the heavily unionized East Bay cities of Oakland and Berkeley with the primarily residential communities of Lafayette, Orinda, and Walnut Creek. The two regions are separated by a range of hills or ridges and a number of contiguous parks. The socioeconomic climate and the relative risk of encountering an effective union drive are very different at each end of the tunnel. Yet the tunnel is only 300 yards long and connected to major freeways at both ends. If a nonunion company were looking for a location for a warehouse and distribution center or a transportation company were looking for a terminal site in the area, this could be a valuable piece of information.

Another local peculiarity may result from union jurisdictional lines. Because of differences in the abilities and ambitions of local union leaders and/or the traditions of different locals or because of the pressures of already unionized employers, some local unions are more aggressive at organizing than others. Every state and large city is sectioned into a maze of jurisdictions by the various unions. At its simplest, a local will have the whole city or county. This is the case in the construction industry when the city is not contiguous with another city. At its most complex, there may be a line, visible only to the union organizer, which places one side of the street in the jurisdiction of one local and the other in the jurisdictional of another local. Moreover, in the case of the Teamsters, such jurisdictional lines vary from company to company in some metropolitan areas.

Such jurisdictional arrangements can be of considerable importance to the company trying to remain nonunion. However, it is almost impossible for an outsider to identify the various jurisdictional lines and make an effective determination of the best location for a new plant in a particular city. A local labor attorney or consultant knowledgeable about the local labor movement should be consulted before the decision is made.

For the sake of completeness, we should note that another way of avoiding American unions altogether is to leave the country. While this may sound extreme (if not downright treasonous), it is exactly what some companies have done. The location of many electronics assembly plants in Southeast Asia, the many manufacturing operations in the Free Trade Zone in Mexico, and the registration of American-owned ships under the flags of Liberia and Panama are partially motivated by a desire to avoid American unions.

LEGAL JURISDICTION

A third way of raising the cost and risk of organizing to the union is by ensuring that the contest will take place under a set of groundrules that are favorable to the employer. Perhaps it would be more accurate to say under groundrules that are the least unfavorable to the employer. Although of limited applicability, the tactic of moving the company from one legal jurisdiction to another that offers certain advantages should not be overlooked.

Under any circumstances, it is important for a company intent upon remaining nonunion to determine the jurisdiction within which a potential representation election will take place. The first question that must be asked in addressing any industrial relations problem is: What law covers the situation? The answer to this question will provide valuable information on the employer's rights and duties. As will be developed, there is much that the company can legally do to strengthen its position before and during the union campaign. However, before the company can determine that a particular situation will support a preferred bargaining unit claim or that a certain employer action or statement constitutes a violation of the law, the applicable statute (or common law) must be identified.

The importance of making this determination early cannot be overstated. Imagine discovering that a strategy based on a bargaining unit structure allowable under one set of rules is worthless because the case falls under the coverage of a different law with different criteria. Imagine discovering that the way in which a demand for recognition was handled or the way in which employees were questioned about their union attitudes was presumed to be within the range of legal activity under, say, state law but now constitutes illegal activity that will require setting aside an election in which the employer prevailed. Or imagine discovering that the election was lost because the company mistakenly thought it was under the National Labor Relations Act when it actually could have taken advantage of certain rights allowed under state law.

46

In the great majority of cases, determining which law controls the situation will be simple and clear-cut: most companies will find that they fall within the jurisdiction of the National Labor Relations Act. Thus, throughout most of this book, it will be assumed that the situation under discussion is covered by the NLRA. This is usually a safe assumption. However, the possibility of avoiding the National Labor Relations Act, with its unfair labor practices, representation procedures, and eager staff, should not be overlooked.

Other laws that may apply are the Railway Labor Act, various public-sector laws, and, most important, state law. The determination of coverage will be made by the administrative agency of the federal law (National Mediation Board or National Labor Relations Board). If the federal agencies decline to assert jurisdiction over a private-sector matter, it will normally fall under the statutes and/or common law of the state or states within which the employer does business. However, this does not rule out the knowledgeable employer's having some influence in this decision.

The Railway Labor Act applies to common carriers in both the railroad and airline industries. If the company is a common carrier in interstate commerce in either industry, there is little question that it will be covered by the RLA. However, between the jurisdictions of any two laws there is a gray area in which the question of coverage is less clear and may offer room to maneuver. Consider a company that contracts with an airline to clean and service its aircraft in a particular city. What if the company also contracts to do the janitorial work of the airport, and the same employees are used in both operations? What if it does similar work in other industries as well and has a policy of shifting employees from one job to another? Note that the employer controls the degree of interchange and the markets in which it will offer its services as one company. The details of this question need not detain us,[2] but it does illustrate some of the complexities involved and the potential employer control over a seemingly simple jurisdictional question.

The NLRB defers to the National Mediation Board on jurisdictional matters.[3] That is, if the NMB asserts jurisdiction, the NLRB will accept that assertion. Should a party insist on petitioning the NLRB for an election, the Board will conduct a hearing and then submit the record of the hearing to the NMB for its determination. Thus, in those cases in which the matter could fall under either the Railway Labor Act or the National Labor Relations Act, the jurisdictional standards and procedures of the National Mediation Board will prevail.

In most cases the employer will prefer to be covered by the National Labor Relations Act rather than by the Railway Labor Act, since the former is less cumbersome and more predictable and its interpretive case law more developed over a wider range of possible business situations. More attorneys and employee relations specialists are familiar with the NLRA than with the RLA. Questions such as the employees' right to strike and the equally important employers' right to take a strike are more firmly established under the National Labor Relations Act.[4]

There is usually little question of whether an operation is in the public or private sector. Governments are in the public sector and corporations and other for-profit organizations are in the private sector. Most of what lies in between would be considered religious or charitable nonprofit (or not-for-profit) organizations over which the Board usually declines to assert jurisdiction on policy grounds beyond the extent to which they are engaged in purely commercial operations.[5] Regulated utilities are within the private sector.

There is little movement from one sector to another, and any movement that does take place is usually pretty clear-cut. It is well established that when a transit system shifts from private to public ownership (as many of them have done in recent years), the employees become public servants and are covered by the relevant public-sector law unless special legislation is passed for them.[6] And if, say, a local trash collection operation moves from municipal government to private control, it becomes covered by the appropriate private-sector law.

The vast majority of jurisdictional questions involve whether the case falls under federal (usually NLRB) or state jurisdiction. This matter will hinge on whether the employer (not the union) is in one of the exempted categories, or whether it has a substantial impact on interstate commerce as defined by the NLRB.

If the unit in question is in agriculture, it is excluded from federal coverage and falls under state law. With the important exception of California, which has its own Agricultural Labor Relations Act, this lack of federal coverage almost always ensures no effective unionization. However, the same gray area exists here as exists between the Railway Labor Act and the National Labor Relations Act. Agriculture applies to fishing and forest products as well as to farming and ranching. Over the years, numerous questions on jurisdiction have been raised. When does the fish in the ocean become a can of tuna in interstate commerce? When does the tree in the forest become lumber? There are now well-established answers

48

to these questions which have greatly limited the extent of this gray area. However, new cases continue to arise and the question of legal jurisdiction should not be overlookd in a preventive labor relations strategy.

Another dimension to the jurisdictional question involves whether the employer's business "affects commerce." This translates into whether the dollar volume of the company's activities in interstate commerce is "substantial." Section 14(c)(1) of the NLRA authorizes the Board to decline to exercise jurisdiction when the size of the enterprise is not "sufficiently substantial" to warrant its attentions, provided that it does not decline jurisdiction in a labor dispute over which it would have asserted jurisdiction prior to August 1, 1959.

The NLRB's jurisdictional standards vary by industry. They are summarized on the following pages. The determination is made by the regional office of the NLRB and is based on the commerce data provided by the employer after the union has filed its petition for a representation election. Should the employer refuse or fail to provide this information, the Board may assert jurisdiction without regard to whether the jurisdictional standards have been met. This is known as the Tropicana rule.[7] Thus, if an employer intends to demonstrate that it does not meet the Board's standards, it must furnish the relevant information as early as possible.

Inflation has reduced the importance of such exclusions from NLRB jurisdiction and promises to continue to reduce its applicability in the future. However, if it is determined that there are substantial advantages to state law (and this will vary from state to state), it may be possible to avoid NLRB jurisdiction by separately incorporating operating units, using independent contractors to perform some operations, or writing franchise agreements in such a way as to demonstrate control by the franchisee. This is a complex area that is beyond the limits of the present discussion. However, when the operating units are small and independent, when there are no important economies of scale, and when there are important advantages to remaining under state law, it would be worth asking counsel for an opinion on this matter. Of course, the decision must be made early—long before the union shows up—because it may require changes in the articles of incorporation, capitalization, and management and operation of the enterprise. For legal and operational reasons, these changes cannot be made after the union starts its drive.

In case of doubt, any regional office of the National Labor Relations Board will give an advisory opinion as to whether an enterprise falls

NLRB JURISDICTIONAL STANDARDS

Nonretail Business: Annual outflow or inflow, direct or indirect, across state lines of at least *$50,000*. Nonretail includes manufacturing.

Retail: Gross annual volume of business of at least *$500,000*. When the gross volume standard is applied (as opposed to the direct or indirect outflow or inflow used in nonretail operations), proof of the NLRB's legal jurisdiction based on out-of-state purchases (inflow) or sales (outflow) is required.

Office Buildings: Gross annual revenue of at least *$100,000,* of which at least $25,000 must be derived from enterprises whose operations meet any of the current jurisdictional standards, except the indirect outflow and inflow standards. Shopping centers are treated the same as office buildings for jurisdictional purposes.

Apartment Houses: Gross annual revenue of *$500,000* or more.

Transportation: At least *$50,000* in annual gross revenue from providing passenger or freight transportation service in interstate commerce or providing such services valued at at least $50,000 to enterprises over which jurisdiction would be asserted under any of the current standards, except one based on indirect outflow or inflow. Transportation includes all enterprises that function as essential links in the transport of passengers and freight in interstate commerce except for those covered by the Railway Labor Act.

Transit Systems: Annual gross volume of business of *$250,000* or more. In contrast to the standard applicable to transportation, this standard covers enterprises engaged in intrastate operations that affect interstate commerce to a substantial extent.

Taxicabs: At least *$250,000* in annual volume of business.

Public Utilities: At least *$250,000* total annual volume of business or $50,000 of direct or indirect outflow or inflow of goods, materials, or services across state lines.

Newspapers: At least *$200,000* total annual volume of business.

Communications: Gross annual volume of business of at least *$100,000*.

Hotels and Motels: At least *$500,000* in gross annual revenue.

Restaurants: At least *$500,000* in gross annual volume of business. This is the same as the retail standard. It also applies to private clubs and the amusement and gaming industries.

Proprietary Hospitals: At least *$250,000* in annual gross revenue.

Proprietary and Nonprofit Nursing Homes: At least *$100,000* in gross annual revenue. This standard also applies to "related facilities" such as homes for the aged and extended facilities. Jurisdiction is asserted over nursing homes and related facilities regardless of their religious or nonprofit character.

Private Colleges and Universities: Gross annual revenue from all sources (except certain limited-use grants) of at least *$1 million*. This standard also applies to symphony orchestras.

National Defense: Any enterprise affecting commerce whose operations have a substantial impact on national defense, irrespective of the Board's other jurisdictional standards. No annual gross volume of business or other dollar value need be demonstrated.

Note: When an enterprise falls under more than one of the standards, jurisdiction will be asserted if it satisfies any one of them.
Source: Office of the General Counsel, National Labor Relations Board, *An Outline of Law and Procedure in Representation Cases,* Washington, D.C.: U.S. Government Printing Office, 1974, pp. 2–15.

within the NLRB's jurisdiction. However, in almost all cases, a glance at the NLRB's jurisdictional standards, as listed on the preceding pages, will answer the question—and that answer will usually be that the company is covered by the Act. If the issue is at all close, assume that the company is covered, since inflation will soon eliminate the difference. However, it should not be thought that study of this area has no practical application. An example will demonstrate that under the right conditions an organization can move from one jurisdiction to another with important results.

In 1951 Columbia University, with the support of other private universities in the state of New York, successfully argued that it was not in interstate commerce to a substantial enough extent to warrant the assertion of federal jurisdiction.[8] Columbia and its sister institutions therefore remained under New York state law, which was then more favorable to the employer. By 1970, however, the state had passed legislation that was at least as favorable to the unions as the National Labor Relations Act and did not contain union unfair labor practices as does the federal law. At that time, Cornell University, with the support of the other universities, proved beyond a shadow of a doubt that it was involved in interstate commerce to an enormous extent.[9] The NLRB then reversed itself and asserted jurisdiction over private universities and colleges with over $1 million in gross revenue.

RESTRICTING ACCESS

It has been observed that anything the employer does either to increase the cost of organizing a group of employees with a given probability of success or to increase the chance of failure for a given expenditure of union resources will alter the union's perceived cost-benefit relationship in favor of the company. If the union's cost and/or risk becomes too great for whatever benefit it is seeking, it will not initiate an organizing drive or will not aggressively pursue an invitation from the employees. Should the union act irrationally under such circumstances and accept the higher probability of failure, the advantage also accrues to the employer.

This critical aspect of a preventive labor relations program is easy to overlook, since its impact is subtle and often invisible. The union is deterred, not defeated. It quietly decides to go elsewhere, or it budgets its resources in such a way as to preclude an effective organizing drive against the more prepared and more difficult targets. It follows that the employer should do everything possible to raise the cost and risk to the union.

This section will examine a number of things that the company can do to reduce the union's access to the employees, the employees' access to the union, and the flow of union information within the workplace. It will be noted that many of the techniques described have little or no cost. Some may even provide certain benefits to the employer independent of their preventive labor relations value. However, in combination they can add greatly to the union's cost (risk) of attempting to organize a particular target.

One important reason for restricting the union's access to the workplace is to hinder it from identifying the appropriate bargaining unit. The critical importance of the bargaining unit in preventive labor relations is developed in the next chapter. Suffice it to say here that if the union misgauges the unit and organizes, say, one department when the appropriate bargaining unit is actually the whole plant or company, it has little chance of winning the election (other things being equal). If, on the other hand, it can correctly determine the appropriate bargaining unit, it can more effectively allocate its resources and estimate the best time to petition for an election.

Another important reason to restrict the flow of information about unions is to slow down the organizing drive. As will be discussed, the union has the considerable advantage of choosing the time to initiate the organizing drive and present its demand for recognition to the employer or file a petition with the NLRB. It is most important that the company have enough time to present its side of the story to the employees before the election is held and make the tactical responses necessary to counter the union's campaign. To respond effectively, the company must have advance warning that a drive is in progress. The longer it takes the union to proselytize the employees, the better, for it increases the company's chances of discovering the drive in time to do something about it.

Remember that we are talking about raising the cost (risk) of the union's organizing drive, not completely cutting off the employees' source of information on unions. The restriction will never be complete, nor should it be. Employees have ready access to information on unionism from friends, newspapers, and other outside sources, in addition to what they learn on the job. They are free men and women with a right to such information. This is especially important, since it is *they* who will decide whether the union wins the representation election, should it come to that. Therefore, even if it were possible to restrict access to union information completely, this would present a serious ethical question in light of our political institutions and traditions. Employees cannot rightfully be denied the information they need to make an intelligent choice.

There are three main types of union presence from which the nonunion company should protect itself. The first, and the easiest to deal with, is the outside union organizer—typically a business agent or other professional staff member of the union. The organizer could be an "old hand" with a great deal of experience or a newly hired college graduate who has done little more than read the union's organizing manual. In most cases, the outside organizer, working without an invitation from the employees and without access to an inside group of union supporters, is not very effective. This is especially so when the company has established and enforces a no-solicitation rule.

The second general type of union presence is the unionized employee of another company with whom nonunion employees come into contact in the course of their work. This may take the form of the truck driver making pickups and deliveries at the nonunion plant, the employees of an in-dependent contractor hired to perform some service in the nonunion plant, or employees from a part of the company that has already been unionized. While such people may be actively organizing for the union, it is much more likely that the threat will be posed by the comparisons nonunion employees make with the compensation and conditions of union employees. Such comparisons need not be accurate. Nonunion employees may overlook important benefits that they receive (such as greater job security) or disadvantages that the union employees have (such as union dues and a strike every few years). They may also ignore such important economic facts as the skill and responsibility levels involved and the labor intensity of the industry. All this does not matter. If the nonunion employees come away from such a comparison with a feeling that they are not getting all they should, the company has a problem.

The third type of union organizer is the employee already on the payroll who, for one reason or another, is promoting the union from within. This is the most serious form of union presence to the employer. It is also the most difficult to restrict.

The three types of union presence mentioned may overlap or change in nature. And, of course, they may operate in combination. A union organizer could be hired by the company and thus become an inside problem. A union member from another firm could become a direct conduit for union information and an aggressive organizer in response to requests from nonunion employees or from the union. And an employee already on the payroll could turn into a serious union proponent in response to an incident or personnel action in the plant.

There is a long list of things the employer can do to restrict the access and movement of union organizers. The tactic that has received the most attention and generated the most litigation is the so-called no-solicitation rule. As the term suggests, this is a rule which prohibits the solicitation of employees for union or other purposes while they are at work. It is obvious that such a rule will go a long way toward restricting the union promoter. However, there are important legal restrictions on what an employer may do in this area.

A no-solicitation rule should always be reviewed by counsel before it is established. Existing rules should also be reviewed for their legality under NLRB (or other) doctrine. If a no-solicitation rule is too broad or is enforced in the wrong way, it could easily ruin an otherwise successful counterunion campaign.

A company has no obligation to allow outside union organizers to use its premises to solicit employees unless the union can show that it has no other way to reach employees. This qualification applies to logging camps, merchant ships, resort hotels, and similar situations where the workforce is physically isolated from the general population. In most other situations it is permissible to keep union organizers off the employer's property, provided it is done right.

To be effective, a no-solicitation rule must be supportable by the company's production or operating requirements rather than by an obvious desire to keep the union out. This means that the rule must be established before the union appears and, certainly, before it petitions for an election or presents a demand for recognition. It would be difficult to defend a new no-solicitation rule whose adoption just happened to coincide with a union drive when the company was able to operate without it for years.

It is also important that the rule be enforced against all solicitation, not just union solicitation. If, for example, the company regularly allows solicitation for charities, baseball pools, and the like, it would be difficult to convince an objective observer that union solicitation was in some way more disruptive of the employer's business than other forms. Therefore, a no-solicitation rule must prohibit all forms of solicitation.

The no-solicitation rule is an effective way of keeping the outside organizer away from the employees while they are at work. The employer's property, in this regard, begins at the point beyond which only employees may pass to enter their place of work.[10] This includes parking lots, provided they are not the same lots used by the public (such as in a shopping center).

Should the unionized employees of another firm start soliciting the employees for union or other reasons—say, while making deliveries—they too would be in violation of the company's no-solicitation rule. Under such circumstances, it is highly appropriate to register a complaint with the other company, just as if the outside employees had violated any other house rule or safety rule. It is not unreasonable to insist that the other company impress upon its employees that they are there to make deliveries and not to campaign for the union or to engage in idle conversation.

It is considerably more difficult to restrict solicitation by employee union supporters than by outside organizers. The long-established position of the Board and the courts is that a prohibition against employee solicitation *during working time* is presumptively—and only presumptively—valid. If it extends to nonworking time (lunch periods, breaks), it is presumptively invalid. In addition, it is permissible for department stores to prohibit solicitation on the sales floor during nonworking time.[11] The Board's position reflects a balance between the employees' rights to communicate information for or against unionization deemed necessary for an informed exercise of their rights and the employer's need for uninterrupted production.

A distinction must be made between solicitation and the distribution of union (or antiunion) literature. An employer may restrict the distribution of literature in work areas even during nonworking time if it can be shown that the material creates litter or interferes with production. However, union authorization cards (to be discussed) are considered "speech" in this regard and may not be banned.

To summarize, an employer may usually prohibit outsiders from soliciting employees, provided the rule is established early and enforced against all solicitation. Employees may be prohibited from soliciting their fellow employees during working time, but not during nonworking time (except on the sales floor of department stores). The distribution of union and other literature may be restricted in work areas even during nonworking time. However, union authorization cards are considered speech rather than literature and may not be prohibited in work areas during nonworking time.

A word of caution: don't overdo it. An overly strict no-solicitation policy could constitute illegal interference even though it falls within the guidelines outlined if it interferes with the employees' right to solicit for or against the union. Moreover, there are limits beyond which an overly stringent no-solicitation policy will affront the sensibilities of the employees. Should the company appear too heavy-handed in this area, it may indicate to some employees that they need a union. Finally, no-solicitation rules do not stop union solicitation; they only slow it down and drive it underground. If it is completely driven underground, the company may be denied the early warning of an organizing drive that is so important to an effective counterunion campaign. This is not to say that no-solicitation rules should not be adopted and seriously enforced. They definitely should be. However, their importance lies in slowing down union communication rather than completely cutting it off. A no-solicitation policy can be more effective when used in conjunction with other techniques to thwart the flow of union information.

Anything the company can do to reduce the easy access of the outside union organizer, the unionized employee of another firm, or the inside employee union supporter to nonunion employees will reinforce the effectiveness of a no-solicitation rule. In fact, the no-solicitation rule per se and the various measures to be discussed should be viewed as complementary parts of the same system.

The union organizer who is not an employee of the company is a member of the public and has no special right to the employer's premises. This argues strongly for separate parking facilities for the employees. If such facilities are fenced or posted and effectively policed, they will minimize communication between the outside organizer and nonunion employees as they arrive for and leave work. This will also prevent the leafleting of parked cars by outsiders. Multiple entrances and exits to and from the lot will make it more difficult to leaflet the employees on their way in or out. Multiple parking lots will have the same effect.

The most effective way to minimize contact between unionized employees of other firms and the employees of the nonunion company is to do business with other nonunion firms. This should be taken into account when deciding on a contractor for such activities as painting, janitorial service, machinery repair, light construction, and modification of the plant. When this is not possible because of a lack of nonunion firms in the market, it may be better to have the work done by company employees, have the work done when company employees are not working, or have the work done off the premises insofar as possible.

It may be more difficult to control contact with unionized truck drivers making pickups and deliveries at the plant. When such contact is unavoidable, it should be minimized. An efficient shipping department will help. Facilities should be designed with enough capacity, and scheduling should be done in such a way as to minimize the amount of time the trucks and their drivers are waiting with nothing to do. Drivers should be prohibited from entering the work area and should normally communicate only with supervisory personnel. This may require providing a separate toilet facility with access from the dock. Company personnel should not be allowed to use the loading dock or the immediate area as a place to eat lunch or take coffee breaks.

Union communication within the company can be reduced by such measures as providing a number of small lunchrooms (say, one on each floor or in each department) as opposed to one centralized facility. Multiple drinking fountains, washrooms, time clocks, and exits will have the same affect. Staggered lunch hours, coffeebreaks, and starting and quitting times will reinforce the effect. Similarly, employees should not be allowed to wander around the plant unless they are on approved company business.

It may also be wise to restrict the use of bulletin boards to official company business. If employees are allowed to post personal nonunion items, they must also be allowed to post union notices.

Christmas card lists, call-in lists, and home telephone directories should be discouraged or prohibited. Should such material fall into the hands of the union, it could prove very useful. Attention should be paid to the security of payroll and data processing units for the same reason.

Note that most of the tactics mentioned above either make sense independent of the company's preventive labor relations efforts or cost little to implement. This is especially so if they are taken into account when the plant is being built or reorganized. It should also be noted that, if fully adopted, these measures will result in a very fractured or segmented workforce. While this will undoubtedly hinder the flow of union information and strengthen the company's no-solicitation rule, it could also have a negative impact. Constructive communication will be restricted along with that initiated by the union. This could be costly if it is important for employees to coordinate their efforts with those of employees in other units of the company. Such segmentation could also reduce identification with and loyalty to the company and contribute to a sense of alienation and dissatisfaction on the part of the employees. The response could well be union organization.

Obviously, a balance must be struck between running an efficient company, which requires a certain level of employee communication and interaction, and restricting the flow of union information. In this regard, two things should be remembered. The first is that the employees of the company are men and women who share a sense of fairness and the democratic political traditions of the United States. There are limits beyond which a no-solicitation policy and the various measures that can work to reinforce it become dysfunctional. The second is that such a policy is only one element in a fully developed preventive labor relations program. It is not necessary that it be completely effective in shutting off the flow of union information. In fact, as mentioned, this is usually impossible. The most it will do is force union information underground, which may work to the disadvantage of the employer by concealing an organizing drive until it is too late to do anything about it. For this reason, the company should err on the side of leniency in its efforts to restrict employee solicitation and the flow of union information. Of course, the correct balance and combination of measures used will vary from company to company and must be chosen with operating requirements in mind.

NOTES

1. A somewhat different version of this table first appeared in John G. Kilgour, "Preventive Labor Relations, Part I: Before the Union Knocks," *Personnel Journal,* April 1978, p. 190.
2. The interested reader is referred to Office of the General Counsel, National Labor Relations Board, *An Outline of Law and Procedure in Representation Cases,* Washington, D.C.: U.S. Government Printing Office, 1974, pp. 18–19. Hereinafter NLRB, op. cit.
3. Ibid., p. 18.
4. The Railway Labor Act does not prohibit the strike. Rather, it establishes a lengthy and complex set of procedures that must be exhausted before a strike is legal. We should remember that the employees' right to strike carries with it the employer's right to take a strike. This is an important management prerogative that—in the opinion of the author—should not be given up lightly.
5. NLRB, op. cit., pp. 19–20. (Nonprofit hospitals are covered by the Act.)
6. The Urban Mass Transportation Act of 1964, as amended, places certain requirements on the public-sector employer in regard to employee protections as a condition of receiving federal grants under the Act.
7. Tropicana Products, Inc., 122 NLRB 121, 123.
8. Trustees of Columbia University, 97 NLRB 424.
9. Cornell University, 183 NLRB 329.
10. M. Scott Myers, *Managing Without Unions,* Reading, Mass.: Addison-Wesley, 1976, p. 143.
11. NLRB, op. cit., pp. 316–318.

3

BARGAINING UNITS

The most potent yet little appreciated instrument of preventive labor relations is the effective use of the bargaining unit. In legal terms, a bargaining unit is a group of employees who are eligible to vote in a particular representation election. Should the union win the election, these employees are the ones for whom the employer and the union have a statutory duty to bargain. Once an agreement has been reached, the bargaining unit may best be thought of as the employees (or jobs) covered by the labor agreement.

The terms "unit" and "union" must not be confused. The bargaining unit exists before the certification or recognition of the union and is independent of any particular labor organization (or "bargaining agent"). Perhaps the best way to think of the bargaining unit is as economic or industrial "space." A particular union may enter or exit that space, but the space remains (unless the company and union mutually agree, or the NLRB decides, to change its dimensions).

The bargaining unit has both a lateral and a vertical dimension. The lateral dimension pertains to the departments, plants, stores, employers, and so forth contained in the unit. The NLRB refers to this dimension as the *scope* of the unit. The vertical dimension pertains to the jobs or employee categories that will be included. This is referred to as the *composition* of the unit. The distinction between scope and composition should be kept in mind when considering a bargaining unit question. For example, the scope of an appropriate unit may be the entire plant, and its composition may be all production and maintenance employees up to, but not including, first-line supervision. Or the scope may be all the drugstores of a particular chain in a metropolitan area, and its composition may include all employees in the stores exclusive of the store manager and registered pharmacists.

SCOPE

Bargaining units vary greatly in size and complexity. They may range from two people in a single location to almost all the longshoremen on the Pacific Coast to the over 400,000 General Motors employees in the GM Council of the United Automobile Workers.

Section 9(b) of the National Labor Relations Act charges the NLRB to determine the appropriate bargaining unit in the course of conducting a representation election. Specifically, it states:

> The Board shall decide in each case whether, in order to assure to employees the fullest freedom in exercising the rights guaranteed by this Act, the appropriate unit for the purpose of collective bargaining shall be the employer unit, craft unit, plant unit, or subdivision thereof: Provided. . . .

The NLRB has wide latitude in its determination. In fact, it may even order a multiemployer unit since, at an early date, the Board interpreted the term "employer unit" to encompass multiemployer units as well. This was known to the Congress in 1947 when the Taft-Hartley Act was passed, and it was allowed to stand.[1]

The only statutory constraints upon the Board (and consequently upon the parties) pertain to professional employees (Section 9(b)(1)), craft units (Section 9(b)(2)), plant guards (Section 9(b)(3)), and the extent of organization (Section 9(c)(5)). The Board may not determine that a unit consisting of both professional and nonprofessional employees is appropriate

61

unless a majority of the professional employees vote to be included in such a mixed unit. It is also prohibited from determining that a proposed craft unit is inappropriate simply because a larger unit has already been decided upon unless a majority of the craft employees vote against the establishment of a separate unit. This language allows for so-called "craft severance." Its impact has been greatly reduced by NLRB and judicial interpretation and it need not detain us. Plant guards may not be included in bargaining units containing other employees. In addition, the Board may not certify a labor organization in a separate guard unit if the union has any nonguards as members or is affiliated (directly or indirectly) with an organization that admits nonguard members. Finally, the Board may not establish a bargaining unit *solely* on the basis of the extent of union organization (although it may take this into account along with other factors).[2]

Within these constraints, the Board has wide statutory discretion in determining appropriate bargaining units. However, this latitude has been limited by two important facts. One is the accumulation of over 40 years of NLRB and judicial precedent, with which the Board's current decisions must be reasonably consistent. This has resulted in the development of a number of well-known standards or principles. The second is that the employer can usually structure the business organization in such a way as to take advantage of these standards.

As a practical matter, the bargaining unit is usually effectively established by one or both of the parties rather than by the Board. This can occur in a number of ways. One is that the union may gain recognition from an unsophisticated company by convincing or bluffing it into voluntarily recognizing the union on the basis of a majority (or claimed majority) of signed authorization cards. In such a case, it is the union that unilaterally determines the effective bargaining unit with the aid of the employer's ignorance. A second arrangement occurs when the employer wants a particular union to win and knowingly grants recognition on the basis of cards. In this situation, the bargaining unit is tacitly agreed upon by the parties. We do not know how many voluntary recognitions take place in the United States each year. No doubt, the number is large. Most are in small units and involve a relatively weak employer and a large or strong organizing union. Some are in larger facilities, such as new plants, where a knowledgeable industrial relations staff decides to give recognition to a union with which it is doing business elsewhere rather than expose the new facility to the risk of being organized by a less desirable union. Such arrangements take place quickly and quietly and generate no statistics.

Another important arrangement occurs when the bargaining unit is stipulated or agreed to voluntarily by the parties in the course of an NLRB-conducted election. This is the case in about 80 percent of the elections. If the parties can come to a voluntary agreement on the unit, the NLRB is likely to accept it, unless it violates the letter or spirit of the law or is clearly inappropriate. This seldom happens. After all, it is the parties and not the Board which will have to live with the arrangement after the election, and they are presumably in the best position to know what will work best.

Finally, the employer often determines the bargaining unit, knowingly or unknowingly, for better or for worse, long before the organizing drive begins. While the Board considers all factors surrounding a bargaining unit decision—including any history of bargaining, the wishes of the employees, and the extent of union organization—the most important determinant is the "community of interest" of the employees. As will be developed shortly, the components of "community of interest" are almost fully under the control of the company. Within the limits allowed by technological and operational constraints, management can structure the company in such a way as to favorably influence the Board's decision. Moreover, when the work is done right, a union may conclude that the probable unit is not organizable and go elsewhere.

Before we get into the technicalities of structuring the bargaining unit, an important question must be raised: what is the best bargaining unit for preventive labor relations purposes? In almost all cases, the larger the unit, the better from the employer's point of view. Union organizers thrive on small units; large units are almost impossible to organize without the employer's cooperation.

Bargaining Unit Size

In 1976, unions won about 48 percent of all representation elections.[3] This reflects a decline from 57 percent as recently as 1968 and from more than 60 percent a decade earlier. Table 3-1 depicts the trend. However, as is often the case, such numbers hide more than they reveal. Table 3-2 disaggregates the data for 1976 by bargaining unit size. Note the large number of elections in small units. In 1976, there were a total of 446,978

TABLE 3-1. RESULTS OF NLRB-CONDUCTED ELECTIONS, 1958–1976.

Year	Elections Resulting in Certification	Collective Bargaining Elections Held	No. of Elections Resulting in Certification Won by Union	No. of Coll. Barg. Elections Held Won by Union	Percentage of Elections Resulting in Certification Won by Union	Percentage of Coll. Barg. Elections Held Won by Union
1958		4,337		2,636		61
1959		5,428		3,410		63
1960		6,380		3,740		59
1961		6,354		3,563		56
1962		7,355		4,305		59
1963		6,871		4,052		59
1964		7,309		4,229		58
1965		7,576		4,608		61
1966		8,103		4,995		62
1967		7,882		4,722		60
1968	7,857	7,618	4,495	4,412	57	58
1969	7,993	7,700	4,367	4,268	55	55
1970	8,074	7,773	4,458	4,367	55	56
1971	8,362		4,445		53	
1972	8,923		4,787		54	
1973	9,369		4,786		51	
1974	8,858		4,425		50	
1975	8,577		4,138		48	
1976	8,638		4,159		48	

Note: There is a discontinuity in the data as indicated by the overlapping columns.

Source: 30, 35, and 41 NLRB Annual Reports (Chart 12), (1965, 1970, 1976); pagination varies.

TABLE 3-2. EFFECT OF INCREASED BARGAINING UNIT SIZE ON THE OUTCOME OF NLRB-CONDUCTED ELECTIONS, 1976.

Number of Employees in Bargaining Unit	Total Elections	Number Won by Union	Percentage Won by Union
0–10	2,007	1,177	58.6
10–19	1,858	1,031	55.5
20–29	997	468	46.9
30–39	669	319	47.7
40–49	434	192	44.2
50–59	325	154	47.4
60–69	228	103	45.2
70–79	202	85	42.1
80–89	158	62	39.2
90–99	128	50	39.1
100–199	581	223	38.4
200–299	180	63	35.0
300–399	108	28	25.9
400–499	41	14	34.1
500–599	29	6	20.7
600–799	37	12	32.4
800–999	19	5	26.3
1,000–1,999	23	1	4.3
2,000–2,999	3	0	0.0
Total	8,027	3,993	49.7

Note: The number of elections won by unions equals the total elections minus elections in which no union was chosen. Thus percentages may differ slightly from those reported in Table 3-1 and elsewhere.

Source: Derived from 41 NLRB Annual Report 250 (Table 17) (1976).

employees eligible to vote in 8,027 elections conducted by the NLRB. That represents 55.7 employees per unit. As Table 3-3 shows, this figure was somewhat below normal for recent years. The typical NLRB-conducted election takes place in a unit of about 60 employees and a consistent and substantial majority of elections over the years have occurred in units of fewer than 30 employees. These are not very large numbers, suggesting that unions concentrate their organizing efforts on the smaller units.

Note further in Table 3-2 the rapid decline in the percentage of elec-

TABLE 3-3. AVERAGE BARGAINING UNIT SIZE AND
PERCENTAGE OF ELECTIONS CONDUCTED IN UNITS
OF LESS THAN 30 ELIGIBLE VOTERS, SELECTED
YEARS.

Year	Number of Employees Eligible to Vote	Total Elections	Average Number of Employees per Unit	Percentage of Elections in Units with Fewer Than 30 Employees
1960	483,964	6,380	75.9	54.9
1965	531,971	7,576	70.2	58.1
1970	588,214	7,773	75.7	57.0
1975	545,103	8,061	67.6	58.7
1976	446,978	8,027	55.7	60.8
1977	528,866	8,635	61.2	57.0
1978	432,264	7,435	58.1	57.9

Source: 25, 30, 35, 40, 41, 42, and 43 NLRB Annual Reports, Table 17 (1960, 1965, 1970, 1975, 1976, 1977, 1978); pagination varies.

tions won by the union as the bargaining unit size increases. Remembering that unions avoid less promising targets and invitations, and that in a fair number of NLRB elections the employer does not resist (and may even help) the union, it is safe to say that once a bargaining unit gets above a few hundred employees, it is almost unorganizable.

The effect of bargaining unit size can sometimes be reinforced by geographical or spatial dispersion. A unit of, say, 50 employees located on one property, with a lot of interaction and communication, is not only an inviting target to the union but also relatively easy to unionize. One or two inside contacts can effectively communicate the union message, and if the other ingredients necessary for "combustion" are present, the plant can be effectively penetrated and organized in a short time. If, however, the 50 employees are segmented into five departments along the lines discussed in Chapter 2, organizing will be a more difficult and slower task. If the 50 employees are located at five geographically separate locations (but still in the same bargaining unit), the organizing campaign will require a much larger investment on the part of the union. Note, however, that the payback to the union remains the same: 50 dues payers. Assuming rational decision making on the part of union leaders, it is likely that the union will decide to invest its efforts in a more promising target.

Operating Considerations

It follows that in most cases the nonunion company should endeavor to "engineer" the largest and most dispersed potential bargaining unit possible. There are important exceptions to this generalization. When the union has a good chance of winning the election (and this possibility should always be explored), the company must consider the fact that it may have to live with the union after the election. If that is the case, the boundaries of the bargaining unit may create constraints on such things as the transfer and promotion of personnel, the assignment of work, and the continuance of a workable compensation program. Although the larger bargaining unit may still be preferable, the decision should be carefully reviewed for potential operating problems.

The Strike Unit

Another consideration is that, in the event of a union victory, the bargaining unit will in all probability become the strike unit. That is, a work stoppage will most likely be coextensive with the bargaining unit. The ability to withstand a strike is one of the most important factors in any labor–management relationship. In addition to its direct impact on the company, it influences the whole collective-bargaining process. One of the factors in the company's ability to weather a strike is its capacity to continue to operate at the same location with nonstriking personnel or at other locations that are nonunion or organized by a different union (or possibly the same union but with a different contract expiration date). The ability to operate during a strike at the same location is largely a function of the composition of the unit and will be discussed below. At this point we will focus on matters relating to the scope of the unit.

If the production process is nonintegrated, the company will be in a better position to continue to operate during a strike if it keeps its operating facilities in separate bargaining units. For example, if Plant A and Plant B manufacture men's suits independently of each other and supply them directly to distributors or retailers, the company should spare no effort to keep them in separate potential bargaining units. That way, if the unionized plant is shut down, the employer can continue to operate with the nonstruck plant. By having employees work overtime and drawing upon inventory, the company may be able to continue to serve its customers and protect its market position. On the other hand, if Plant A produces only jackets and Plant B only pants, there would be no reason to keep them in separate units. Indeed, there would be a strong reason for combining the two properties into the same bargaining unit for strike purposes independent of other considerations.

Most of the retail industry represents a nonintegrated operation as far as the individual stores are concerned. While it is usually preferable to create a large, multilocation bargaining unit in retail and similar situations to deter unionization, under certain conditions it is better to isolate the union presence in a single location and render it impotent by denying it the ability to strike effectively. The trade-off is clear: a large unit is better for fighting unions; a small unit is better for rendering a victorious union harmless.

A third consideration when a union victory is likely is the possibility of decertifying the union at a future date. Decertification is the procedure whereby the employees may vote out a union with which they are dissatisfied. The details of this subject will be covered in Chapter 13. At this point, it is enough to note that it is easier for the employees to decertify a union in a small bargaining unit than in a larger one. The reasons are the same as those applying to the organizing of a small unit. Thus under some circumstances it may be best to opt for the smaller unit and attempt to keep the union's influence isolated until a decertification election can be arranged. This will be at least 12 months after the representation election.

Much of this conflicts with earlier recommendations. The employer cannot enjoy the advantages of a larger unit and a smaller unit at the same time, and often a trade-off must be made. While it is difficult to generalize about such a decision, the controlling factors include the value of the larger unit in the employer's efforts to remain nonunion, the chances of success, the ability to keep the organized unit isolated from the rest of the company, and the likelihood that the employees in the unit will want to decertify the union after the election. All these factors in turn will be influenced by the organizational structure and physical layout of the plant or company, the degree of union support in the unit (and in the rest of the company), the labor turnover rate in the organized unit, and the company's ability to prevent the union from "looking good" and carrying out its campaign promises after the election.

These comments aside, when in doubt, go for the larger unit. It is such a powerful preventive labor relations tool that it should never be relinquished unless there are clear signs that the smaller unit will be more advantageous. But since the important work in structuring the bargaining unit must be done long before there is a union on the scene, the employer would not have the information needed to decide to seek a smaller unit when the matter should logically be under review.

Community of Interest

Remember that the major NLRB criterion in defining the appropriate bargaining unit is the "community of interest" of the employees. This leads to the important question: How can the employer create community of interest? The most important factors to be taken into account are described below.[4]

1. *Degree of functional integration of the plant.* How integrated is the work being done by the employees? If the efforts of two departments are necessary to produce a product or render a service, this would argue in favor of a single unit as opposed to two separate units.

2. *Common supervision.* Employees under the direction of the same supervisor or supervisory structure by definition share many important job-related interests. This would argue in favor of a common unit for collective-bargaining purposes. However, different supervision is not in itself a sufficient reason for excluding a group of employees from an otherwise appropriate unit.

3. *The nature of employee skills and functions.* Other things being equal, craft or skill level is an important ingredient in community of interest. Clerical and secretarial personnel have different interests from the salesforce. Medical technologists have different interests from nurses, and registered nurses have different interests from practical nurses, even though they work for the same employer and perform overlapping services. Whether or not quality control would be sufficiently distinct from production and maintenance or whether journeymen machinists and their apprentices would be sufficiently different from production workers in a paper mill is a more difficult question and depends on the particular situation.

4. *Interchange and contact among employees.* If the personnel of two departments or locations regularly move back and forth (interchange) or interact with each other, this argues in favor of a single bargaining unit. For instance, if warehouse and shipping-department personnel are regularly transferred across departmental lines or if sales personnel are assigned to different stores in response to demand or to cover

absences, this would argue in favor of a single unit. Similarly, if the shipping department interacts with the finishing department, or materials handling with production, a contention of common interest will be supported. This is especially so if employees are normally allowed to transfer or if promotion lines cross departmental or proposed bargaining unit lines. If, for example, the company allows lift-truck operators to transfer to open jobs in the shipping, warehouse, or materials handling department, or if it promotes from one department to another, it would be hard to argue that they should be in separate units.

5. *Work situs.* Employees working in the same location have a natural set of common interests that must be taken into account in a bargaining unit decision. It would be dysfunctional, to say the least, to have two unions negotiating on working conditions for employees in the same office. It would be almost as bad to have a union representing only, say, full-time employees in a department store. On the other hand, employees who are located on different properties have, almost by definition, a claim to separate representational status.

6. *General working conditions.* Other things being equal, employees who share the same working conditions will have many interests in common that will be the locus of collective bargaining. Of course, this factor overlaps extensively with work situs and interchange of employees.

7. *Fringe benefits.* Common administration and funding of benefit plans is a strong argument in favor of a single unit. If, for example, the employer has been contributing to a funded (specified benefits) pension plan on behalf of the employees, it would be difficult and disruptive to sever only the unionized employees from the plan. Not only would such a move affect their accrued rights under the plan; it would affect the remaining nonunion employee-participants as well.

8. *Central control of labor relations.* When the employer operates several plants or stores under personnel and labor relations policies that are centrally determined, it argues in favor of a multilocation unit. By contrast, when there is a high degree of local management autonomy, it militates toward separate units.[5]

In most cases the plantwide, single-location unit is presumptively appropriate.[6] That is, in the absence of a history of bargaining or influence by one or more of the factors outlined above, the plantwide or storewide unit will be favored by the Board. This works to the advantage of the employer with fairly large operating units and is an especially important consideration for department stores. It would be fairly easy for the Teamsters, or another union, to organize some of the nonsales personnel in a retail store. But when such employees are grouped in a bargaining unit with the "safer" sales staff, whatever union proclivities the nonsales employees may have are swamped, and this area of employer vulnerability is effectively neutralized. (This topic is further discussed in Chapter 4 from the point of view of employee selection.)

The presumption that a single-plant unit is usually appropriate operates to the disadvantage of the employer with small operating units. However, if the employer starts early enough, this disadvantage can often be offset by the effective use of some of the standards and tests discussed above to establish a multilocation unit.

Note that *all* the factors influencing community of interest are under the direct control of the employer. Management decides how, when, and where the work is to be done. Management decides whether to use traditional craft workers hired from outside or to design jobs and train and promote from within. Management decides how supervision and compensation plans will be structured, what the working conditions will be, what interchange and contact to allow or encourage, whether or not to promote and transfer across departmental lines, and the extent to which the company will have common personnel and labor relations policies and practices. There is *nothing* that goes into the community-of-interest equation that is not under the control of management within the limits allowed by technological and operational requirements. Of course, these limits are real. A ship has to be assembled (if not built) in one shipyard, and a retail outlet cannot be larger than the market will support. However, a great deal can be done to reduce or increase the bargaining unit size by the judicious use of the NLRB criteria.

The importance of an early start in this area cannot be overstated. To wait until the union has started its campaign or filed a petition for an election to begin restructuring the company will not work. Whatever the company goes into a union drive with in regard to the determinants of a bargaining unit decision is what that decision will be based on. Given the importance of the size of the bargaining unit to the outcome of representation elections, a company intent on remaining nonunion would be shortsighted not to review its operation with this in mind. It may be found that the company can *greatly* improve its chances of deterring serious union activity or increase its chances of winning a representation election with

71

little or no cost. In fact, some companies that have evolved to their present stage and structure would benefit from such a review independent of its preventive labor relations ramifications.

COMPOSITION

Thus far we have directed our attention to the *scope,* or lateral dimension, of the bargaining unit. We now turn to its *composition,* or vertical dimension. Within a given company, plant, or subdivision, there are important decisions to be made about which employees are to be included in or excluded from the unit.

The appropriate unit will usually include all employees except those excluded for one reason or another. While the employer may have less control over the composition of a unit than over its scope, and while it is more difficult to determine where the advantages lie, there may be room to maneuver in a given situation.

Supervision

A common area of contention between the union and the company is whether certain employees are "supervisors" and therefore to be excluded from the bargaining unit, or nonsupervisors and therefore to be included. The outcome of such a dispute can have an important impact on the election results and/or on the ability of the employer to continue operations during a work stoppage should the union win.

Section 2(11) of the National Labor Relations Act defines a "supervisor" as

> any individual having authority, in the interest of the employer, to hire, transfer, suspend, lay off, recall, promote, discharge, assign, reward, or discipline other employees, or responsibility to direct them, or to adjust their grievances, or effectively to recommend such action, if in connection with the foregoing the exercise of such authority is not of a merely routine or clerical nature, but requires the use of independent judgment.

Obviously, there is room for interpretation in this definition, especially in regard to the "effectively to recommend" and "independent judgment" provisions. Often a company has a group of employees designated as "leadmen," "gang bosses," "floor girls," "trainers," "assistant managers," and so on, whose duties are quasi-supervisory in nature. That is, they work alongside the other employees most of the time but have some

72

coordinating, reporting, training, or other duties for which they are responsible and usually compensated. Such employees are typically chosen from the employee group, and the assignment may be viewed as a steppingstone to first-line supervision.

Are such employees supervisors or not? The answer depends on whether they possess *any one* of the authorities listed in Section 2(11) of the Act. There are no firm rules that apply to this determination beyond the important distinction between the exercise of independent judgment and the routine following of instructions.[7]

Whether or not an employee is a supervisor under the Act is independent of exempt or nonexempt status under the Fair Labor Standards Act and is not influenced by such things as title or payroll status (salaried versus hourly). It is determined only by the on-the-job authority vested in the employee by the company.

The company has control over how much supervisory authority is to be delegated to such quasi-supervisory personnel. Thus it can increase or decrease the number of supervisors to be excluded from the bargaining unit within a fairly wide range. Of course, this decision must be made well in advance of the union drive and cannot be made on preventive labor relations grounds alone, since it involves the important organizational questions of span of control, closeness of first-line supervision, and the number of levels of supervision and management desired by the company. Turning quasi-supervisors into supervisors could conflict with other employee relations objectives of the organization.

The quasi-supervisors can play an important role in an election. However, it is impossible to know in the abstract how the respective parties will perceive that importance. In some situations the union may view them as additional dues payers and want them in the unit for that reason. In other situations, it may want them in or out of the unit because of the way they will probably vote or because of their importance to the employer in a future strike. The company should always have an established position on this issue, determined well in advance of the organizing drive and supported by an appropriate delegation of authority.

If the quasi-supervisory personnel are chosen from among the more dependable, company-oriented, long-service employees, they may be the least interested in, or most firmly opposed to, unionization. This is especially so if they consider themselves to be "management" or promotable to supervision. If there are a fair number of such employees and if they are likely to vote for the company or against the union (which is not quite the same thing), then it may be better to have them in the proposed bargaining unit. If the quasi-supervisors are respected by their fellow employees and are effective communicators, they may be valuable promoters of the company cause as well. In addition to controlling whether such employees are supervisors for election purposes, management can have considerable influence over the attitude of these employees by the way in which it rewards and relates to them.

A word of caution is in order. If quasi-supervisors are to be included in the bargaining unit, they are "employees" under the Act. The employer may not threaten, promise, or question them without running the risk of committing an unfair labor practice or jeopardizing an otherwise successful representation election. Similarly, if such employees are to be excluded from the unit as supervisors, they must be given adequate training to ensure that they do not commit unfair labor practices in acting on behalf of the employer.

In making this determination, the company should consider two important questions: whether a strike (or a series of strikes) can be expected if the union wins the election and whether the production process lends itself to continued or partial operation with supervisory personnel during a work stoppage. If the answer to both questions is yes, then the appropriate response is to have the quasi-supervisors excluded from the bagaining unit. As supervisors, they are not entitled to the protection of the Act, and support of a strike or other union action would not be considered "protected activity." The employer can handle such problems as disciplinary matters in an appropriate manner. It goes without saying that all supervisory employees should be informed of their legal position during a union campaign, representation election, or work stoppage well in advance of the event.

Of course, the company cannot have its cake and eat it too. Quasi-supervisors are either "employees" and included in the bargaining unit or "supervisors" and excluded. Which of these positions the company takes will depend on the situation and the company's objectives. Regardless of the position taken, this matter must be considered early and handled as an integral part of the company's overall preventive labor relations program.

Professional Employees

A distinction must be made between supervisors and professional employees. Supervisors are excluded from coverage of the Act. That is, they are not "employees" and do not have the various rights and protections guaranteed by the law. While they are not prohibited from joining unions or forming their own organizations, and the employer is not prohibited from bargaining with them, such activity is not "protected." Thus, refusing to bargain with a union of supervisors or discharging supervisors for their union activity does not constitute an unfair labor practice. Similarly, a company may expect and demand that its supervisors participate in its preventive labor relations efforts as a part of their regular duties. Nonsupervisory professional employees, on the other hand, are "employees" under the Act. They have the legal right to organize and choose a union, and the employer may not interfere with that choice.

Many companies have employees whom they consider to be part of management and therefore safe from unionization. However, if such employees are not supervisors as defined in Section 2(11) or managers as narrowly defined by Board policy, they are "employees" under the Act, with all the rights and protections of production and maintenance workers.

While the Act makes no mention of managerial employees, they are defined by Board policy as "employees in executive positions who have authority to formulate, determine, or effectuate employer policies with respect to employee relations matters or whom other employees could reasonably believe to have such authority."[8] Thus it is possible for a firm to employ a number of quasi-managers who occupy a position similar to the quasi-supervisors discussed above. Again, the situation may allow room to maneuver for preventive labor relations purposes, since the company controls most of the factors that distinguish a manager from a nonsupervisory professional employee.

Section 2(12) of the Act defines "professional employee" as

(a) any employee engaged in work (i) predominately intellectual and varied in character as opposed to routine mental, manual, mechanical, or physical work; (ii) involving the consistent exercise of discretion and judgment in its performance; (iii) of such a character that the output produced or the result accomplished cannot be standardized in relation to a given period of time; (iv) requiring knowledge of an advanced type in a field of science or learning customarily acquired by a prolonged course of specialized intellectual instruction and study in an institution of higher learning or a hospital, as distinguished from a general academic education or from an apprenticeship or from training in the performance of routine mental, manual, or physical processes; or

(b) any employee who (1) has completed the course of specialized intellectual instruction and study described in clause (iv) of paragraph (a) and (ii) is performing related work under the supervision of a professional person to qualify himself to become a professional employee as defined in paragraph (a).

Note that the determination of a professional employee in paragraph (a) is based mainly on the work that is done rather than on the person's qualifications. This is not to say that the Board will not look at the backgrounds of the employees involved as an indication of whether or not their work requires "knowledge of an advanced type." But the primary and controlling consideration is job content and responsibility, as opposed to individual qualifications. Even in paragraph (b), which is directed primarily at the individual, the definition requires that the person be "performing related work."

As is the case with supervisors, professional status is not influenced by title, method of compensation, or exempt status under the FLSA. Thus engineers, lawyers, doctors, and other professionals who often identify with and are considered to be part of management may be employees for collective-bargaining purposes.

The law requires that professional employees be treated differently from other employees in a representation election. Section 9(b)(1) stipulates that they not be included in the same bargaining unit with nonprofessional employees unless a majority of the professional employees vote for such inclusion. Procedurally, this is done through an NLRB-conducted self-determination election, often called a Sonotone election.[9] In such an election the professional employees are asked (1) whether they wish to be included in the same unit as nonprofessional employees and (2) which union they prefer. If a majority of the professional employees choose to be included in the larger unit, their votes are counted along with those of the other employees. If not, they are counted separately to determine which union, if any, will represent the employees in the separate professional unit. However, if the proposed unit is *predominately* professional, no self-determination election is required.[10]

If the company starts early enough, it can have some influence on the determination of a professional unit. However, to do this effectively, the company must first determine what arrangement would work to its advantage.

In most cases, one relatively large bargaining unit is preferable to two or more smaller ones, since smaller units are easier targets for the union. In addition, a relatively large unit will have a more mixed group of employees, which usually works to the disadvantage of the union. Should the union win the election, it will still generally be to the advantage of the employer to have one unit, since this precludes the possibility of "whipsawing" (each union using the other's settlement as a floor in its negotiations) or the increased militancy that can result from two or more unions trying to outdo each other. There is also the advantage of having to administer only one labor agreement and face one expiration date. Thus, in most cases, the employer should be opposed to a separate professional (or other) bargaining unit.

There are two important exceptions to this generalization. A separate unit may be preferable (1) when the employer is fairly certain that the professional employees will not vote union (even after the production workers have done so) and the production process allows for partial operation by supervisory, managerial, and other nonstriking employees during a work stoppage, or (2) when the work of the professional employees can go on uninterrupted by the strike. If either the professional employees are likely to go union (now or in the future) or production cannot be continued during a strike, or if the professional employees cannot continue their activities during a strike, it would be to the employer's advantage to have a single unit.

One way to avoid the problems associated with a separate professional unit is not to hire professionals. This may require designing and staffing jobs in such a way as to minimize the need for professional employees. Or it may be possible to turn the professional employees into "supervisors" by assigning them duties that conform to Section 2(11) of the Act.

Notice that, as with most of the preventive labor relations strategies described, lead time is essential. The company cannot wait until the union is at the gate to start restructuring itself.

Plant Guards

Section 9(b)(3) of the National Labor Relations Act states in part:

> . . . the Board shall not . . . (3) decide that any unit is appropriate for such
> purposes if it includes, together with other employees, any individual
> employed as a guard to enforce against employees and other persons rules to
> protect property of the employer or to protect the safety of persons on the
> employer's premises; but no labor organization shall be certified as the
> representative of employees in a bargaining unit of guards if such organization
> admits to membership employees other than guards.

This direct prohibition against including guards and nonguards in the same bargaining unit is sensibly designed to prevent conflicts of interest among the ranks of the plant guards during a work stoppage. This is an important provision for the company that intends to continue operation during a strike. Not only are the guards most needed at such times to protect company property, but their presence may also be important reassurance to employees and customers crossing a picket line. Security personnel are also important to preventive labor relations in keeping unauthorized personnel, including union organizers, off the premises and restricting the unauthorized movement of employees within the plant, as discussed in Chapter 2.

While guard status is usually clear-cut, there are some situations under which "watchmen" or similar job classifications may not be considered guards. The determination is based on their duties. When in the course of making their rounds, the watchmen also "enforce company rules and prevent unauthorized individuals from entering plant property," they are considered guards by the NLRB. When their responsibilities are limited to checking for fire hazards and the like, they are not guards.

Note that the duties of guard and watch personnel are determined by management. The firm intent on remaining nonunion or weathering a strike should it become unionized is well advised to make sure that it has enough security personnel on hand to protect its property and working personnel during a strike. On the other hand, if the company hires a significant number of older, relatively "safe" individuals as watchmen, it may be better to have them in the unit for election purposes. Additional guards can be hired as needed from agencies that specialize in such services.

Confidential Employees

Board policy excludes certain employees who have access to confidential labor relations information from the bargaining unit. The term "confidential" is restricted to "only those employees who assist and act in a confidential capacity to persons who formulate, determine, and effectuate management policy in the field of labor relations."[11] While this is a narrow definition and the Board has refused to expand it over the years, there may be room for maneuvering under the right circumstances.

Confidential status may extend to employees who substitute for regular confidential secretaries. In addition, the secretaries of vice presidents and of the secretary treasurer of a company were found to be confidential because of their presence on occasion at meetings where labor relations matters were discussed.[12] Of course, management determines which secretaries fill in for others during absences. The employer also determines which managers are involved in meetings where confidential labor relations matters are discussed and which managers receive such written information.

While there are limits to the confidential-employee exclusion, it should not be overlooked as a preventive labor relations tool under the right circumstances. I once worked in an office that had about ten secretaries. Five of them were clearly confidential for representational purposes: one worked for the labor relations staff; the other four worked for division vice presidents who were regularly informed of and involved in confidential labor relations matters. A sixth secretary worked for a regional traffic manager who was regularly consulted on labor relations matters concerning several Teamsters contracts and may also have been excludable. Human nature being what it is, it is unlikely that the remaining four secretaries would have been willing to pay union dues, possibly go on strike, and incur the other costs and risks of unionization for the benefit of the whole group. In addition, the attractiveness of the office as an organizing target from the perspective of a union was greatly reduced. There was little chance of that office ever being organized; and even if it was, the employees in the remaining bargaining unit would not have been in a position to mount an effective strike.

While this was a regional office of a large corporation and may represent an extreme example, the possibility of excluding a number of employees from an office unit should not be ignored. Under the right circumstances, such exclusions can improve the company's chances of deterring or defeating the union or enhance its ability to withstand a work stoppage should the union prevail.

Independent Contractors

Another group of employees who may be excludable from the bargaining unit is independent contractors. Section 2(3) of the Act, in defining "employee," excludes "any individual having the status of an independent contractor." The term was left undefined, and the NLRB and the courts have followed a policy of determining independent-contractor status on a case-by-case basis according to the common-law principles of agency. The major principle relied upon by the Board is the right-to-control test.[13] Under this test, an employer–employee relationship exists when the company controls not only the end to be achieved but also the means to be used in achieving it. If, on the other hand, the control is limited to the result sought and the party performing the work is free to do the job as it thinks best, an independent-contractor relationship exists.

The above statement oversimplifies the matter. In making its determination, the Board balances all the evidence relevant to the relationship. It is specifically not controlled by such things as a written agreement between the parties defining one of them as an independent contractor, the fact that the company does not make payroll or Social Security tax deductions, or the fact that the claimed independent contractor is free to solicit business on its own. Rather, the Board looks at the total relationship in empirical terms in light of the common-law principles of agency.

It is impossible to generalize about the independent-contractor relationship. If it appears that the employer may benefit from having a group of individuals considered independent contractors for representational purposes, advice of counsel should be sought. The following discussion will be limited to those situations in which an independent-contractor relationship may be desirable.

One situation that often leads itself to the independent-contractor relationship is trucking. A company may be able to farm out its pickup and delivery or interplant transport functions in such a way as to remove the drivers involved from the employee classification. In practice, this removes them from the employ and control of the company rather than simply removing them from a larger potential bargaining unit, since such people would normally be considered to be in a separate unit anyway. The arrangement usually results in a number of independent owners–operators rather than a group of employees. This almost guarantees the absence of labor problems in the company's trucking operations and may preclude the necessity of dealing with the Teamsters. The possible costs of such an arrangement are twofold. One is that the company loses control of its trucking activities. If scheduling or customer contact by drivers is important, the cost may be prohibitive. The second is that if the company farms out only part of its operation, the drivers who become independent contractors are removed from the remaining potential bargaining unit. This would make the remaining unit smaller and possibly easier to unionize.

A second, and related, activity that lends itself to the independent-contractor relationship is installation and service. This activity is important in nongrocery retail establishments, especially department stores, where major appliances, drapes, carpeting, and many other products are sold with installation and some degree of warranty or service provided. Farming out such work often makes sense from a purely operational point of view. In addition, it removes from the generally safer sales population a group of employees who may be more inclined to unionize.

Other situations in which independent-contractor relationships have been found include newspaper distributorships, gas station lessees, freelance photographers, and musicians. The Board has declined to find such a relationship for certain salesmen, cab drivers, and car transporters. Again, the determination is made on an empirical basis and hinges on the principles of agency, especially on the degree of control retained by the company.

Part-Time and Temporary Employees

There are often bargaining unit questions concerning part-time, temporary, student, probationary, casual, seasonal, and on-call employees. Beyond noting that part-timers will usually be included in the unit and that the status of the other groups hinges on their relationship to the employer, it is difficult to generalize in this area. The point to be made is that the employer who hires significant numbers of nonregular employees would be wise to consult an attorney on the bargaining unit status of such employees early enough to make any changes needed to get them into or out of the bargaining unit as appropriate.[14]

SELECTED INDUSTRY PATTERNS

This section will examine a number of industry bargaining unit patterns and principles developed by the Board over the years. Caution is urged. For every generalization or recognized "rule," there are numerous exceptions based on the particulars of the situations.

Construction Industry

The NLRB has a long history of approving separate craft units in the construction industry. That is, bargaining units consisting of all plumbers, all carpenters, and other craft groups are usually deemed appropriate.[15] This pattern is supported by the craft form of unionization, which is all but universal in that part of the construction industry which is organized. Bargaining unit questions usually concern the appropriate division between crafts and have limited application to preventive labor relations.

Drivers

When a union petitions for an election for a group of drivers, the single-terminal bargaining unit is presumptively appropriate. When a petition is made to include the drivers in a larger bargaining unit or when the drivers do not constitute a homogeneous group, the matter becomes more complicated.[16]

Prior to 1961, the NLRB included drivers and driver-salesmen in larger production and maintenance units in the absence of an agreement by the parties to do otherwise or another labor organization seeking to represent them. In 1962 the Board abandoned this policy and adopted what is known as the Koester rule,[17] under which driver unit determinations were to be based on:

> 1. "Whether the truck drivers and plant employees have related or diverse duties, the mode of compensation, hours, supervision, and other conditions of employment."
> 2. "Whether they are engaged in the same or related production processes or operations, or spend a substantial portion of their time in such production or adjunct activities."[18]

Thus the determination of driver units is now based on community of interest. As a result, a unit determination can go either way, depending upon the facts. The Board has held that drivers should be included in plantwide (terminalwide) units when:

> 1. The drivers spend much of their time performing the same duties as other employees at the terminal.
> 2. Some of the terminal employees perform some driving duties.
> 3. Drivers have the same supervision, common compensation plan, and substantially the same conditions of employment as other employees.

Under almost all circumstances it will be to the advantage of the non-union employer to have drivers included in a unit with other terminal or production and maintenance employees. A separate unit of drivers is usually vulnerable to the union organizer. If the production and maintenance employees go union, it is unlikely that a group of drivers will remain nonunion for long. And if, after the election, the production and maintenance employees engage in a strike, it will usually be of little value to have the drivers in a separate unit and still on the job (assuming that they do not honor the picket line of the other employees). Note that the company controls the determinants of community of interest, as outlined above. As usual, the company must start early.

The Board has found separate units for drivers and driver-salesmen when the driving duties of the latter were incidental to the sales function. Driver-salesmen have also been excluded from plantwide units. Similarly, local drivers and over-the-road drivers have been held to be in separate units. As usual, community of interest is the major determinant.

Hospitals

The Board has a history of finding that all nonprofessional employees in a proprietary hospital usually belong in the same bargaining unit. Professional employees constitute appropriate separate bargaining units. In 1974 Congress extended the coverage of the National Labor Relations Act to not-for-profit hospitals.[19] This has resulted in a great deal of recent organizing activity and election-related litigation concerning hospitals.

The Board has given considerable weight to a successful history of bargaining where one exists and where the existing arrangements do not seriously violate the spirit of the Act or established Board policy. This is an important consideration, since many of the newly covered hospitals have units that were voluntarily recognized or established by various state agencies, which can complicate the bargaining unit determination.

In the absence of a history of bargaining, the Board has usually held against the creation of numerous small units. However, the situation is so fluid and there have been so many exceptions and dissenting opinions by Board members that it is difficult to generalize.[20] The Board has recently reaffirmed its position that bargaining unit decisions in hospital cases will be based on community of interest and a Congressional admonition against unit proliferation.[21]

Nursing Homes

The Board asserted jurisdiction over proprietary nursing homes in 1967. The bargaining unit question is usually simple and noncontroversial in such cases, with the exception of licensed practical nurses. In recent years the Board, observing that the duties of the licensed practical nurses vary considerably from one nursing home to another, has both included and excluded them depending on the nature of their duties and community of interest.[22]

Manufacturing

The manufacturing plant is the standard against which most other business organizations are compared for representation purposes. Most of the considerations discussed above either originated in manufacturing or apply to manufacturing along with other industries.

In general, the single-location, plantwide unit is presumptively appropriate. This will be modified by the exclusion of supervisors, guards, certain professionals, and other employee groups with a separate, identifiable community of interest. In addition, a single-plant unit will sometimes be incorporated into a larger multiplant or even multiemployer bargaining unit because of the particulars of the situation.

Retail

Preventive labor relations is particularly important in the retail industry. Because of that, and because of the enormous size and complexity of the industry, it has generated a considerable amount of material on bargaining units. The basic rule in retail is that the single-location, storewide unit is presumptively appropriate. However, there are numerous questions and qualifications that surround this generalization.[23]

1. *Multilocation units.* The general rule is that the single-location unit is presumptively appropriate unless the employees involved have been merged into a larger unit by a history of bargaining or are so integrated with the personnel of other stores (plants) as to have lost their separate identity.

At one time the Board had a policy that retail outlets in a chain were to be included in a bargaining unit coextensive with the employer's administrative structure or geographical area of operation. In 1962 the policy was changed. Today the rule is that the proposed retail unit will be considered either appropriate or inappropriate in light of all the circumstances in the case.[24]

This shift in Board policy is important for preventive labor relations purposes. While it does not rule out the possibility of multilocation units in retail, it does reduce the employer's chances of getting such a unit. For all practical purposes, the single-store unit has become the standard. Of course, it is easier for a union to organize one store in a chain than several stores that are spread over a wide geographical area.

2. *Selling and nonselling employees.* As mentioned, the storewide

84

unit is presumptively appropriate. However, separate units for nonselling employees may be allowed under various circumstances. In the absence of a history of bargaining or agreement among the parties, the matter hinges on the now familiar community-of-interest considerations.

In almost all cases, the so-called wall-to-wall, storewide unit is most effective for preventive labor relations purposes. One reason for this is the inherent safety of a large unit, as discussed earlier. It is easier for a labor organization to organize a relatively small, concentrated, and homogeneous group of employees than the entire store. In addition, a typical nongrocery retail operation will employ a number of different employee types. As will be discussed in Chapter 4 some employee types are easier to unionize than others. A work group made up of prime-age males who install tires and mufflers or unload trucks is, other things being equal, extremely vulnerable. However, if these employees are incorporated into a comprehensive storewide unit, their pro-union potential can be offset by the larger number of sales employees, who may have been chosen in part for their relative safety.

As usual, it is the employer who is in command of the determinants of community of interest upon which such unit questions are based. Care should be taken not to create a separate unit (or a number of separate units) of nonselling employees. This can be done by establishing common supervision, compensation plans, and working conditions and by regularly transferring, promoting, and interchanging personnel across potential bargaining unit lines. For example, major appliances usually require a certain amount of backroom setup and preparation work in addition to the actual selling. If both sales and backroom employees are placed in the same department under the same supervision, and if it is common for the sales employees to engage in some backroom work and for the backroom personnel to engage in some customer contact, or occasionally be promoted from setup to sales, it would be impossible for a union to claim or the NLRB to find that the nonsales employees constituted an appropriate separate bargaining unit.

This is an important and by no means academic matter for a retail establishment. The Board has found separate units for employees working in alteration departments (tailors), bakeries, carpet workrooms, display departments, restaurants, and appliance service centers in some department stores. It is likely that, had the various employers structured their organizations in such a way as to create more community of interest between these employee groups and the remainder of the workforce, the smaller units would not have been found appropriate and the unions would have been almost automatically defeated.

3. *Warehouse units.* A special case of the selling–nonselling employee problem involves warehouse personnel. The general rule is that a separate warehouse unit is appropriate when (1) the warehouse is geographically separate from the store; (2) there is separate supervision; and (3) there is no substantial integration between warehouse and other employees. Given the kind of personnel needed for most warehouse jobs and their regular contact with unionized employees of other companies (drivers), a warehouse that meets these three criteria is vulnerable.

The solution is obvious. Warehouses should be located near retail outlets whenever possible, supervision should be overlapping, and there should be some transfer, promotion, and/or interchange of personnel between the warehouse and stores. Note once again that such arrangements are entirely under the control of the company, provided it starts early. In the case of locating a warehouse, an especially early start may be needed.

This situation raises one of the many interesting conflicts that run through preventive labor relations. Retail outlets must be located where the customers are, which often means in cities. However, it may be safer to place a warehouse or distribution center in a more remote location where the chances of remaining nonunion are better. Although there is no easy solution to this dilemma, a company should go into a warehouse location decision with at least an awareness of the trade-off involved.

4. *Licensed departments.* Licensed departments are common in department and discount stores. Under such an arrangement the licensor (or lessor) leases space, services, and the right to merchandise certain products to a licensee (or lessee). Thus what appears to the public to be the hardware, liquor, or pharmacy department is in most respects an independent business.

The general rule under such circumstances is that the licensor and licensee are joint employers when the licensor is in a position to influence or control the licensee's labor policies. When the agreement reserves to the licensor the actual control of labor relations, or when the licensor has the right to dissolve the relationship and retains overall management control and/or the right to establish the manner and methods of work performed, a joint employer relationship will usually be found.

The importance of this matter is that if an establishment consists of 20 different employers, it may logically consist of 20 different bargaining units. Thus a union could petition for an election for a handful of employees who work in, say, the hardware department. The potential for industrial-relations chaos is obvious. Fortunately, the problem is easy to avoid; indeed, under most circumstances the parties would have to go out of their way to create such a problem. It would be unusual for the licensor not to retain control over employment matters, at least to the extent of requiring minimum standards of wages, hours, conditions, employee selection, and discipline. To do otherwise would be to invite problems under state and federal wage and hour laws, the Occupational Safety and Health Act, and the Civil Rights Act, not to mention the National Labor Relations Act. And since the public perceives the store as a single entity, the performance of the employees in one licensed department reflects upon the rest of the store and the entire chain.

A special case involves the employees of a licensee who do not normally work on the premises. For example, in the greeting cards section an employee of the licensee may show up every week or so to straighten out and restock the display. The licensee may have many such operations and have a number of employees who do this kind of work. An individual licensor would have little or no claim to the control of employee relations of such a licensee. Thus if a union petitioned for an election for the employees of the licensee, the unit would be small and the chance of a union victory large. Under the right circumstances this could create a situation similar to the unionized subcontractor or delivery truck driver discussed in Chapter 2. The same precautions and solutions apply.

NOTES

1. Office of the General Counsel, National Labor Relations Board, *An Outline of Law and Procedure in Representative Cases,* Washington, D.C.: U.S. Government Printing Office, 1974, p. 158. Hereinafter, NLRB, op. cit.
2. Ibid., pp. 130–131.
3. This discussion and its supporting data exclude decertification, deauthorization, and a few other types of NLRB-conducted elections. That is, it is limited to the so-called RC and RM petition elections.
4. NLRB, op. cit., p. 132.
5. Ibid., p. 151.
6. Ibid., pp. 129 and 149.
7. Ibid., p. 225.
8. Ibid., p. 246.
9. Sonotone Corporation, 90 NLRB 1236.

10. NLRB, op. cit., pp. 238 and 269–271.
11. Ibid., p. 243.
12. Ibid., p. 244.
13. Ibid., pp. 217–219.
14. For additional information, see ibid., pp. 256–266.
15. Ibid., pp. 168–169.
16. Ibid., pp. 169–175.
17. E. H. Koester Bakery Co., Inc., 136 NLRB 1006.
18. NLRB, op. cit., p. 170.
19. Public Law 93-360, 88 Stat. 395. The exclusion worded "or any corporation or association operating a hospital, if no part of the net earnings inures to the benefit of any private shareholder or individual" was deleted from the definition of "employer" in Section 2(2) of the Act.
20. 41 NLRB Annual Report 49–60 (1976).
21. National Labor Relations Board, News Release, "NLRB Defends Unit Approach to Health Care Industry, States Unit Proliferation Has Been Avoided," December 24, 1978. To date, the Board has found units appropriate for physicians, registered nurses, all professionals except physicians and registered nurses, technical employees, office and clerical employees, and service and maintenance employees. Narrower units for powerhouse and maintenance employees have also been approved.
23. Ibid., pp. 149–151, 182–184, 189–193.
24. Sav-On Drugs, Inc., 138 NLRB 1032.

4

EMPLOYEE SELECTION

A question central to the subject of preventive labor relations is: Which employee types or groups are most inclined to join or support unions *voluntarily* and why? If a nonunion company had reliable information on this, it could greatly improve its chances of remaining nonunion by simply selecting a safe workforce and/or by eliminating those causes of union interest that are important to employees. Many companies do exactly that, often with a high degree of success. However, this matter is by no means simple, and there are many myths and conventions abroad that must be treated with caution. Recent study suggests that there is no segment of the population that can be consistently counted on to vote for or against unionization when job conditions warrant.[1]

One of the problems that the nonunion firm faces in this area is that it may not discriminate on the basis of union membership or sympathy in its hiring or personnel decisions. Section 8(a)(3) of the National Labor Relations Act makes it an employer unfair labor practice to discriminate "in regard to hire or tenure of employment or any term or condition of employment to encourage or discourage membership in any labor organization. . . ." Clearly, refusing to hire known union members or supporters because of that membership or support would constitute an unfair labor practice. Discriminating on the basis of probable union attitude would probably also violate the law; however, as a practical matter it would be most difficult to identify and prove such discrimination.

The practical effect of this prohibition is to constrain what an employer may ask on an employment application or in an interview. However, these matters have been so constrained by equal employment and affirmative action requirements that the union-related restriction is not very troublesome. An experienced employee relations manager can obtain needed information from indirect questions or from voluntarily submitted material. When the information needed to make an informed decision is not available, the prudent company should decide *not* to hire. From a preventive labor relations perspective, it is better not to hire ten applicants who may have turned out to be "safe" than to hire one union supporter or organizer. Of course, such a policy will require additional expenditure on recruitment and selection or higher wages and benefits in order to get a workforce of the same quality. Discrimination, for whatever reason, costs money. The elimination of part of the applicant pool must be offset either by a decline in the quality of the employees hired or by an increase in the resources allocated for recruitment and selection and possibly compensation in the long run.

The more difficult question is who to hire. That is, what constitutes a "safe" hire? This is one of those questions that grows in compexity the more it is examined. Perhaps the best thing is not to look too closely. Many practitioners have a feel for what constitutes a "safe" hire, and their track record indicates that they know what they are doing. However, their decisions are often based on assumptions that are at least questionable when applied to the general situation. This is not to say that they are inaccurate. An assumption that may be valid in, say, banking may be less valid in retail and completely unsupportable as a generalization for the whole economy. There may also be important differences between parts of the country or the degree of urbanization of particular labor markets. Thus a profile developed in the Southern textile industry which may be highly predictive in that environment could prove totally inaccurate for a chain of discount centers in Los Angeles.

There is general agreement within the employee relations community that some employee types are more difficult to organize than others. Union organizers share these beliefs. In brief, it is held that women are more difficult to organize than men; older, and especially long-service, workers more difficult to organize than younger new hires; and people from middle-class backgrounds more difficult to organize than those identifiable as working class. Job applicants who have previously belonged to unions are considered especially dangerous. There are also observations about race, ethnicity, religion, and political affiliation that are less in vogue than they once were but that may still influence some hiring decisions. Finally, it is widely held that white-collar and part-time or temporary workers are more difficult to unionize than their blue-collar and full-time counterparts.

While there may be some validity to these beliefs, examination produces more questions than answers. The problem seems to lie in the assumption that such relationships are stable over time and independent of context.

The highlights of this conventional wisdom, with appropriate comment, are outlined below. It is recognized that this discussion has a strong "strawman" quality. Few practitioners believe in all the generalizations mentioned, and many have never explicitly "thought through" the factors that go into a conclusion that a particular employee type is, or is not, relatively safe. Many of the generalizations on the subject are questionable and must be tempered with informed judgment. However, since it would be impossible to discuss the preventive labor relations aspects of employee selection along such lines, the "strawman" will serve as an expository convenience.

WOMEN

It is often heard that women are more difficult to organize than men. This is untrue, and most of the research available that supports the myth is dated or questionable.[2] If women ever were less inclined to join unions than men, the reason lies in labor force attachment and the other factors surrounding the employment relationship, not in any inherent attitudinal difference. As those factors have changed over the years, the assumption that women are "safe" has become seriously dated. A recent study reports that 40 percent of the female employees of nonunion establishments would vote for a union, as compared with 30 percent for employees in general.[3] Of course, the 30 percent includes the women, so the difference is even more pronounced than would appear at first glance.

Historically, women have been concentrated in less skilled and less strategically placed occupations than men. An important theme running through the history of labor in America is that the more highly skilled craft-type employees were the first to unionize and usually the only ones who could sustain effective organization. Because of sociocultural attitudes and the usual child-related need to withdraw from the labor force, women were seldom given the training for such occupations. The more recent industrial type of union organization made possible by the passage of the National Labor Relations Act in 1935 was concentrated in manufacturing and in occupations dominated by men. In both cases, unions were able to organize and remain organized because of their ability to exert meaningful economic pressure on the employer. In the absence of such an ability it is considerably more difficult for a union either to force effective recognition or successfully perform for its members. It may also have been the case that male-oriented unions have been less effective in communicating their message to women.

Both conditions have changed. Women are increasingly found in nontraditional work situations; and many unions, especially those with an interest in industries that employ large numbers of women, use more female organizers. Moreover, women's liberation (or feminism) has spread to the union movement. Many women in traditionally female occupations now perceive unions as instruments to redress the wrongs of sexual discrimination. This has become a particularly potent issue in campaigns to organize office employees, where the unions have been quick to recognize and exploit an often valid complaint on the part of female employees. This development at least calls into question the generalization about women being hard to organize. Indeed, it may have reversed it.

Another important consideration is that a disproportionate number of women work part time. In 1976, almost 70 percent of the 11 million employees voluntarily working part time in the United States were women.[4] For reasons that will be discussed separately, part-time employees (male or female) tend to be difficult to organize.

In 1976 there were 84 million people employed in nonagricultural establishments in the United States. Women comprised 35 million, or about 41 percent, of this civilian labor force.[5] In 1976 the membership of unions and employee associations was 26.7 percent female (22 percent for unions alone). The percentage of total membership was up from 25 percent for unions and associations from 1974.[6]

It may appear from the above that the female portion of the labor force is less well organized than the male. However, it must be remembered that we are looking at the accumulated results of history. While data on the number of women who are presently being unionized are not available, a glance at the unions experiencing the most rapid growth in membership suggests a different picture.

From 1966 to 1976, eight labor organizations grew by more than 100,000 members. As indicated in Table 4-1, six of them reported substantial to high proportions of women members.[7] This suggests that women account for much of the recent growth in the more effectively organizing unions. The picture is complicated by the fact that women are

TABLE 4-1. FEMALE MEMBERSHIP IN THE MOST RAPIDLY GROWING UNIONS (IN THOUSANDS).

	Membership		Increase		Women Members in 1976	
	1964	1976	Number	Percent	Number	Percent
State/county employees	281	957	676	241	300	44
Teachers (AFT)	125	446	321	257	268	60
Teamsters	1,651	1,889	238	14	NR*	—
Steelworkers	1,068	1,300	232	22	163	13
Service employees	349	575	226	65	201	35
Communications workers	321	483	162	50	266	55
Laborers	475	627	152	32	6	1
Retail clerks†	500	699	199	40	336	48

*NR means not reported.

† Merged with Amalgamated Meat Cutters and Butcher Workmen June 7, 1979, to form the United Food and Commercial Workers International Union (AFL–CIO) with a combined membership of 1.2 million.

Source: U.S. Department of Labor, Bureau of Labor Statistics, *Directory of National Unions and Employee Associations, 1975,* Bulletin 1937, Washington, D.C.: U.S. Government Printing Office, 1977, p. 103, App. E. Ibid. 1977, p. 100, App. E-1. Bureau of Labor Statistics, *News,* "Labor Union and Employee Association Membership, 1976," Released Labor Day Weekend 1978 (undated), p. 7, Table 7.

entering the labor force at an increasing rate and are remaining longer. Also, there has been a disproportionate amount of growth in the service and public sectors, which have traditionally employed relatively high percentages of women.

Many of these women, like many of the men, were brought into the labor organizations automatically by the operation of previously negotiated union-shop agreements. However, the evidence indicates that large numbers of women have voluntarily joined unions in recent years. Common sense suggests that this will continue to be the case. In fact, when we consider the areas of the economy that are experiencing growth, along with the changing attitudes on labor force entry and attachment, the changing career expectations of many women, and the explosive social phenomenon of the women's movement, it would be surprising if these changes were not reflected in representation election results in the 1980s.

If the assumption that women were safer than men from a union prevention point of view was ever valid, it is not so today. Other things being equal, women will be *easier* to organize than men during the 1980s.

AGE

It is commonly thought that older workers are safer—more difficult to organize—than their younger counterparts. Again, reservations are in order. A distinction must be made between age per se and length of service. Newly hired 40-year-olds warrant different generalizations than 40-year-olds who have been with the company for 15 years.

Are older job applicants safer than younger job applicants from a preventive labor relations perspective? If there ever was an answer to this question, it is rapidly becoming out of date. For any given job applicant, the answer will depend on his previous experience, work-related attitudes, and expectations.

Not too many years ago the typical older worker had formed his attitudes toward work in the pre-World War II depression period. In many cases this bred a stoicism and appreciation of a steady job that often worked to the advantage of the nonunion employer. Work may not always have been pleasurable, but few people expected it to be. Further, the memories of the massive unemployment of the 1930s and the many protracted strikes of the postwar 1940s left their mark.

The individual who turned 40 in 1980 was born in 1940 and grew up in the relatively affluent 1950s, with the period's attendant high employment and steadily improving standard of living. How will this different frame of reference affect the work-related attitudes of the older job applicant of the 1980s? It will depend on how well the person's experience fits in with his expectations. If such people are seeking a job because of a layoff or involuntary termination, they may be susceptible to the union message. On the other hand, if they are seeking a job because of a desire to improve themselves or a dissatisfaction with their present position, they are likely to be relatively safe. (The question of whether they are coming from a unionized work situation will be discussed separately.)

Long-service employees are a different matter. This segment of the workforce is especially important to preventive labor relations. These employees are in a position to communicate to younger workers that the employer has always been fair and reasonably responsive to their needs, that work has been steady and free of strikes, that they have never needed a union to represent them, and that previous attempts to unionize the plant have not fared well. Of course, if these workers do not hold such favorable opinions, they can do a great deal of damage to an otherwise effective preventive labor relations program.

Nothing will turn a loyal long-service employee from a supporter of a union-free company into a union member faster than rumors of impending loss of work. The Age Discrimination in Employment Act notwithstanding, older people have difficulty finding jobs, especially jobs comparable to the ones they left. One of the most important things that a collective-bargaining agreement gives to the worker is a high degree of predictability. Layoffs, should they occur, follow some system of seniority. Thus the employees can make a fairly accurate assessment of their chances of remaining on the job until retirement. In addition, layoffs and recalls occur in an orderly and predictable fashion that is perceived to be fair by those laid off and by those remaining on the job. Obviously, a sense of relative security is important for maintaining employee morale and for developing feelings of loyalty to the company. This is especially so for long-service employees. When layoffs are handled in a less fair and less predictable manner, important questions are raised: "Will I be next? Will that happen to me when I am 55? And what can I do about it?"

It goes without saying that management should do all in its power to avoid or minimize layoffs. When this is not possible because of seasonal or other predictable reasons, the layoffs should take place among the relatively short-service employees, and those employees should have been hired with the understanding that a layoff was at least possible. When the layoff is not an expected event, the rules on layoffs discussed in Chapter 5 should be followed in order to minimize the impact of the action. Further, management should do everything possible to quell unfounded rumors of a staff reduction before they are blown out of proportion.

A second important personnel concern to older workers is retirement income, a subject that will be dealt with in more detail in Chapter 7. It is dangerous for a company with a significant number of older employees to operate for any length of time without a respectable pension plan. If there is no pension plan in existence or if the plan compares unfavorably with those of unionized plants, the union organizer has a powerful issue that may prove effective with those long-service employees assumed to be among the most loyal to the company. It follows that if a nonunion company employs a significant number of older workers, it must offer them a respectable pension plan. If this is not feasible, it must opt for a younger workforce and generate enough turnover to keep it young. In other words, either the compensation package fits the workforce or the workforce fits the compensation package.

SOCIOECONOMIC BACKGROUND

Given the fluidity of North American society, it is impossible to discuss class attitudes with confidence. The matter is complicated by ethnic, religious, and geographical considerations that render almost any generalization suspect. Nevertheless, common sense tells us that there are important socioeconomic differences among people that influence the way they feel about unionism.

A young person who has grown up in a home in which one or both parents are nonunion is probably safer than one whose parents are union members. If the parents are managers, professionals, or entrepreneurs, it is even more probable. The children of such parents usually inculcate attitudes that make them less receptive to the union message. This is not to say that all young people from union homes are easy to organize. Many are strongly opposed to unions because of a lengthy strike or other unfortunate union experience by a family member. However, the chances are pretty high that a young person whose parent is an engineer will be safer than one whose parent is a steelworker. Note how this observation interacts with the discussion on plant location in Chapter 2.

Similarly, a second-income spouse of a nonunion person is usually safer than the spouse of a union member. Again, the reason is the inculcation of values at home that influence attitudes on the job. The decision to join a union and incur the costs and risks of union membership is often a family decision. The attitudes of the other working spouse will definitely be a factor in the decision.

Level of education may also influence attitudes toward unionism. Education correlates highly with socioeconomic position, and managerial or professional status usually requires university education. More often than not, college graduates marry other college graduates and encourage their children to continue their education. Thus individualistic attitudes are likely to be transmitted and reinforced within an educated family. In addition, educated workers are often more able to see through the sometimes spurious claims of the union organizer or understand the market-imposed limits under which the employer operates.

There are important limitations to any generalization about the impact of background on attitudes toward unions. Many young people from nonunion homes go through a period of experimentation that may include an interest in unionism or other "isms." The "safe" working wife may become convinced that union representation is a necessary adjunct of the women's movement or some other cause. An educated and able person may view union membership as a means to an end or as the only way of dealing with a difficult employment situation. Most important, whole categories of once-safe employees in the public sector have gone union. Given the personal interactions within families, neighborhoods, and social organizations and a certain amount of mobility between the public and private sectors, this will prove important in the years ahead.

ETHNIC BACKGROUND

One occasionally hears comments to the effect that blacks or other minority group members are less difficult to organize than whites, that Catholics of Eastern European extraction are more inclined toward collective action than their Protestant Yankee counterparts, or that Democrats are more inclined to vote union than Republicans. While there may at one time may have been some truth to such statements, it would be difficult to defend them today in the absence of firm proof. Even then, it must be remembered that there are differences in attitude within and between ethnic groups and that these attitudes change over time. To a considerable extent, the "melting pot" has done its job.

Getman, Goldberg, and Herman found a slight tendency for employees who identify with the Democratic Party and for minority-group members to have more favorable attitudes toward unions.[8] Kochan found that a surprising 67 percent of black and other minority-group employees would vote for a union.[9] Thus it would appear that hiring minority-group members, rather than being relatively safe, has become somewhat of a preventive labor relations detriment. Again, caution must be urged; the data probably hide more than they reveal. Moreover, in almost all work situations affirmative action objectives take precedence over preventive labor relations objectives in selection decisions.

On the other side of this issue, many blacks I have talked to have a generally unfavorable opinion of unions, usually because they believe that unions have engaged in racial discrimination and have restricted the entry of blacks into certain trades. While this has been true for some craft unions in the construction and railroad industries, it is not the case in the large industrial unions in manufacturing. Nor is it true in situations where the employer does not hire through a union-operated hiring hall and/or participate in a union-management apprenticeship program. Indeed, in the majority of organizing situations, the union can point with pride at its record of nondiscrimination and blame past employment discrimination on the company. When the workforce is made up of a large number of minority-group members, the union may even present itself as an instrument to press for minority interests. The combination of unionization and racial interest can result in a virulent form of unionism and collective bargaining, as the recent experience in California agriculture attests.

PRIOR UNION MEMBERSHIP

It is widely thought that hiring employees who have previously worked in a unionized setting is particularly hazardous. There is a certain logic to this. Whether or not the new employee is a conscious union supporter, he will be a source of information that may prove embarrassing to the employer. Other employees will have a certain curiosity about compensation and conditions in the unionized shop. If pay and conditions are (or appear to be) better in the unionized shop, problems may ensue. In addition, it is probable that sooner or later a work-related event will occur that will prompt the thought: "That wouldn't have happened at the last place. The union wouldn't have let them get away with it." This thought may arise even if the new employee was an unwilling union member in his previous job and is sincerely unsympathetic toward unionism. We all tend to remember the better parts of our experience and forget the bad.

The above reasoning was not supported by the findings of Getman, Goldberg, and Herman. In the representation elections they studied, 72 percent of the employees who had previous union experience voted *against* the union and gave unfavorable experience with unions as one of their reasons. Overall, previous negative experience with unions was a stronger factor in voting against unions than was positive experience in voting for unions.[10] It might be inferred from this that prior union experience is a desirable employee characteristic for the nonunion company— indeed, it might be if former *unfavorable* union experience could be identified. However, in the absence of other evidence, such a conclusion is unwarranted. The Getman, Goldberg, and Herman study focused on companies that had a union problem serious enough to result in a representation election. Thus it ignored those companies whose preventive labor relations programs were so effective that no problem appeared. Further, the fact that a former union member voted against the union does not mean that he did not contribute to the problem by providing information. It should not be assumed that the beneficial effect of the 72 percent "no union" vote of the former union members offsets the negative effect of the remaining 28 percent. The relationship may be the opposite.

It must be pointed out that in many locations it is impossible to avoid hiring people with prior union experience. Getman, Goldberg, and Herman found that 43 percent of their subjects had previous union experience and that 30 percent had voted in previous representation elections.[11] This should not be surprising. Since 1935, 30 million Americans have voted in 300,000 NLRB-conducted representation elections.[12] Since unions have won roughly half of these elections, resulting in a labor force that has been about one-quarter unionized, there is a good chance that a randomly selected group of job applicants will contain a sizable proportion of people who have prior union experience and/or who have voted in one or more representation elections. Of course, in those states with a high Union Risk Index (see Chapter 2) the chances are higher. Perhaps the best advice to the nonunion company is to avoid hiring people who have been members of those unions actively organizing in its industry. This will reduce the relevancy of the union information the employee brings into the new situation and will decrease the chances of hiring a vocal union supporter or organizer.

RETIRED MILITARY PERSONNEL

A special word is in order about retired military personnel. Other things being equal, such people are usually resistant to unionism. This observation pertains to the career person who retires after 20 or more years, not to the single hitcher. The career soldier or sailor usually develops a set of values that results in his viewing unions with suspicion or hostility.

Retired military personnel can be an important asset to a preventive labor relations program. When it is desirable to hire mature males, either because of the nature of the work or because of customer expectations, retired military personnel are often an excellent choice. Not only do they have a union-free background and the personal qualities resulting from a disciplined life; they also have substantial pensions, access to Veterans Administration health services, and other economic benefits not available to other workers. As a result, they will generally be more satisfied with the level of wages and benefits offered by the company and thus are less likely to be a source of union interest and support.

So far we have discussed characteristics that are specific to the employee or applicant. We now turn to characteristics that relate to the work itself.

WHITE-COLLAR WORKERS

It has long been held that white-collar workers are more difficult to organize than blue-collar workers. This is evidenced by the fact that union membership in the United States has historically been concentrated in the blue-collar occupations.

The terms "blue collar" and "white collar" are conveniences, not precise definitions. The border between them—sometimes aptly referred to as "gray collar"—is ill defined. Moreover, the distinction between blue- and white-collar union membership is usually determined by the responses to Bureau of Labor Statistics questionnaires within labor organizations. No doubt there are important differences in definition among unions and within the same union over time.

The term "white collar" applies to everything from lawyers and accountants to file clerks and sales personnel in grocery and department stores. The same type of white-collar work—say, secretarial/clerical—

may take place under circumstances ranging from the comfortable executive offices of a large corporation to the factorylike conditions of a steno pool to the production floor or loading dock itself. Thus generalizations about white-collar employees must be treated with care.

With the above cautions in mind, it is still possible to learn from the evidence available. As Table 4-2 indicates, white-collar union membership has grown steadily in both absolute and relative terms since 1956. When employee association membership is included in the figures since

TABLE 4-2. WHITE-COLLAR UNION AND EMPLOYEE ASSOCIATION MEMBERSHIP, 1956–1976.

Year	Number of White-Collar Members	Percent of Total Membership
Unions		
1956	2,463	13.6
1958	2,184	12.2
1960	2,192	12.2
1962	2,285	13.0
1964	2,585	14.4
1966	2,810	14.7
1968	3,176	15.7
1970	3,353	16.2
1972	3,434	16.5
1974	3,762	17.4
1976	3,857	18.4
Unions and Associations		
1970	4,917	21.8
1972	5,202	22.6
1974	5,881	24.3
1976	6,460	26.9

Source: 1956–1974: U.S. Department of Labor, Bureau of Labor Statistics, *Directory of National Unions and Employee Associations, 1975,* Bulletin 1937, Washington, D.C.: U.S. Government Printing Office, 1977, p. 67, Table 12. 1976: Bureau of Labor Statistics, *News,* "Labor Union and Employee Association Membership, 1976," Released Labor Day Weekend 1978 (undated), p. 4, Table 4.

1970 (the first year such data are available), the growth is even more impressive.

The figures suggest that much of the recent "growth" in the American labor movement has occurred among white-collar workers. That is, the decline in blue-collar membership has been largely offset by the organization of white-collar employees. This should not be surprising. Much of the growth in employment in recent years has been in the white-collar categories, especially within the public sector. Unions have naturally adjusted their organizing efforts to take advantage of this development. In many cases, union organizing has been facilitated by the passage of new public-sector collective-bargaining laws. While much of this growth has been in the so-called employee associations (which usually develop into unions once collective bargaining is available), a significant amount has been captured by the traditional trade unions.

A number of factors suggest that white-collar workers will be easier to organize in the 1980s than they have been in the past. In many employment situations the treatment of such employees has declined in absolute and especially in relative terms. As clerical operations have grown in size and the work has become more routine, the relationship between the employee and the job has come to resemble that of factory work. Salaried status, improved management style, and more pleasant surroundings cannot eliminate this basic fact for many white-collar employees. Further, as the compensation and conditions of blue-collar workers have improved over the years, the status distinctions between white- and blue-collar employees have blurred. There is nothing inherently wrong with this, provided peoples' expectations change accordingly. However, at some point the skilled secretary begins to wonder why *she* is making only half as much as the lift-truck operator.

Adding to the strength of white-collar unionism in the years ahead is the fact that many white-collar workers are female. As already discussed, the notion that women are safer than men is a myth. It has recently been found that female white-collar workers are more likely to support a union than their male counterparts.[13]

Another factor that will lead to more white-collar unionization in the 1980s is the coming of age of people born during the "baby boom" years. With the emphasis on education and training that has been so pronounced in the United States in the recent past, there will be a glut in the labor market of the 1980s of relatively well-educated people in the age group 25–44.[14] Many of them will be "dead-ended" in jobs that do not utilize all their training and do not meet all their expectations. It should not be surprising if they turn to union representation in greater numbers in an effort to improve their situations.

Finally, the labor relations developments in the public sector in recent years may influence white-collar unionization in the private sector. Many private-sector managers feel that events in government employment have little to do with them. This is a dangerous assumption. As white-collar workers in government agencies improve their terms of employment, either through union representation at the bargaining table or through the political process, their private-sector counterparts will learn from the example.

Table 4-3 depicts the percentage of plant and office employees covered

TABLE 4-3. PERCENTAGE OF PLANT AND OFFICE EMPLOYEES COVERED BY LABOR AGREEMENTS, 1967–1974.

Year	All Industries		Manufacturing		Non-manufacturing		Trans-portation, Communica-tion, and Other Public Utilities	
	Plant	Office	Plant	Office	Plant	Office	Plant	Office
1967–68	68	15	76	13	56	17	93	61
1969–70	67	15	76	13	53	16	92	61
1971–72	65	15	76	13	51	16	91	63
1972–74	63	14	75	12	49	15	90	61

Year	Wholesale Trade		Retail Trade		Finance, Insurance, and Real Estate		Selected Services	
	Plant	Office	Plant	Office	Plant	Office	Plant	Office
1967–68	55	8	37	14	—	2	53	8
1969–70	55	7	35	13	—	2	50	7
1971–72	57	8	33	12	—	2	48	8
1972–74	55	7	31	12	—	2	46	8

Note: Data relate to percentage of workers employed in establishments in which a contract or contracts covered a majority of workers in the respective categories.
Source: U.S. Department of Labor, Bureau of Labor Statistics, *Handbook of Labor Statistics, 1977,* Bulletin 1966, Washington, D.C.: U.S. Government Printing Office, 1977, p. 316, Table 144.

by labor agreements in metropolitan areas for the period 1967 through 1974. These are percentage figures, and they reflect the relative decline in union membership in the United States throughout the period. Of particular interest is the generally low level of unionization of office employees. The great exception to this fact occurs in "transportation, communication, and other public utilities," an industry group with a high degree of union organization among its nonoffice employees, much government regulation, and usually a monopolistic or oligopolistic market position. This suggests that the office employees have a special need for union representation to protect their interests in an otherwise organized setting; that the employers may not vigorously resist the unions because of their value as political allies before the Interstate Commerce Commission, Public Utility Commissions, and other agencies; and that the additional costs of union organization can be passed forward to consumers with the approval of the appropriate regulatory agency. Note how this contrasts with the "finance, insurance, and real estate" industry group, which is virtually unorganized.

PART-TIME WORKERS

A second job condition that is a function of the work rather than the individual is part-time status. Of course, this overlaps with other characteristics, such as sex and age. It is generally agreed that part-time workers are difficult to organize. Although no data exist on the number of part-time workers who voluntarily join or vote for unions, this generalization is supportable by casual observation and common sense.

Part-time employment has enormous importance to the American economy and to preventive labor relations. When the nature of the work lends itself to part-time employment, such as in much of the retail and banking industries, the use of part-timers can be an important part of a preventive labor relations program. Of course, this may be necessary from a purely operational perspective. Part-time employment is often an excellent way to cover peak hours or days and to tap an additional source of labor.

In 1976 there were 65 million people working full time in nonagricultural establishments and an additional 11 million voluntarily working part time.[15] Thus 14.4 percent of the employed nonagricultural workforce consisted of part-timers. As depicted in Table 4-4, 69.1 percent of them were women, and part-timers were concentrated in two industry groups in

TABLE 4-4. DISTRIBUTION OF NONAGRICULTURAL PART-TIME EMPLOYMENT IN 1976.

	Percent of Subtotal by Sex	Percent of Total Part-Time Employment
Sex and Age		
Male:		30.9
16 to 17	8.4	
18 to 24	10.9	
25 to 44	3.4	
45 to 64	3.4	
65 and over	4.8	
Female:		69.1
16 to 17	8.6	
18 to 24	14.0	
25 to 44	24.9	
45 to 64	17.2	
65 and over	4.4	
Industry Group		
Wage and salary workers:		90.4
Construction	1.6	
Manufacturing	5.2	
Transportation and public utilities	2.7	
Wholesale and retail trade	33.7	
Finance and services	44.8	
Other industries	2.4	
Self-employed and unpaid family workers		9.6

Source: U.S. Department of Labor, Bureau of Labor Statistics, *Handbook of Labor Statistics, 1977,* Bulletin 1966, Washington, D.C.: U.S. Government Printing Office, 1977, pp. 66–67, Table 21.

which preventive labor relations is of considerable interest: 33.7 percent in "wholesale and retail trade" and 44.8 percent in "finance and services." The characteristics of the part-time workforce have remained stable over the past decade, but its size in both absolute and percentage terms has grown significantly, as portrayed in Table 4-5. There is no reason to expect this upward trend to reverse. Indeed, given the current attention to leisure-time activities and the inflation-caused need for additional family income, part-time employment is likely to become an even more important factor in the American economy in the 1980s than it has been in the past.

TABLE 4-5. FULL-TIME AND VOLUNTARY PART-TIME WORKERS IN NONAGRICULTURAL ESTABLISHMENTS, 1967–1976 (IN MILLIONS).

Year	Full-Time Employees	Voluntary Part-Time Employees	Percent Part-Time
1967	56.9	8.0	12.3
1968	57.9	8.5	12.8
1969	59.2	9.0	13.2
1970	59.1	9.4	13.7
1971	59.2	9.6	14.0
1972	N.R.*	9.9	—
1973	63.6	10.3	13.9
1974	64.1	10.5	14.1
1975	62.0	10.6	14.6
1976	64.8	10.9	14.4

*Not reported (typographical error in source).
Source: U.S. Department of Labor, Bureau of Labor Statistics, *Handbook of Labor Statistics, 1977,* Bulletin 1966, Washington, D.C.: U.S. Government Printing Office, 1977, pp. 66–67, Table 21.

Part-time employment is of particular interest to the nonunion employer for a number of reasons. First, the part-time employee is often especially resistant to unionization. Many unions charge all members the same dues and fees regardless of the number of hours worked. When there is a reduction in dues for part-timers, it is seldom proportionate to the difference in earnings. The recent move by many unions toward a dues schedule based on a percentage of earnings has been concentrated in those industries with a predominately full-time workforce. This is understandable. It is the full-time industry-committed employees who are the most active and influential in the unions. It is unlikely that they would approve arrangements that benefit the less active and less influential part-timers. Union dues of, say, $15 per month take a significantly larger percentage out of the take-home pay of the part-timer than of the full-time employee. This is usually reinforced by the fact that full-time employees have higher wage rates than part-timers. Thus the relative cost of union representation is significantly higher for the part-time employee.

Second, part-time workers often have interests and needs that the union may not be able to satisfy. The part-timer who is a wife and mother, a college student, or a "moonlighter" may have scheduling needs that can better be met by an understanding employer than by the rigidities of a labor agreement. The case can be made that a union will curtail the employer's flexibility in this area by subjecting scheduling and job assignments to seniority or some other mechanistic procedure. Of course, an employer who has been unresponsive to this need may find that part-timers prefer the predictability of a bidding system that is based on seniority.

Third, the use of part-timers will increase the size of the bargaining unit. As noted in Chapter 3, as the number of employees in the bargaining unit increases, the incidence of representation elections and the percentage of union victories decline dramatically. In almost all cases, part-timers vote on an equal basis with full-time employees in NLRB-conducted elections.[16] If a company with 200 full-time equivalent positions staffs half of them with employees working 20 hours per week, it increases the number of voters in the bargaining unit from 200 to 300. A glance at Table 3-2 indicates that this move alone significantly reduces the company's chances of encountering a union drive and greatly increases its chances of winning a representation election.

TEMPORARY EMPLOYEES

Temporary employees are usually excluded from the bargaining unit and are, therefore, unimportant for representational purposes. However, seasonal workers may or may not be excluded, depending on the circumstances. The important distinction for preventive labor relations purposes lies between those employees who have a long-run commitment to the company and those whose interests in their present employment are essentially short-run. An example of the latter with particular interest for preventive labor relations is the college student working part time as a salesperson in a department or other retail store.

Such short-term employees typically have little invested in the job. Further, their time horizon is short, a few years at most. As a result, the benefits of union membership are reduced for such employees. Most of what they invest in the job—including any effort or financial expenditure they make in support of a labor organization—will be lost when they move on. In a way, they are the opposite of the typical part-time employee. The part-timer pays proportionately more for the same benefit. The short-termer pays the same for reduced benefits, since he will not be there to collect the long-run benefits of union representation.

The costs involved include union dues and any initiation fee the union imposes on new members (sometimes waived during an organizing drive), the risk of employer retaliation, and the risk or actual cost of a strike during or following the organizing drive. The benefits usually include a somewhat higher money wage (partially offset by union dues and fees), improved benefits (such as health and retirement plans), and more predictability and control over the employment situation through a seniority system and a grievance procedure terminating in outside arbitration. As a practical matter, many of the costs and risks of unionism to the unorganized employee are "front end" costs, while many of the benefits are long-run in nature. Assuming rationality and access to accurate information, the short-term employee will not be inclined to join a union. It should be kept in mind, however, that short-term employees are also less affected by some of the consequences of union activity. If, for instance, the short-term employee loses his job as the result of a termination, layoff, or lengthy work stoppage, the cost will usually be much less than it is to the long-service employee. This could result in a greater degree of bravado that may offset the inherent safety.

DIVERSIFICATION

There is no easy conclusion to a discussion of employee selection from a preventive labor relations perspective. Most of the traditional assumptions about certain employee groups are suspect. Yet when the various generalizations are tempered with judgment and are integrated into a larger preventive labor relations program, they seem to work. Historically, blue-collar prime-age males employed full time have been more inclined to join unions than the various employee groups discussed above.

Perhaps the best approach to employee selection for the nonunion employer is to strive for a healthy mix of employee types within the potential bargaining unit. A workforce consisting of employees who differ in sex, age, socioeconomic and ethnic background, work hours, attachment to their present employment, and the like may present the union organizer with an impossible problem. In the absence of an employment-related cause to rally around, how does a union tailor an organizing campaign to appeal to a workforce consisting of part-time college students, elderly women, and retired chief petty officers? Chances are, it doesn't.

Of course, there are operational and labor market limits to this pattern of employee selection. For example, heterogeneity may make it more difficult for the employees to communicate and cooperate with each other. If the tasks are technical or complicated, the training costs associated with using part-timers and short-term employees may be prohibitive. In some locations the employer may not have large numbers of certain employee types to choose from, and in a tight labor market or in relatively low-wage industries the choice may be further curtailed. Finally, and perhaps most important, a heterogeneous workforce makes it more difficult for the employer to offer a compensation package and create a work environment that satisfies most of the employees. Younger and lower-paid employees prefer to take the bulk of their compensation in money wages, while older and higher-paid employees usually prefer it in the form of retirement income or some other tax-sheltered benefit. Younger and more ambitious employees may prefer a faster work pace, stricter supervision, and promotion on the basis of performance and ability, while older workers may prefer an easier, more sociable, and more predictable work environment. Just as, in the absence of an employment-related cause to rally around, the union organizer has difficulty communicating with a mixed work group, so in the absence of some commonality the employer has difficulty motivating employees at a reasonable cost. Just where the limits lie varies from situation to situation and cannot be dealt with in a general discussion. However, it should be kept in mind that at some point the trade-offs involved translate into labor costs.

An analogy to finance may be of interest. An investor can get an average rate of return for less than average risk by diversification. That is, the investor can offset the risk associated with a particular stock by investing in other stocks. This eliminates the unsystematic risk associated with the particular stock while leaving the investor with only the systematic risk associated with the whole market. A similar line of reasoning may be applied to employee selection for preventive labor relations purposes.

If the company does not know the potential union risk associated with hiring particular employee types, it can eliminate the (nonsystematic) risk of a particular employee group by mixing along the lines discussed above. The arrangement will leave the company with the average risk for the labor market. This should logically be related to the local Union Risk Index developed in Chapter 2.

While it is not seriously suggested that random selection be used as a hiring criterion, deliberate diversification in employment decisions, in the absence of sound information on the union risk associated with particular employee groups, has value. This is especially true when a company enters a new area and does not have the contacts or the time to research the labor market for preventive labor relations purposes.

NOTES

1. Thomas A. Kochan, "How American Workers View Labor Unions," *Monthly Labor Review,* April 1979, p. 27.

2. Myron Roomkin and Hervy A. Juris, "Unions in the Traditional Sectors: The Mid-Life Passage of the Labor Movement," Industrial Relations Research Association, *Proceedings of the Thirty-First Annual Meeting,* August 29–31, 1978, p. 219.

3. Kochan, op. cit., p. 25.

4. U.S. Department of Labor, Bureau of Labor Statistics, *Handbook of Labor Statistics, 1977,* Bulletin 1966, Washington, D.C.: U.S. Government Printing Office, 1977, pp. 66–67, Table 21.

5. Ibid., pp. 21–22, Table 1.

6. U.S. Department of Labor, Bureau of Labor Statistics, *Directory of National Unions and Employee Associations, 1977,* Bulletin 1937, Washington, D.C.: U.S. Government Printing Office, 1979, p. 66, Table 10. Hereinafter *Directory of National Unions.* The difference between a union and an employee association is today more a matter of emphasis or degree than anything else. The American Federation of Teachers (AFL–CIO) is a union; the National Education Association (Ind.) an association. Yet they compete vigorously in organizing drives and representation elections, and both operate as labor organizations in those situations in which they have bargaining rights.

7. For information on female membership in other unions see *Directory of National Unions,* p. 100, Appendix E.

8. Julius G. Getman, Stephen B. Goldberg, and Jeanne B. Herman, *Union Representation Elections: Law and Reality,* New York: Russell Sage Foundation, 1976, p. 99.

9. Kochan, op. cit., p. 25.

10. Getman, Goldberg, and Herman, op. cit., p. 99.

11. Ibid., p. 140.

12. 42 NLRB Annual Report, p. 1 (1977).

13. Kochan, op. cit., p. 28.

14. Roomkin and Juris, op. cit., p. 220.

15. *Handbook of Labor Statistics, 1977,* loc. cit.

16. Office of the General Counsel, National Labor Relations Board, *An Outline of Law and Procedure in Representation Cases,* Washington, D.C.: U.S. Government Printing Office, 1974, pp. 256–258.

5

EMPLOYEE RELATIONS

An effective preventive labor relations program must be based on sound personnel practices. Few would argue with this propostion. Yet it is only part of the story. Complete reliance on the employee relations components of preventive labor relations is not enough. It is best to think of the items discussed in this chapter as one dimension of a comprehensive program of preventive labor relations.

It is not necessary to discuss the essentials of personnel administration here, since most readers will already have been exposed to the substantial literature on the subject. Our focus will be on the preventive labor relations aspects of a number of personnel functions that occur after selection. The following two chapters will discuss compensation and benefits administration from a similar perspective. This coverage is by no means exhaustive, and the reader will no doubt think of other personnel functions and subfunctions with preventive labor relations implications.

An important assumption underlying this and the following chapters is that there is a causal relationship between the company's personnel actions and the employees' response. It is unwise to underestimate the ability of employees to evaluate their wages, hours, and working conditions relative to those in other companies. Employees can and usually do. When they cannot do so accurately because of a lack of information, they will speculate in a way that is seldom to the advantage of the nonunion employer. Having made this evaluation, they will respond in a rational and reasonably predictable way. This response may take the form of excessive turnover and absenteeism, lower morale and productivity, disciplinary problems, or interest in and support of a union. It should be remembered that unionism is often a rational response on the part of employees to employment-related problems. It is this rationality that gives the nonunion employer some control over the situation.

The assumption of employee rationality must be qualified by the recognition that we are dealing with perceptions rather than absolute fact. It is the employees' perception of the relative level of their compensation, the fairness of company rules, and the need for certain disciplinary measures that counts. This can work either to the advantage or to the disadvantage of the nonunion employer. If the employees perceive their compensation and conditions to be more favorable than they are—either because the company has done a good job in packaging and marketing itself or because it has effectively restricted access to union information—employees may be less inclined to favor unionism. This will work to the advantage of the employer as long as nothing happens to disturb that perception. On the other hand, if employees perceive themselves to be relatively less well off than they actually are, they will be more inclined to favor union representation. That is, if the benefits package is not adequately communicated to the workforce, the company may end up paying the price in the form of a union drive that could have been avoided. In the absence of continual management attention to this matter, the direction of change will be toward greater accuracy. It follows that the organization should provide a compensation package and a work environment that are as good as its market position allows. It should also communicate this fact to the employees. However, it is far easier to sell a good product than a bad one.

Employee perception is as much a function of packaging and communication as it is of substance. There is a trade-off between the preventive labor relations value of investing in the content of compensation and conditions of employment and in selling or marketing that content. The parallel to the relationship between production and marketing costs is obvious.

It should be noted that within the limits dictated by law and common sense, there is wide latitude in regard to the best course of action to follow. However, two principles should be kept in mind.

1. The personnel practices adopted must fit the needs of the organization and its employees.
2. Personnel decisions and interpretations must be made in a consistent, equitable, and predictable way.

It is especially important for personnel professionals or other managers transferring from one company or plant to another to keep these principles in mind. Sudden changes in management style or in important employee relations matters can undermine an otherwise effective preventive labor relations program

A special word is in order for the small business organization that has outgrown its informal employment practices. From a preventive labor relations point of view, this period is a critical time in the life of an organization. Often the organizational growth causes employment-related strains that can generate union interest before the company has developed the tools needed to cope with a union drive.

The problem of growth is often exacerbated by a change of leadership at the top, the acquisition of the firm by a larger organization, or the hiring of one or more "outside" managers to straighten things out. Should the employees perceive any of these organizational changes as threatening, the company may find itself especially vulnerable to unionization. Under such circumstances, two approaches may be followed. The first, and the one that most behavioral scientists would recommend, is to involve the employees in the decision-making process and thereby gain their support of the new arrangements. The second approach, which is often more practical when a staff reduction or reorganization is necessary, is to make the changes as early as possible, implement them all at once, and then follow up with an explanation of why the changes were necessary and a statement reassuring employees that no additional personnel changes are planned.

The following discussion will focus primarily on the large or medium-size firm that has already weathered the transition to a more professionalized management approach. However, most of what is discussed has relevance to the small but growing organization as well. The main difference is that the smaller company may not as yet have established or formalized the policies and procedures mentioned.

EMPLOYEE ORIENTATION

Once recruited and selected, employees must be introduced into their new employment. This aspect of the personnel function, common to all organizations, is referred to as orientation. In general, the larger and more stable the organization, the more formal the process will be. Orientation is usually part of the personnel function. Its objectives are to reduce early turnover, cut down training time, provide needed information, and aid in the socialization of the new employee. It is also an important element in the company's preventive labor relations program.

There is probably no time when the employee is as receptive to communication from management as during the initial day or two on the job. This is not to argue with the often heard observation that little of the information contained in orientation programs is retained or even received. Of course it is not. Most of the information is either obvious or unrelated to the new employee's immediate needs: how to get along with his new co-workers and stay out of trouble with supervision.

It is unfair to the new employee to leave a question as important as the company's position on unionism unanswered. This information should be included in the literature provided to new employees and should be explicitly stated during the orientation program. Not to do so is to miss an important opportunity to reinforce pro-company or antiunion attitudes on the part of the employee.

A new employee is often forced to decide on the desirability of unionism in general during the first few weeks on the job. This will occur whether or not management raises the subject. If there is no union interest in the company, the employee will have to decide whether or not to "go along with the crowd" on this and related issues. If there is a union organizing drive in progress, the new employee will naturally be viewed as a potential source of union support. He will be approached by union supporters as soon as decency and security allow—seldom on the first day, but usually within the first two to three weeks. If the new employee has a firm pro-company or nonunion attitude, the company has won one. If the employee is already pro-union, someone made a hiring mistake. And if he is indifferent to or equivocal on the subject, he will make the decision at a later date.

It is to the advantage of the nonunion employer to have this decision made early, ideally before the union supporters are able to communicate with the employee. The orientation session is an excellent place to confront the employee indirectly with the choice. The statement that "*we* are a nonunion company and intend to stay that way" helps to establish and reinforce attitudes that may be important later. Care must be taken not to engage in unfair labor practices during the orientation process. Never threaten, promise, or interrogate the employee about unions, and have the company's statement reviewed by counsel.

The attitudes established at orientation may influence the way the employee responds to union information at a later date. We all engage in selective perception to one degree or another. The employee's frame of mind on unionism will influence how much pro-union information he receives and the way it is interpreted. In addition, once an employee has taken a position on a subject, especially if it has been publicly proclaimed, his future decisions, actions, and statements will usually be consistent with that position. This is not to say that people do not change their minds. They do. But they do not do so easily in the absence of important new information.

A second advantage to the employer in forcing an early decision is to help identify a problem before it is too late to do something about it. If the company is hiring pro-union employees, it should be well aware of the fact before a union drive is under way. While it is illegal to take any direct action against pro-union employees (and none is here recommended), it may be desirable to restrict their effectiveness. In addition, the company may seek to convince such employees that a union is not necessary by making a special effort to treat them fairly and openly. Finally, and most important, if the organization is accidentally recruiting union supporters, this is important feedback for those in personnel. If an employee comes out in favor of the union soon after being put on the payroll, it suggests that he brought the attitudes in the door. If, on the other hand, such attitudes surface a year or two later, the cause is less certain. They may be the result of any number of things that have occurred since the employee joined the company and an important piece of feedback on the selection process will have been lost.

INTRODUCTION TO THE JOB

After orientation, the new employee is assigned to a job. This involves an introduction to the supervisor, the work group, and the work. In some situations the new person will be taught the new job through assignment to a trainer, an experienced employee, or a group of employees. The introduction should be taken seriously by the nonunion employer, since the new employee is highly impressionable at this time. The company should make a special effort to use this period constructively by helping the employee adjust successfully to the new environment and protecting him from unnecessary union influence.

The worst approach is to throw the new employee into the work group and let nature take its course. It is generally agreed that this approach contributes to excessive early turnover. The new employee will have many questions and problems. One way for the employee to deal with them is to quit. Another is to rely on new friends and associates who already have the answers. Who should they be? One important new associate is the supervisor. Supervisors should have a standing charge to help new employees during the first few weeks on the job. This involves more than just being available to answer work-related questions. Supervisors should also make a point of approaching new employees regularly to help with questions or problems and to give constructive feedback.

Another approach is to assign the new employee to a "buddy" who is responsible for breaking him in. This task should be reserved for the more dependable, long-service employees and should be treated as an honor to the experienced employee. It should be initiated with a formal introduction away from the work area to emphasize its importance. The new employee should be informed that the buddy will be available to answer questions and help with problems that may come up. The experienced employee should be instructed to introduce the new employee to the work group, help with the training, and generally be responsible for his welfare. All this should be done in complimentary terms, while impressing the new employee with the high regard the company has for the buddy and impressing the buddy with the importance of the new responsibility.

Of course, buddies should be chosen with care. In addition to being safe from a preventive labor relations viewpoint, buddies should be respected members of the work group. Every supervisor knows who these people are.

It is a good idea to spread the buddy responsibility around. That is, use several most likely candidates rather than *the* most likely. This will make the matter more of a novelty and less of a chore. It will also spread the honor over a larger number of people and prevent one employee from monopolizing the role. Using a single employee as buddy could present a problem if the experienced employee's attitudes toward the company or unions change. It is less serious to stop selecting one out of six people for such work than to shift the task from a single person to another.

PLACEMENT, PROMOTION, AND TRANSFER

The decision of *where* to place new employees has important preventive labor relations ramifications. In a small company or organizational unit which does its own staffing, this question may not come up. Similarly, the technology or skill needs of the job to be staffed may preclude such a question. If, for example, the company needs only one electrician, that person must be hired from without. It would be impossible to place such a new employee in any job other than the one for which he was hired. In many employment situations, however, the company regularly hires relatively large numbers of people and then trains and promotes from within. This at least raises the question of whether the organization can be structured in such a way as to contribute to its preventive labor relations objectives.

Operating requirements will always be paramount. Reorganization should not detract from the efficiency of the production process and other important functions of the company. However, within that constraint there is often considerable latitude as to how the organization places its members. For example, a plant may consist of three production departments, a finishing department, and a shipping department. One approach to staffing such a plant is to hire directly into each department. A second is to hire into a common production group and separately into finishing and shipping. A third is to hire into a general labor pool and then assign and promote into all five departments as needed.

The last approach has advantages from a preventive labor relations perspective. It keeps new employees relatively isolated and, therefore, less available to inside union organizers and supporters during those first few weeks with the company when important attitudes are formed. This relative isolation can be reinforced by some of the methods recommended in Chapter 2: separate lunchrooms, parking facilities, entrances, and so on. Another advantage to this approach is that it prevents a union organizer or supporter hired by mistake from coming into regular contact with the rest of the employees. If a hiring mistake is made, it can be identified and dealt with before any harm is done. Finally, only those employees who demonstrate a high degree of dependability need be promoted into positions with particular union vulnerability—such as in the shipping department, where contact with unionized truck drivers is common. Alternately, if union support or interest is concentrated in a particular department, it may be desirable to assign especially safe new employees to that unit on a regular basis to dilute the union's strength.

Close attention should also be paid to all interdepartmental promotions, transfers, and temporary assignments. Placement, promotion, and transfer policies are interrelated and are an integral part of the company's preventive labor relations program.

MANAGEMENT STYLE

Over the past several decades a great deal of attention has been paid to management style in the business literature. It may be the single most researched and written-about management topic. Popular interest in the subject began with reports of the now famous Hawthorne studies in the 1930s, although there are antecedents in Frederick Taylor's scientific management movement and other early schools of thought. The subject has since evolved through two generations of behavioralists, human relators, and proponents of Theory Y, System 4, management by objectives, the managerial grid, and various other recipes for humanizing the workplace. The general recommendation has been away from an exaggerated authoritarian management style associated with the past toward a participatory approach in which all members of the organization make their contribution and thereby gain fulfillment, satisfaction, and self-actualization. The adopters of such programs often hope that this will be done without the aid of a union.

It is hard to argue with the wisdom of such an approach. An overly authoritarian management style will conflict with the values of most American workers. Most employees will cooperate with those organizational decisions about which they were consulted and to which they may even have contributed. Furthermore, an organization can always learn from the experience of its members. There is little question that an enlightened, people-oriented management style is appropriate for a company operating in the United States of the 1980s. However, this should not blind us to the potential dangers of such an approach from a preventive labor relations perspective.

A management style must fit the needs of the organization and must be

118

applied with consistency and predictability. The danger is in the adoption of a program that does not meet the demands of the company, even though it may have been successful in other organizations. As many companies and managers have learned, a little MBO or System 4 improperly introduced can do a great deal of harm. However, it is the nature of management literature that we hear more about the success stories than about the failures. This is unfortunate, for we often learn more from our mistakes than from our successes. Of course, it is even better to learn from the mistakes of others.

While the complex subject of management style is beyond the scope of this book, a number of cautions are offered. They are particularly important for a company thinking of introducing one of the many "canned" programs on the market or engaging in a little organizational development on its own.

1. *Does the proposed management style fit the task?* Some activities require timely and decisive action that may call for sacrifice by the members of the organization. An extreme example is a military unit in a combat situation. However, it is equally unreasonable to expect much democratic decision making in the building of a bridge or other major construction project. In general, when the task is done only once (or has a long production cycle), when the employees do not have access to the needed information, or when the costs of mistakes or delay are high, a relatively authoritarian management style is necessary. Under such conditions the cost, if any, of the resulting employee dissatisfaction can be offset with additional compensation and benefits or absorbed in the form of additional turnover, absenteeism, or pro-union sentiment.

2. *Does the proposed management style fit the workforce?* In his interesting and highly successful book *Making Unions Unnecessary,* Charles L. Hughes classifies employees into six types: Tribalistic, Egocentric, Conformist, Manipulative, Sociocentric, and Existential.[1] He reports that the various personality types behave in ways essentially consistent with their respective value systems and that this has significance for employee motivation and satisfaction. Such trait or categorizational theories are often suspect; however, Hughes's thesis has a certain intuitive appeal. People do differ in their psychological makeup. Allowing for numerous exceptions, some personality types seem to seek out and remain in certain lines of work. And some employers, either consciously or unconsciously, seem to seek out and retain certain types of employees. Do not overlook the possibility that a proposed management style may

not fit the employees involved. Remember, the present workforce is as much a result of the employees' decision to remain on the job as of the company's decision to retain them.

Some employees may prefer an old-fashioned, relatively authoritarian management style to the uncertainties of change. A sudden invitation to participate in making decisions that have traditionally been made by management may be viewed as an imposition once the novelty is over. In addition to feeling uncertain and insecure, employees may feel that the change in management style should cover other matters that the company does not wish to share. It is not inconceivable that such feelings could translate into increased union interest.

There is nothing inherently wrong with any approach to management provided it is fair, consistent, and accepted as legitimate by the employees. This is not to say that a different approach is not called for in many situations. However, from a preventive labor relations perspective, any change as important as the way in which the company relates to its employees must be carefully studied before it is adopted.

3. *Does the company really mean it?* Never underestimate the employees' ability to see through a sham. It takes only one person in the work group to figure things out and communicate the truth to the others for the best-designed charade to fail.

There are always limits to the scope of decision making that management is willing to share with the employees or to the weight it is willing to give to employees' ideas. If those limits are too narrow or the weight too light, the employees will know it and react accordingly. This will at the very least reduce the effectiveness of the new program. It may also cause resentment and suspicion if employees believe the company is attempting to manipulate them. A participatory management program that is less than genuine raises questions about the employer's sincerity and trustworthiness that could carry over into a counterunion campaign.

4. *What are the hidden costs?* Every management decision carries hidden costs. To the extent possible, these costs should be identified and taken into account before the decision is made. One cost of a change in the company's management style is that it replaces the old system. Although this sounds axiomatic, it is an important fact of life. If the organization has operated successfully in the past, it should not abandon a good thing without study and caution. Someone should always ask: "What have we gained from the existing system?"

A second cost of organizational change is the break in continuity. The new approach may change attitudes and expectations in such a way as to make reversal impossible. To the extent that tradition and consistency are important in employee relations, the adoption of a new approach for a short period of time may undermine an effective program. For instance, if a company has a principle of always backing its first-line supervisors in disputes with hourly employees, a departure from this policy, even for a short time, could cause long-run problems with the morale of the foremen and the expectations of the employees.

A third possible cost associated with the adoption of a particular concept or program is that the company uses up its best opportunity to correct a problem and demonstrate its good faith to the employees. If the company adopts plan A, by definition it does not adopt plan B. Should it turn out that the wrong choice was made, the shift to plan B may be more difficult than it would have been initially.

This is not to say that a company should resist the newer approaches to management. When the concept meets the needs of the organization and its employees, when it is sincere, when it does not carry prohibitive hidden costs, and when the existing situation calls for change, the adoption of a new management style can pay handsome rewards. This has been repeatedly documented. However, today so many new programs are being sold with such enthusiasm in the marketplace that a word of caution is warranted. Management style is a serious matter and an integral part of any effective program to remain nonunion. The nonunion firm should approach anything as important as a change in the way it relates to its employees with caution.

DISCIPLINE AND REVIEW

Nothing is as important to the maintenance of good morale and the contribution that it makes to a union-free environment as sound discipline. For every employee who appreciates getting away with something, there are many more who would rather see the offender caught and fairly dealt with.

When one employee breaks a rule and is not penalized for it, other employees feel a sense of inequity. If employees perceive rule breaking as a positive benefit, and especially if they believe that conforming to the rules is a cost (one that is not offset with additional reward), their perception of the relative benefits of work will be altered. In compensation administration this line of reasoning is called "equity theory." It predicts that when there is a perceived imbalance in the ratio between the contributions (inputs) and the rewards (outcomes) of employment, the employee will adjust in such a way as to restore that balance: reduce inputs and/or increase outcomes. Ignoring several important psychological adjustments, the employer who fails to enforce reasonable shop rules essentially forces the nonviolating employees to engage in unproductive work behavior. If, for example, some workers are allowed to get away with excessive tardiness, insubordination, or pilferage, other employees will have strong inducement to emulate that behavior. Not only will employees conclude that it is safe to engage in such activity, but they will observe that the miscreants are contributing less to or gaining more from their employment experience. The consequences of such observations can be serious.

Most people prefer fairly strict discipline at work. This does not mean that there is no room for compassion or flexibility in the exercise of shop rules. Often extenuating circumstances arise that must be taken into account. It is also important to distinguish between those cases that call for coaching and counseling and those that demand disciplinary action. Beyond that, the guiding principles in shop discipline should be reasonableness and consistency.

One of the most important things that a union obtains for its members is a fair and predictable shop disciplinary and "judicial" system. In a unionized setting, personnel and disciplinary actions are subject to review through a formal grievance procedure. Those problems not resolved in the grievance process may be submitted to final and binding arbitration by a third party independent of both the union and the company. Decades of grievance reviews and arbitration have forced unionized employers to demonstrate that they handle all disciplinary matters fairly and consistently. Many managers agree that an effective grievance system and labor relations program work to the advantage of the company as well as the employees.

The nonunion company must recognize the importance of sound discipline to personnel administration in general and to preventive labor relations in particular. Its disciplinary standards and procedures should be at least as fair and predictable as they would be in a unionized setting. While the specifics will vary with the type of work, the setting, and the management style of the company, a number of general recommendations are offered.

1. *Work rules should be formally promulgated and made known to*

122

the employees. The best way to promulgate work rules is to include them in a personnel manual or employee handbook *and* post them. It is not enough to describe the rules during an orientation session or bury them in an employee handbook and then expect the new employee to remember them or get the information from other employees. In addition to its communications value, the posting of rules will yield important feedback to management. If employees view a particular requirement as unreasonable, they will have something firm to complain about. If they consider a rule too restrictive (or too lenient), management should know this and make changes when justified. If employees raise no objections, it may be assumed that the posted rules are tacitly accepted.

2. *The penalty for an infraction of the rules should be officially promulgated when appropriate.* This is especially important for serious violations which call for a heavy penalty on the first offense. For instance, if the penalty for smoking in a restricted area or fighting on the job is automatic suspension or termination, employees should be informed of this in no uncertain terms. Such fair warning will not only make the penalty more acceptable but help communicate the seriousness of the offense.

3. *Work rules do not exist in a vacuum.* Rather, they are an integral part of the company's relationship with its employees. The content, promulgation, and enforcement of rules must be consistent with the company's managerial style. Other things being equal, a participatory work environment will call for fewer and less restrictive work rules. Moreover, the members of the work group will be involved in their development and, *perhaps,* in their enforcement. A more authoritarian management attitude is likely to work in the opposite direction.

To be most effective, work rules should be viewed as necessary and functional by the employees. A no-smoking, no-talking, or no-solicitation policy must be obviously called for; otherwise it should be explained to the work group. If a work rule cannot be justified, it is probably unnecessary and is doing more harm than good. In such a case, the rule should be modified or abandoned.

The objective of work rules is cooperation and communication. If a rule is broken too often, questions arise about its appropriateness and about the company's relationship with its employees.

4. *Rules must be enforceable and enforced.* A company should not maintain more rules and regulations than necessary, but it should enforce those that are needed. Obsolete and unenforceable rules, dealing with

such things as hair length, should be dropped before they result in unnecessary litigation or before management finds itself having to overrule a supervisor who attempts to enforce them. No rule or regulation should exist that cannot be defended in court, before an arbitrator, or to the employees. Particular attention should be paid to those requirements that apply differentially to men and women or to different age groups.

5. *All disciplinary action should be reviewable.* At the request of the employee, a higher management level with the authority to overrule the supervisor should review disciplinary actions. This suggests review by line rather than personnel or other staff management.

Another approach that has certain advantages is to create a review committee (either ad hoc or permanent) with representation from line management and supervision, the personnel staff, and *perhaps* the employees. Employee representation, if included, should be handled with care, and the advice of counsel should be sought on the legal implications involved. In general, the employee member or members should be appointed by management, not elected by the work group. This does not preclude consulting the employees or appointing the representatives they probably would have elected. However, from a preventive labor relations perspective, elections are dangerous. They generate attitudes that are too closely associated with unionism. Such an arrangement can give an articulate union supporter an opportunity to obtain information, gain visibility, and exploit management mistakes. In addition, the committee may begin to engage in negotiation over the matter under review. If this should occur on a regular basis with the participation of duly elected employee representatives, the situation could become dangerously close to collective bargaining. Such an arrangement could even be considered "concerted activity" and, therefore, protectable under Section 7 of the National Labor Relations Act.[2]

Whether or not the review procedure involves employee participation, it must be perceived as fair and objective by the employees and by supervision. This will increase the acceptance of disciplinary action and will also tend to improve the performance of supervisors. It is not suggested that the reviewing manager or committee make it a practice of overturning disciplinary decisions. Indeed, this should be a rare event. To overdo it would be to weaken the position of supervision in the workplace and inhibit supervisors from enforcing those rules and regulations that the company needs enforced. The importance of maintaining supervisory authority, credibility, and morale cannot be overstated.

6. *Discipline should be constructive and progressive rather than punitive.* Other than in the most serious cases involving discharge, disciplinary action should be considered educational and directed at improving the job performance of the employee and of the work group in general. Fair notice should be given of the behavior expected and the consequences of not living up to expectations. A first infraction should be dealt with more leniently than a subsequent one, with the penalty increasing for repeated offenses. The action, the reason for the action, and the probable result of a repeat violation should be explained to the employee both verbally and in writing. This communication, along with other relevant documentation, should be retained for a reasonable period of time (one to three years, depending on the seriousness of the offense) and then destroyed. Documentation is important in the event of a discharge and/or subsequent litigation or administrative proceedings. If there are no repeat infractions within a reasonable period of time, the matter should be forgotten. The employee should be informed that the documentation has been removed from his personnel file and should be congratulated on his improved performance.

DISCHARGE

The ultimate disciplinary action is discharge. It has often been referred to as industrial "capital punishment." While that description may be a little overdrawn, it does highlight the importance of the action.

It must be remembered that discharge for cause is a very different matter from layoff or involuntary termination for reasons beyond the employee's control. In the case of a layoff, the employee may collect unemployment compensation and can usually expect to be recalled to the job. In many industries layoffs are common because of seasonal demands or model changes and become an accepted part of the job. An involuntary termination is somewhat more serious for the employee. However, the employee can usually obtain unemployment compensation and use the former employer as a reference. For the discharge, in contrast, unemployment compensation is not available. Generally, the employee cannot use the company as a reference without informing a prospective employer of the reason for the discharge. The dischargee is under great pressure to get a new job while being in a disadvantageous position in the job market. Therefore, on strictly human grounds, a discharge should be considered an extreme measure. This does not mean that employees should not be discharged when the situation warrants. It does mean that the discharge must be handled appropriately.

The most important aspect of a discharge for the nonunion employer is its impact on the rest of the workforce. It is imperative that other employees perceive the action as fair and necessary. In a unionized situation, this is all but guaranteed because of the grievance procedure and arbitration provision. Almost all discharge cases are processed as grievances (commonly in an expedited fashion); cases where the discharge is questioned often go before an outside arbitrator. Since the burden of proof is generally on the company in a discharge arbitration case, it is imperative that the unionized employer handle the discharge properly. The employees know that the company must have good cause for discharging an employee; otherwise the person will be reinstated with back pay. Alternately, if the union chooses not to pursue the matter to arbitration, it can be assumed that on review of the facts the union has concluded that the company would be upheld. The nonunion company has no such built-in guarantee of the fairness and legitimacy of a discharge.

From a preventive labor relations point of view, the company should approach a discharge as though the case were going to be reviewed by an outside party. It should engage in progressive discipline along the lines developed above, with particular attention to documentation and to communication with the employee. In all but the most serious cases calling for immediate separation from the company, the employee should have one or more formal warnings or a series of progressively serious disciplinary actions short of discharge. This will communicate to the rest of the workforce that the company made an effort to ''save'' the miscreant and that it discharges only as a last resort. In addition, when it is necessary to get the offender out of the plant as soon as possible, it is best to suspend the employee pending a review of the matter rather than to discharge him immediately. If, upon reviewing the facts, the company decides that permanent separation is called for, the suspension can be changed to a discharge. If, on the other hand, the company decides that a discharge is too severe or involves legal complications, the penalty of a suspension of appropriate length can be assigned.

This approach has two important advantages to the company. First, it allows time for consultation and an objective review of the facts away from the heat of the incident. Second, it simplifies the process of compensating the discharged employee. Many states require that a discharged employee be given all due compensation at the time of discharge or within

126

so many hours of discharge. The process can become rather hectic as management attempts to compute vacation eligibility, taxes to be withheld, and the like.

It should always be assumed that a discharge will result in litigation and/or an administrative proceeding. At the very least, the company should be prepared to demonstrate before a hearing officer (administrative law judge, referee, whatever) that the discharge was for cause in case the dischargee files for unemployment compensation. The same documentation may be required if the employee claims that the discharge resulted from union activity and files an unfair-labor-practice charge with the National Labor Relations Board—a charge that is of special interest to the nonunion employer. The dischargee may also file charges of ethnic or sexual discrimination with the Equal Employment Opportunity Commission (EEOC) or a state-level Fair Employment Practices Commission (FEPC). It is safe to assume that the practical, if not legal, burden of proof is on the company. Thus progressive discipline and documentation are all the more important.

LAYOFFS

It goes without saying that any responsible employer should go to great lengths to minimize the need to lay off employees. However, when a reduction in staff in a nonunion setting is necessary, three simple rules will go a long way toward minimizing problems.

1. *Layoffs should take place all at once and at as early a date as possible.* This will minimize the spread of rumors. The action should be followed immediately by a communication explaining why the layoffs were necessary and assuring employees that no additional layoffs are planned.

2. *Layoffs should not be used to correct past personnel mistakes.* Training, motivational, or disciplinary problems should be handled as they arise. To wait for a layoff to "weed out the deadwood" is to invite charges of arbitrary or discriminatory personnel actions. Whenever possible, a staff reduction should be based on some objective, explainable, and defendable criterion. In the great majority of cases, this boils down to seniority. The employer can often make the action more palatable by specifying how length of service applies to certain departments, locations, or job classifications.

3. *Layoffs and terminations should be handled as humanely as pos-*

127

sible. There are few things in life more personally devastating than losing one's job. In addition to the financial crisis that may ensue, termination can be very ego-deflating. All employees identify themselves in occupational terms, especially long-service employees. Losing that identification can be painful.

The employer is in a position to soften the impact of a layoff or not-for-cause termination. Providing information on unemployment insurance (usually required), known job openings or other opportunities, and job-hunting techniques can reduce the financial problems of the employee. It may also reduce the impact of some terminations on the employer's unemployment insurance experience rating or reserve account. An explanation of why the layoff or termination was necessary, an assurance that it was not for cause, and an offer to recommend the employee to other employers will go a long way toward reducing the personal blow. It may be helpful to put this in writing to aid the employee in his job hunting and in explaining the event at home.

EMPLOYEE COMMUNICATIONS

To a great extent, management is communication, and employee relations management is communicating with employees. Communication is also the centerpiece of the employee relations aspect of preventive labor relations. As noted earlier, what the employees think or perceive is often more important than the facts. If a company has fair and necessary work rules but they are perceived as otherwise, it has a problem. If it has arbitrary and unrealistic rules but this fact has not been discovered by the employees, it may continue to operate effectively until the fact is recognized. The difference is the access to and interpretation of information by the employees.

It should not be inferred from the above that communication can operate in place of sound personnel practices over the long run. Such propaganda can be effective only in a closed system where access to accurate information is denied and dissenting opinion controlled. No workplace in the United States fits these conditions and hopefully never will. There are important limits on the degree to which the employer may exaggerate or distort the facts. The watchword in this area is not to underestimate the employees' ability to see through a statement or position that is less than accurate.

The usual situation in the target company is that it provides a good place to work with reasonable compensation and treats the employees with fairness and respect. The problem is that they do not perceive the situation as it is and they are, therefore, vulnerable to the union organizer or supporter who may make misleading comparisons between the best that exists in unionized shops and what the employees think they have. The employee-communications task then becomes one of selling the company to the employees. The marketing suggestion is obvious and deliberate. The company is in the position of selling a product to a particular public. As in marketing, the firm will have difficulty if it tries to market an inferior product. And the more inferior it is, the more difficulty it will have. On the other hand, it is easy to sell something that is good.

Another way of looking at this is to recognize the trade-off between putting money into the product and putting it into packaging and marketing that product. Within the constraints of a given budget, the company will allocate in such a way as to maximize sales or revenue. There are few conditions under which it would put all its resources into either product or marketing. The same thing applies to selling the company to the employees. While it is unwise for a nonunion employer to attempt to operate for any length of time with less than adequate compensation and conditions, it is also unwise to ignore the important function of communicating their value to the employees.

One of the most important jobs of employee communications in a nonunion firm involves explaining how the company's compensation and conditions compare with those in other—especially unionized—firms. If they compare favorably, management should communicate this fact to the employees regularly and effectively. This will usually involve keeping supervisors informed so that they can effectively field questions on the subject. It may also be appropriate to include such information in newsletters and other written communication, provided the wording and tone of the message are chosen with care. If the nonunion company does not compare favorably, then the reason why it is below standard should also be made known. If, for example, the nonunion firm is just starting or does not have the economies of scale of its unionized competition, this information should be provided to the employees directly or indirectly. This is especially so if a successful union organizing drive would put the company out of business or force it to curtail employment. Not to provide such information is to invite the employees to come to the conclusion that they can improve their terms of employment with little or no cost to themselves by simply voting in a union. The employer has an obligation to correct such an impression before it can do a great deal of harm. Of course, care must be taken so as not to engage in unlawful threats or promises.

If a nonunion company does not have a reasonable explanation for not paying as much as its unionized competition, it is asking for trouble. There should be no reason for a nonunion firm to pay lower wages or provide poorer working conditions than it would if it were organized by a union or than currently being offered by unionized firms in the same industry. If it makes sense to remain nonunion, as it almost always does, it follows that there are savings involved. The nonunion employer, free of the direct and indirect costs of unionization, should be in a position to meet, if not exceed, the compensation and conditions of unionized firms. If that is not the case, it raises serious questions about the effectiveness of the management of the nonunion firm.

Should the nonunion company elect not to meet the standards of unionized firms for one reason or another, it must either invest more heavily in the other aspects of preventive labor relations or accept a higher probability of being unionized. While the values in this equation will vary with industry, location, and employee type, the trade-off remains.

Communication is a two-way process. It is not enough to inform the employees that their compensation is as good or better than that of other firms in the area or industry. It must also be established that they have received that communication and accepted it as accurate. It is possible that such a piece of information buried in a newsletter or employee handbook goes unnoticed. It may also be the case that it is received but discounted as employer propaganda. If the company is unaware of such a breakdown in its employee communications, it could overestimate the strength of its position. It is therefore important that the nonunion employer develop upward communication in the form of attitude surveys, supervisory reporting, and, perhaps, an informal grievance mechanism. These matters will be discussed in Chapter 8. In a unionized setting the union automatically provides the employer with such feedback. It also keeps the employees informed of their relative well-being in the course of its representational functions. The nonunion company should do at least as much for its employees.

Employee communications start with recruitment and do not end until the employee retires or otherwise leaves the company. Of course, their content will change with time and with the employee's position in the organization. Much of them will be strictly work-related technical or general information that has no relevance for preventive labor relations. Some communications, however, will be central to the company's efforts to remain nonunion.

As mentioned, it is especially important for a company to establish its position in regard to unions and make it known to the employees, supervisors, and prospective employees. This should be done formally and in such a way as to leave no doubt. This simple fact will have the effect of inducing some potential pro-union applicants to go elsewhere and, more important, help influence attitudes of incoming members of the organization in the right direction. There is no excuse for an employee or supervisor not knowing the company's position on so important a matter.

It is important that the company let the employees know what is expected of them and what the consequences of not meeting those expectations will be. This relates, in part, to the discussion on discipline and discharge above. However, it is more than that and involves the entire employment relationship. One of the important things that a union gains for its members is a high degree of predictability and control of the work environment. The employees of a nonunion employer should have the same. That is, without destroying the advantages of nonunion operation, the company should do all it can to keep the employees informed of what will happen next.

Another, and very important, function of employee communications is to dispel rumors. As mentioned in our discussion of older employees in Chapter 4, there are few things as threatening to an otherwise effective preventive labor relations program than rumors of layoffs or some other unwelcome event.

NOTES

1. Charles L. Hughes, *Making Unions Unnecessary,* New York: Executive Enterprises Publications Co., 1976, pp. 45–53.
2. Among other things, Section 7 grants employees the right to "engage in other concerted activities for the purpose of collective bargaining or other mutual aid or protection."

WAGE AND SALARY ADMINISTRATION

Compensation decisions are central to the life of any business organization. People accept and remain on jobs to a great extent because of the monetary compensation provided. They are motivated; induced to accept transfers, promotions, more arduous or dangerous work; and rewarded—and sometimes punished—through the compensation system. Nonmonetary factors such as status, authority, and more pleasant surroundings and interesting work tend to correlate positively with monetary compensation. When a company does an effective job in compensation, it has gone a long way toward creating a healthy organizational climate. When a company has compensation problems, they tend to have a negative impact on all related areas. Needless to say, compensation decisions are central to a company's preventive labor relations program.

This chapter will review the preventive labor relations aspects of wage and salary administration. Chapter 7 will examine benefits administration from the same perspective. Again, it is important to recognize the role of perceptions. From a preventive labor relations point of view, it is not wages and benefits per se but the employees' perception of those wages and benefits that is important. If that perception compares well with the employees' expectations and their concept of equity, the company has gone a long way toward removing a main cause of union interest. If, on the other hand, the comparison is not favorable or the employees feel that the system is less than equitable, the company has problems that can result in unionization.

WAGE AND SALARY ADMINISTRATION: AN OVERVIEW

The details of wage and salary administration are beyond the limits of this discussion. The interested reader is referred to any of the standard books in the field.[1] After a superficial review, we will limit our attention to the preventive labor relations aspects of the subject. A typical wage structure is depicted in Figure 6-1. The horizontal axis relates jobs (not people) to each other in terms of their relative worth to the organization by a procedure called "job evaluation." There are various ways of doing this. The most common for nonexempt personnel is the "point system," which assigns a number of points to each job on the basis of what are known as "compensable factors" (education, experience, effort, initiative, working conditions, and so on). We will assume a point system of job evaluation throughout this discussion. The vertical axis translates the point values into wage rates. This operation is termed "pricing the jobs," or "monetary conversion." It locks those jobs with standard content and titles (lift-truck operator, tool and die maker), usually referred to as "benchmarks" or "key jobs," into their appropriate position in the labor market. For production personnel this market is local. For engineers and professionals, it is regional or national.

If there is a single rate for each job, the wage structure can be presented as a straight line, such as *AA* in Figure 6-1. However, it is more common for each job to have a range of rates. This allows the company to compensate for experience and tenure on the job and to reward employees for successful performance. It is also customary to group jobs with approximately the same number of points (say, between 300 and 350 on a 500-point scale) into a single classification or job grade for administrative convenience. This results in the rectangular boxes presented in Figure 6-1. The horizontal dimension of the box represents the group of jobs with similar point values that will receive the same wage rate, and the vertical dimension represents step increases based on merit and/or time on the job.

As a practical matter, the nonunion company has control over the *mechanics* of its wage and salary program. Of course, there are constraints demanded by the labor market, legal requirements, and the company's important operational objectives such as minimizing unwanted labor turnover and remaining nonunion. Turnover and union organizing drives are often closely related. Turnover is one way of responding to dissatisfaction; seeking union representation is another. Consequently, from a wage and salary perspective, responding to turnover or potential turnover problems is often an effective proxy for responding to potential union problems. However, judgment is called for. Turnover rates are sensitive to labor market conditions. When unemployment rates go up, it is

FIGURE 6-1. HYPOTHETICAL WAGE OR SALARY STRUCTURE.

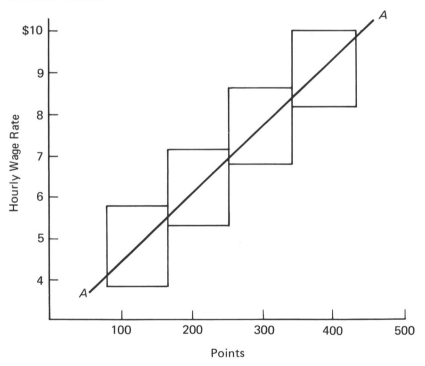

reasonable to expect employees to improve their lot by means other than quitting.

It is up to the company to decide what jobs to include in a particular wage or salary program or, alternatively, whether to have one overall wage and salary program or separate programs for different employee groups (for example, separate programs for production and maintenance, clerical, supervisory, different plants, and so on). Remember, this decision can be important to the company's bargaining unit strategy discussed in Chapter 3. The company must also decide what compensable factors to use, their relative worth (number of points assigned), and how to translate those points into money wages. The only internal constraint is that the program must be explainable to and accepted, at least tacitly, by the employees to whom it applies. This acceptance is an important objective of any wage and salary program and is critical to preventive labor relations.

There are four main problem areas in wage and salary administration to which the nonunion firm should be especially sensitive: wage levels, wage structures, internal relationships, and wage adjustments.

WAGE LEVEL

In deciding how to price jobs, the company makes one of its most important decisions. Should it be a high-wage employer and attract the "cream" of the market? Or should it be a relatively low-wage employer and offset the effect of this with greater recruitment and selection expenditure, more training and employee development, lower productivity, more turnover, and, perhaps, a higher probability of being unionized? There are few questions of equal importance to a business organization.

Employees seldom recognize the existence of this trade-off, and there is no way of sharing it with them. It would be foolish to tell employees that they should accept a lower wage than they expect because they are qualitatively below employees of competing firms. Indeed, few managers are willing to think of their personnel decisions in such terms either. Yet, the trade-off exists and must be recognized by those involved in compensation and personnel administration. In the long run, you get what you pay for. This does not mean that there are no bargains or mistakes. But given a large enough number of purchases or hiring decisions, the bargains and the mistakes cancel out. Another way of expressing this is that error is random. The company that adopts a low-wage policy must expect to offset the savings in wages in some other way. This is especially important for the company intent upon remaining nonunion. While high wages do not guarantee the continuance of nonunion status, paying wages that are perceived by the employees as too low is to ask for trouble.

Actually, determining the overall wage level is a relatively simple matter. The company decides to be high, low, or somewhere in the middle in regard to its starting or average wage rate or salary. A more complex matter from a preventive labor relations point of view involves the characteristics of the wage structure.

WAGE STRUCTURE AND EXTERNAL COMPARISONS

From a purely technical point of view, the designer of a wage and salary program who is unencumbered by union or employee participation can achieve any wage structure desired by the choice of compensable factors and the way in which points are assigned to those factors. That is, by deciding to include or exclude working conditions, or a particular working condition (such as noise level), the designer can upgrade or downgrade certain kinds of work. Or by deciding to assign 200 points to working conditions and only 100 to education, the designer can alter the point totals of the various jobs, and hence their position in the job structure. Of course, if the program is to pass the test of acceptability by the employees, there are limits to the extent to which this can be done. Moreover, many personnel professionals would consider such manipulation unethical and unprofessional. A more honest way of attaining the same result is to do an objective and fair job evaluation and then adjust the wage structure to obtain the results needed in regard to its slope and/or linearity.

Wage structures always have a positive slope. That is, as the total number of points increases, the wage rate increases. To design the system differently would not make sense. However, the characteristics of that slope carry important implications for the organization and for its preventive labor relations program.

Figure 6-2 shows various hypothetical wage lines that could be adopted by an organization. Diagrams A and B depict linear or arithmetic relationships between the number of points (and therefore the skill level and value to the organization) of the jobs and their monetary wage rate.

Note that diagram A represents a much steeper progression from one job or group of jobs to the next than does B. Another way of saying this is that *AA* reflects a wage structure with more skill differential than *BB*. Assuming that both Firm A and Firm B hire at the bottom only, promote from within, and have the same average wage rates, the difference suggests that Firm A hires at a lower starting rate but is more generous with its long-term employees who progress from one job to the next. This approach may mean that Firm A is accepting lower-quality employees and then investing more in employee development, or that it is spending more on recruitment and selection. In comparison, Firm B hires at a higher initial rate but pays less for progression from one job to the next. Other things being equal, we may infer from this that the more senior and presumably more skilled employees in Firm A arc rclatively better off than are their counterparts in Firm B.

What are the implications of this for the preventive labor relations programs of the two firms? It suggests that Firm A is in a stronger position. At least it is less vulnerable to problems caused by dissatisfaction among its long-service employees. Of course there are limits and trade-offs in regard to the slope of the wage structure and a company's skill differential. The more money the company puts at the high end of the wage dis-

FIGURE 6-2. VARIOUS HYPOTHETICAL WAGE LINES.

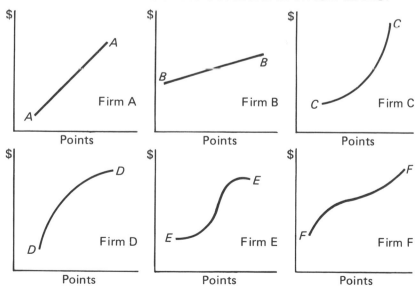

tribution, the less it can put at the lower end. If it overdoes its wage strategy, it will have difficulty attracting the number of high-quality employees needed. Thus, at some point the costs of labor turnover and reduced quality of new employees (or the training costs associated with compensating for the turnover and qualitative difference) would prohibit additional progression.

Diagrams C and D in Figure 6-2 present a somewhat different picture. Here the relationship between point values and wage rates is nonlinear. Both have the same minimum and maximum rates. However, the wage experience of an employee's moving from bottom to top is quite different in the two companies. In Firm C, the employees experience relatively modest monetary increases as they begin to move up and then receive more substantial raises with later promotions. In Firm D, similar employees would experience a more rapid wage advance early in their careers, with less impressive raises later on. Thus, in Firm C, the skill differential is relatively more pronounced among the more highly skilled employees than among the newer or less skilled. In Firm D, in contrast, there is a greater difference between the rates for the jobs at the lower end of the distribution, and this difference diminishes as the top is approached. Assuming that the wage lines apply to identical or similar jobs, the employees at the higher end of the distribution in Firm C should perceive their situation as being more advantageous relative to those at the bottom end. In Firm D, those in the middle of the distribution are better off relative to both those below and those above them, assuming they accept the job structure.

It should be noted that diagrams C and D do not assume the same average wage rate. If the lowest and highest rates are the same, then the average wage will be significantly lower for Firm C than for D. It will also be noted that the average wage or total wage bill will be influenced by the number of employees in each job or group of jobs. If the bulk of the workforce is concentrated in the lower half of the job structure (horizontal axis), the wage bill for Firm C will be lower than for Firm D. However, it will have the same minimum and maximum rate. If the employees tend to make wage comparisons at the bottom and the top of the range, and if turnover is not a problem at the middle because of an industry or trade practice of hiring only at the bottom, then the nonunion employer may find a wage structure as depicted by CC advantageous. If, on the other hand, a highly visible and easily compared job, such as lift-truck operator, is located in the middle of the wage structure, the company may have a problem. This would be especially so if a large number of employees were in that classification.

Diagrams E and F represent refinements on a simple curvilinear wage structure. Curve *EE* may be appropriate for a firm with a potential turnover or morale problem in the middle of its job structure. For instance, in a trade with apprentices, such as printing, the trained journeymen are often both highly mobile and influential as opinionmakers in the shop. The unskilled workers and apprentices are less of a loss to the company if they move on, and they usually have a lower status on the job. The relatively few employees above the skilled journeymen in such a work situation are usually no more of a turnover problem and no more influential than the journeymen. The nonunion company may, therefore, be particularly concerned with the middle range of its job structure and adopt an S-shaped wage structure such as *EE*. Alternatively, if a company's turnover and morale problems are at the bottom and the top of its skill distribution, it may find a wage structure resembling *FF* appropriate.

The nonunion company should be cognizant of how its wages and salaries relate to those of other companies with which the employees make comparisons. This is especially important if some of those companies happen to be unionized. One of the most common mistakes in wage and salary administration is for the company to confuse its position in the labor market with its position in the product market. Managers usually think in product-market terms. They compare their costs, including labor costs, with those of other companies with which they compete in the product market. A furniture manufacturing company compares its operation with other companies in the furniture industry, a bank with other banks, a printing plant with other printing plants. In those situations where the skills involved are industry specific (aircraft maintenance) or where the labor market is regional or national (nursing, university faculty), this may be appropriate. However, where the employees involved make a comparison that is different from that made by management, it can create problems. For example, the employees in a furniture plant are more likely to compare their compensation with that of the employees in the paper mill or oil refinery down the road than with that of employees in a company hundreds of miles away with which their employer competes. The data processing employees in a bank will compare their compensation with that of people doing similar work in the local area rather than employees in banks in other cities. The employees in a nonunion industrial printing (folding carton) plant may compare with the local commercial printing industry. The reason for this is that to the employees the relevant market is the area about which they have information and within which they would reasonably expect to work should they change jobs. Credit clerks in Chicago seldom have information on or interest in the wage rates of credit clerks in Houston. They are better informed about and more interested in clerical wages in the firm down the street, which may be unionized.

If the employer does not compare well with the companies with which the employees make their comparisons, this could result in excessive turnover, other employment problems, and increased interest in unionization. The logical thing to do is to pay high wages. However, it may be that the company cannot afford to pay the wages that such comparisons suggest. This may be due to the competitive nature of the product market, the degree of labor intensity in the production process, or any number of other economic facts of life. If that is the case, then the important question becomes: What can the company do about it?

The first thing the company should do is identify and get accurate information on those companies with which it is compared. This may not be as easy as it sounds. Different employees or employee groups may make different comparisons, and many companies are reluctant to exchange compensation information. However, an attitude survey, employment and exit interviews, and reports from supervisors will usually provide adequate information on the relevant companies. Wage information, if not directly available, can usually be gleaned from the help-wanted section of the local newspaper and from information provided by new hires. If the other company is unionized, a copy of the labor agreement can almost always be obtained. Such specific information may be supplemented by government-generated data. The Bureau of Labor Statistics of the U.S. Department of Labor collects and publishes a great deal of wage and salary information, such as Area Wage Surveys. This information can be obtained either free or at a nominal charge from the regional office of the Department of Labor (white pages of your phone book under United States Government).

If it is discovered that the employees' wage information is inaccurate or misrepresented, as often happens, the company should tactfully correct the inaccuracy. The best way to do this is to provide supervisors with appropriate information on a continuing basis so that they are in a position to counter any claims that the company is paying low wages. Another approach is to involve one or more hourly employees in the design and/or administration of the wage and salary program. While this has costs and hazards, it does serve as an effective way of communicating with the rest of the workforce.

A second thing that can be done is to make it more difficult for the employees to make the wrong comparisons and to arrange the wage structure in such a way that it contributes to the employer's preventive labor relations objectives. This can be done in part through the judicious use of job titles. A machine operator should not be called a "machinist" or a person who operates duplicating equipment a "printer" or "pressman." Inflated job titles may get the company a little mileage in the way of morale, but they also lend themselves to inflated comparisons. The term "machinist," for instance, is used to describe a wide range of jobs and should be avoided unless the particular work in question is at the top of that range.

Special attention should be paid to the job titles of local higher-wage industries and to unionized plants in the same area and industry. If a local high-wage employer has "quality control technicians," the nonunion firm should have "inspectors." If the labor agreement of a unionized firm refers to "stationary engineers," the nonunion company should have "power plant assistants." The title differences can be reinforced by ensuring that the duties performed are somewhat different. Some of the quality control work can be performed by production workers or by supervisers while the quality control personnel can be assigned enough production, clerical, or materials-handling work to make it impossible to compare them with the "quality control technicians" of the other company. Similarly, power plant employees can be assigned other nonpower plant, operating, or repair and maintenance duties while some of the more technical power plant functions can be performed by supervisers. All this will make it more difficult for employees and union organizers to make a comparison between their rates and those of other companies.

A third thing that can be done is to pay those jobs that cannot be "camouflaged" at a competitive rate. This matter was touched upon in our discussion of S-shaped wage structures. If a particular job is highly visible and standardized, such as medical technologist in those states with a certification or licensing requirement, then the nonunion employer may have to pay the going rate or accept the costs and risk of doing otherwise. Of course, paying that rate may cause the kind of internal problem to which we now turn.

INTERNAL RELATIONSHIPS

Thus far we have emphasized the problems associated with wage level comparisons with other companies. We now examine the question of internal relationships. One of the most important objectives in the design of a formal wage and salary program is the elimination or minimization of perceived inequities within the employee group. If the company is small and just getting started, it may be appropriate to have personal rates of pay and adjust to special needs with informal arrangements. However, once the organization is large enough to employ one or more personnel professionals and worry about unions in a serious fashion, it invariably needs a more objective approach to its compensation decisions. Moreover, one of the most potent employee complaints, and one that can easily translate into union interest, is that of "favoritism." Questions of personal fondness aside, this often means that in solving one personnel or compensation problem, the employer makes one friend and ten enemies.

Wage and salary systems that have been allowed to evolve over the years often contain inequities. These inequities may have originated innocently enough. Old Joe may have really deserved that extra 25 cents per hour back in 1968 because he was the only guy in the shop who knew how to weld or because he kept the production records. But by now the company has three full-time welders and a plant clerk, and Old Joe's quarter has been subject to several percentage wage increases. The other employees may have a legitimate gripe at the inequity.

Another common source of wage inequity of special concern to the nonunion employer is the employer's attempt to adjust to a labor market phenomenon along the lines suggested in the preceding section. If a skill is in short supply or a job in a low-wage nonunion firm is easily compared with its counterpart in other firms, it may be necessary to assign it a relatively high wage rate. While this may make sense in terms of external comparisons, it can cause internal problems. If it is necessary to pay sheet-metal workers disproportionately more than production employees because they are in short supply or because of the visibility of the job, it may cause feelings of resentment among the other employees.

Feelings of inequity also occur when part of the employer's operation is unionized. It is common for a manufacturing company to have all or part of its production and maintenance personnel represented by one or more unions while its office and sales staff remain nonunion. Or one or more locations could be organized while the rest of the company remains nonunion. Under such circumstances, the employer who ignores or is unresponsive to the needs of the nonunion employees is asking for trouble.

WAGE AND SALARY ADJUSTMENTS

Another wage and salary area that may create feelings of inequity is the handling of merit raises. Such raises are usually tied in with a performance appraisal system. Although excellent in concept, such arrangements are often poorly executed and cause more trouble than they are worth. At the very least they should be carefully monitored and regularly evaluated from a preventive labor relations perspective.

One of the problems associated with merit increases during periods of inflation (which have become continuous and permanent) is that they become maintenance increases rather than true merit increases. That is, the company uses them to maintain the employees' purchasing power as prices go up. As tempting as this may be to the employer who wishes to motivate or retain employees through the compensation program, it destroys the policy of rewarding on the basis of performance. Even worse, when someone is denied a merit salary increase, it is accurately perceived as a real wage cut and as punishment. The personnel problems resulting from such incidents can be serious and long lasting, for they change the role of the supervisor from that of a coach rewarding employees for good work to a judge involved in a punitive process. It is better to call maintenance increases what they are and use whatever is left over for true merit raises.

Admittedly, such advice is easier to give than to follow. When step increases reflect a skill difference resulting from added experience and the company has a tradition of moving people through the steps with the use of merit salary increases, adopting such advice may cause serious "compression" of the wage structure. If allowed to continue, this could cause severe problems to the company's entire compensation program. I have no solution to the problem other than to budget more of the organization's resources for money wages. Of course, this presents most companies with a serious dilemma.

The second difficulty with merit salary increases, from a preventive labor relations point of view, is that they are often associated with a performance appraisal system. Proclamations to the contrary, if the merit salary increase (MSI) is really based on merit, the two actions are inseparable in the eyes of the employees and of most supervisors—a high performance evaluation results in a merit increase; a low evaluation does not. Using two different forms, signed by the same supervisor, doesn't change anything. If the merit increases have evolved into maintenance increases, the same thing applies except that the emphasis is on the negative.

Except from a few personnel managers, who may have had a vested interest in the subject, I have heard few kinds words about performance appraisal programs. The problems associated with their design and operation are legion and need not detain us. As viewed by the employees, it would appear that there are few well-run performance appraisal systems in existence. When not associated with merit increases, they are perceived as less important than the day-to-day feedback from the supervisor. When merit increases are associated with the performance appraisal, they are often considered no less unfair, prejudicial, and arbitrary than the performance appraisal itself. If this view is held by a significant number of employees, it can provide the union organizer with a powerful cause.

Another thought on wage and salary increases involves the size of the increase. It has long been thought that a wage increase or a differential between rates must be sizable in order to be perceived as significant by the employees. Fifteen percent is an often heard value. The other side of the argument is that two 6 percent raises are more effective from a motivational and reinforcement standpoint than one 12 percent raise.[2] This may be true, but it leaves unanswered an important preventive labor relations question: What is the optimal wage increase, and what is the optimal time between raises? These are really two sides of the same coin. The more often wage adjustments are granted, the smaller they will be.

It is safe to say that wage adjustments must be made at least annually. It is also safe to say that adjustments that occur more often than quarterly would be administratively prohibitive and probably dysfunctional from a motivational point of view. Thus, while a company may get more mileage out of two 6 percent raises than one raise of 12 percent, it is not at all clear that it would get even more from four 3 percent raises, and it is certain that twelve 1 percent raises would be viewed as ridiculous.

This is by no means a simple matter. One of the factors involved in the decision is the rate of inflation. Perceptions of money wages have changed drastically over the last few years. The American people have become aware of the difference between real and money wages. Workers assume that their employer will, in one way or another, protect their incomes from inflation. At this writing the inflation rate stands at over 10 percent, and there is no indication that it will go down appreciably in the near future. This means that a 10-plus percent annual wage increase, however packaged, is necessary just to maintain purchasing power. Wage increases are no longer an extraordinary event granted as a reward for successful performance or as a token of the employer's appreciation. To a great extent they have come to be viewed as an expected right that is necessary to maintain real wages. In many labor agreements this has been institutionalized in the form of so-called escalator clauses or cost-of-living allowances (COLA). In nonunion settings the matter is handled less formally and less rigidly. However, the need to stay abreast of inflation is just as important to the nonunion employer as to the unionized company.

What has inflation done to the perception, and therefore the preventive labor relations implications, of wage adjustments? One thing is that the typical annual adjustment has increased in size. Whereas it was difficult to divide a 3 percent annual increase into more than one raise without losing its motivational effect, a 10 percent annual adjustment can be cut in half or even quarters without becoming insignificant. It may also be argued that more frequent adjustments are called for during a period of high inflation to protect the employees' purchasing power.

On the other hand, there are two arguments in favor of having one large annual wage increase rather than two or more smaller ones. The first is that the raise will be more noticeable and, presumably, more appreciated by the employees. This may be strengthened by the fact that they may have fallen behind more than they would have with more frequent adjustments. The second is that the employer will save money by delaying wage increases as long as it is practical. In the terminology of labor relations, "back loading" is cheaper than "front loading." A wage increase granted in the first quarter of a budget year must be paid out for the remainder of the year. This can be expensive and uses funds that may be better employed elsewhere. An example is in order.

Assume that a nonunion firm expects to grant a 10 percent wage adjustment this year to offset the effects of inflation. It has average straight-time hourly earnings (ASTHE) of $5, which we will use as a base, and a work year of 2,080 hours (or 520 hours per quarter). If it grants the full 10 percent increase at the *end* of the budget year, the ASTHE will go from $5 to $5.50 at that time. However, if it divides the 10 percent by four and grants quarterly increases of 2.5 percent each, the situation shown in the accompanying table will result. To put this into perspective,

Quarter	Old Rate	New Rate	Hourly Difference Times Hours	Additional Wage Cost to the Company
I	—	$5.00	—	—
II	$5.00	$5.13	.13 × 520	$ 67.60
III	$5.13	$5.38	.38 × 520	$197.60
IV	$5.38	$5.52	.52 × 520	$270.40
			Total Difference	$535.60

the $535.60 per employee for the year converts to about $.26 per hour across the board ($535.60/2,080 = .2575). Using the initial ASTHE of $5.00, this translates into 5.15 percent. Using $5.52 as a base, it is 4.66 percent.

The reader should also note that in the example given, the compounding effect of quarterly increases adds $.02 to the year-end ASTHE. While this may not seem important, it should be remembered that this will be added to and compounded quarter after quarter. Of course, it is not "real money," since the nonunion employer can withdraw it in the future by reducing the magnitude of future wage adjustments.

A word of caution may be appropriate at this point. The costing of labor agreements and related phenomena is more of an art than a science. The preceding example, and others that will be used, are for expository purposes. They do not always withstand objective analysis. The assumptions may be questionable and the result challenged for one reason or another. However, so long as the same assumptions are used consistently and the mathematical license is not too outrageous, such techniques can provide the personnel professional with a powerful analytical tool. In the example discussed, it is not important that the numbers be precise. If they are reasonable approximations, they throw a considerable amount of light on the question under examination.[3]

There is no general answer to the question of whether or not it is better to grant one large annual wage increase, four quarterly ones, or something in between. However, it should be kept in mind that multiple increases cost more and will, other things being equal, result in higher payroll costs. They will also result in higher administrative costs, since adjustments must be made that much more often. Whether or not this is the best use of those funds depends on the situation. In my opinion, when in doubt, opt for the single annual adjustment.

Another inflation-caused problem that we should at least be aware of involves the effect that repeated wage adjustments can have on the wage structure. It will be recalled that the slope of the wage structure can have important preventive labor relations implications, since it reflects the skill differential and other interrelationships among the various jobs and their wage rates. If the wage structure gets out of line, serious personnel problems can ensue.

If wage adjustments are made on a cents-per-hour basis instead of a percentage basis, they will compress the wage structure (unless the cents per hour are graduated with the base rate). That is, they will reduce the slope of the wage line. Given the certain high rates of inflation in the American economy throughout the 1980s and the necessary wage and salary adjustments, the potential problem from this quarter is quite large. The solution is obvious: grant percentage wage increases.

Finally, a word on wage and price controls. The nonunion employer has the advantage of unencumbered discretion in wage and salary administration. This freedom can come to a sudden end with the imposition of controls.

Wage and price controls were in effect in the United States from 1971 to 1973. At this writing, there are no controls per se. Rather, there are "voluntary" restraints that hold little promise of halting the massive inflationary pressure that has built up in recent years. The president of the United States does not at this time have the authority to impose mandatory controls without going to Congress. Since a straightforward national debate on this subject would touch off additional inflationary pressure as various parties attempt to protect themselves from impending controls, it will be necessary for Congress to give some sort of stand-by discretionary authority (as was granted to President Nixon) to the president before real controls are again imposed.

Should the administration be given the authority to establish a forceful wage and price controls program, the nonunion employer must not be taken by surprise. It is important that the company not be caught with below-standard wage and salary levels when the controls program begins. While some may think that a controls program is a handy excuse for not granting sizable wage increases, it should be remembered that such savings are short run at best, whereas damage done to the company's compensation system may produce long-run problems. The employee response to perceived substandard wages will be the same regardless of the cause. Further, if the controls program is structured in such a way as to allow already negotiated improvements in labor agreements to go into effect or in some other way favors unionized employees (as may well occur as a way of gaining political support and cooperation from organized labor), it will create a strong new argument in favor of unionization.

A word of advice and prophecy: When the Administration starts loudly proclaiming that it has no intention of using the discretionary authority that Congress has given it, get your compensation program in order.

NOTES

1. David W. Belcher, *Compensation Administration,* Englewood Cliffs, N.J.: Prentice-Hall, 1974 (formerly published as *Wage and Salary Administration,* 1955 and 1962), has commanded the field for so many years that it has become must reading for anyone with an interest in employee relations.

2. Thomas M. Rohan, "Would a Union Look Good to Your Workers?" *Industrial World,* January 26, 1976, p. 37.

3. The reader interested in the costing of wage and benefit adjustments is referred to John G. Kilgour, "Wrapping the Package of Labor Agreement Costs," *Personnel Journal,* June 1977, pp. 298–299, 313.

7

BENEFITS ADMINISTRATION

Employee benefits have become an important part of the compensation package. They now make up from 20 to 40 percent of total compensation, depending on the company and industry, what is included in the term, and how the arithmetic is done. Anything of this magnitude has considerable importance to preventive labor relations.

Employee benefits can be divided into three groups as viewed by the nonunion employer: (1) those that are legally mandated, (2) those the employer establishes voluntarily, and (3) those required by the nature and/or location of the work.

There is a trade-off among the various employee benefits programs and between such benefits and money wages. All are components of labor costs. Whether mandatory or discretionary, employee benefits cost money. Assuming that a relatively fixed amount of the organization's resources is devoted to labor costs in a given period, whatever is spent on one program cannot be spent on another. Further, the cost of a particular benefits program is a function of both the money value of the benefits, or the protection given to the employees, and the administrative costs of running the program. The preventive labor relations value of a benefits program can be greatly influenced by the efficiency with which the program is administered. As with so many things, an efficient personnel operation is an important element in an overall preventive labor relations program.

GOVERNMENT-REQUIRED BENEFITS PROGRAMS

Legally required benefits include such important programs as unemployment insurance, Workers' Compensation, and Social Security. Their significance to preventive labor relations is that they cost money and that they may allow the nonunion employer an opportunity to get some "mileage." Very importantly, if the employer is unaware of their significance and the opportunity to make substantial savings in their administration, such programs can cost more than necessary and thereby absorb resources that could be better used elsewhere.

Unemployment Insurance

The federal government effectively requires that the states operate unemployment insurance programs that conform to minimum standards. The specifics of the programs and the orientation and efficiency of their administration vary from state to state. This fact alone can mean a considerable difference in the cost of the program for an employer with a given level of unemployment.

In all but three states (Alabama, Alaska, and New Jersey) the employer pays the entire cost of unemployment insurance. This is done in the form of a payroll tax on all or a portion of each employee's wages. The wage base and the tax rate differ substantially from state to state. As of January 1977, covered wages ranged from the first $4,200 in many states to $10,000 in Alaska and to all wages in Puerto Rico. The tax rate varies with the employer's experience, from 0.0 to 2.7 percent in South Dakota to 3.9 to 5.1 percent in Massachusetts. Michigan has the highest maximum rate, 6.6 percent. Benefit amounts also vary, from a low of $15 to $63 in Texas to a high of $14 to $162 per week in Massachusetts. Moreover, the maximum duration of unemployment compensation benefits (independent of any federally funded extensions) ranges from 26 weeks in numerous states to 36 weeks in Utah.[1] These data, along with

150

the maximum employer payment per employee and the maximum amount an employee could collect in 1977 (assuming he earned enough to warrant the maximum weekly benefit amount and remained unemployed for the full period) are computed for each state in Table 7-1.

Table 7-1 is not intended to be taken at face value. By the time these words are in print, numerous changes will have been made. Further, because of experience-rating provisions, not all employers pay the maximum tax. Also, many employees collect less than the maximum possible benefit, and most remain unemployed for less than the maximum number of weeks for which they are eligible to collect benefits. With these cautions in mind, Table 7-1 does illustrate a number of important points. The first is that there are enormous differences in the cost of the benefit among states. The employer contribution equals the wage base times the tax rate as determined by the employer's individual experience rating. Assuming the company has a poor record in this regard and is therefore subject to the maximum tax rate, its annual payment per employee (assuming all employees earn the full wage base) can range from $113 in Mississippi, Oklahoma, South Dakota, and Virginia to $480 in Alaska. Perhaps a more appropriate upper limit for comparison purposes is Michigan with $356.

Lest the importance of these numbers be missed, $113 per year translates into $.054 per hour and $356 into $.171 per hour across the board (using a work year of 2,080 hours). Assuming $5 average straight-time hourly earnings (ASTHE), these figures amount to 1.1 and 3.4 percent of the hourly rate, respectively.

Other things being equal, the employer contribution is three times greater in Michigan than in the states with the lowest rates. More significantly, the maximum employer payment in Michigan of $356 is substantially above neighboring Ohio's $181 and Indiana's $139. Such cost differences are important enough to be taken into account in a location decision. This would be especially so for a company in a seasonal or cyclical industry that is subject to regular layoffs. Such an employer would be subject to the highest tax rate.

The unemployment insurance systems in two states, New York and Rhode Island, allow employees to collect benefits while on strike. New York requires a seven-week waiting period and Rhode Island six weeks (instead of the usual one week for both states). This controversial arrangement results in the state effectively requiring the employer to pay striking employees "strike benefits." In 14 states benefits may be col-

TABLE 7-1. SELECTED FEATURES OF STATE UNEMPLOYMENT INSURANCE PROGRAMS AS OF JANUARY 1977.

State	Employer Contributions Applied on Wages up to	1976 Tax Rate Min.	1976 Tax Rate Max.	Maximum Employer Payment per Employee	Maximum Weeks of Benefits	Weekly Benefit Amount	Total Possible Benefits
Alabama	$ 4,800	0.5%	4.0%	$192	26	$15–$90	$2,340
Alaska	10,000	2.3	4.8	480	28	18–120	3,360
Arizona	6,000	0.1	2.9	174	26	15–85	2,210
Arkansas	6,000	0.5	4.4	264	26	15–100	2,600
California	7,000	1.4	4.9	343	26	30–104	2,704
Colorado	4,200	0.0	3.6	151	26	25–116	3,016
Connecticut	6,000	1.6	4.5	270	26	15–174	4,524
Delaware	4,200	1.6	4.5	189	26	20–125	3,250
Florida	4,200	0.7	4.5	189	26	10–82	2,132
Georgia	6,000	0.05	4.03	242	26	27–90	2,340
Hawaii	9,300	3.0	3.0	279	26	5–120	3,120
Idaho	8,400	0.5	3.6	302	26	17–99	2,574
Illinois	4,200	0.1	4.0	168	26	15–135	3,510
Indiana	4,200	0.3	3.3	139	26	35–115	2,990
Iowa	6,000	0.7	4.7	282	39	20–116	4,524
Kansas	4,200	0.0	3.6	151	26	25–101	2,626
Kentucky	4,200	0.4	4.2	176	26	12–87	2,262
Louisiana	4,200	0.7	3.3	139	28	10–120	3,360
Maine	4,200	2.4	5.0	210	26	12–119	3,094
Maryland	4,200	2.8	3.6	151	26	10–89	2,314
Massachusetts	4,200	3.9	5.1	214	30	14–162	4,860
Michigan	5,400	0.8	6.6	356	26	16–136	3,536
Minnesota	6,500	0.9	6.0	390	26	18–113	2,938

Mississippi	4,200	2.7	1.3	113	26	10–80	2,080
Missouri	4,500	3.2	0.5	144	26	15–85	2,210
Montana	4,800	3.1	1.5	149	26	12–97	2,522
Nebraska	4,200	3.7	0.1	155	26	12–80	2,080
Nevada	6,500	3.5	1.1	228	26	16–94	2,444
New Hampshire	4,200	4.15	2.4	174	26	14–95	2,470
New Jersey	5,800	6.2	1.2	359	26	20–104	2,704
New Mexico	4,200	3.6	0.6	151	30	17–83	2,490
New York	4,200	5.2	1.5	210	26	20–95	2,470
North Carolina	4,200	4.7	0.3	197	26	15–105	2,730
North Dakota	4,200	4.2	0.9	176	26	15–107	2,782
Ohio	4,200	4.3	0.6	181	26	10–161	4,186
Oklahoma	4,200	2.7	1.2	113	26	16–93	2,418
Oregon	8,000	4.0	2.6	320	26	28–102	2,652
Pennsylvania	4,200	4.0	1.0	168	30	13–141	4,230
Rhode Island	4,800	5.0	3.2	240	26	26–120	3,120
South Carolina	4,200	4.1	1.3	172	26	10–103	2,678
South Dakota	4,200	2.7	0.0	113	26	19–89	2,314
Tennessee	4,200	4.0	0.4	168	26	14–85	2,210
Texas	4,200	4.0	0.1	168	26	15–63	1,638
Utah	8,800	2.8	1.3	246	36	10–110	3,960
Vermont	4,200	5.0	1.0	210	26	15–96	2,496
Virginia	4,200	2.7	0.55	113	26	20–103	2,678
Washington	7,800	3.0	3.0	234	30	17–102	3,060
West Virginia	4,200	3.3	0.0	139	26	14–128	3,328
Wisconsin	6,000	5.2	0.5	312	34	23–126	4,284
Wyoming	4,200	3.86	1.16	162	26	10–95	2,470

Source: U.S. Department of Labor, Employment and Training Administration, Unemployment Insurance Service, "Significant Provisions of State Unemployment Insurance Laws, January 3. 1977" (1976).

lected if the work stoppage is caused by a lockout (often a difficult distinction to make). And in Michigan, strikers who take a short-term job with a friendly employer and then lose it are allowed to collect, and the struck employer is charged for the benefits. This, along with the increasing availability of food stamps and welfare payments to strikers, is a most disturbing development. It can only lead to more strikes, longer strikes, and more costly settlements.[2] Its importance to the nonunion employer is that it reduces one of the costs or risks of unionization to the employee: the financial impact of going on strike. The expectation that a strike may follow an organizing drive and representation election is one of the great deterrants to unionization.

The column headed "Total Possible Benefits" in Table 7-1 shows how much a former employee can collect if he is entitled to the maximum weekly benefit and is unemployed for the total number of weeks allowed for each state.[3] Again, the numbers provided are intended only as approximations. Although the mechanics vary from state to state, the employer always ends up paying the cost of unemployment benefits. This is usually in the form of having a reserve account charged, which is then reflected in the company's experience rating and a higher future tax rate. Such indirectness and delay often result in managers not thinking of such costs as real money. This is wrong.

No one enjoys challenging unemployment claims. It is unpleasant work. However, management, especially personnel management, has an obligation to dispute all questionable claims. To do otherwise is to impose a cost upon the company that could have been legitimately and ethically avoided. The importance of this is that if, say, $1,000 is unnecessarily expended on a fraudulent or avoidable unemployment insurance claim, it is not available for other purposes. The company gets no preventive labor relations value from payments to former employees who are not on temporary layoff or will rejoin the company for some other reason. It is better to convert such funds into wages or other benefits for those still on the payroll and eligible to sign authorization cards and vote in NLRB-conducted elections.

This is not to recommend that the company dispute obviously legitimate claims. If an employee is involuntarily laid off, he has every right to collect unemployment benefits for as long as he is actively seeking work or until those benefits are exhausted. If, on the other hand, the person is terminated for cause, or quits voluntarily, or is not actively looking for work, management has an obligation to challenge the claim.

The usual procedure is that the last employer and the base-period employer(s), whose accounts will be charged, are notified when a claim is filed. In many cases the last employer and the base-period employer are the same. The company then has a number of days in which to respond with information germane to the case. Such information may be that the person was discharged for cause or quit voluntarily. If the claimant is charging that the quit was motivated by harassment or some other reason that would justify approval of the claim, the company should present its side of the story. Following the initial determination by the administrative agency involved, there may be a conference or other proceeding. Someone in the organization should become familiar with the law and the review procedure through the initial review level. All questionable claims should be contested as a matter of policy. This will not be a cost item. If the company wins a reasonable percentage of the cases, it will end up saving money. Indeed, a firm that employs large numbers of relatively short-term employees (as is common in retail and fast-food businesses) will find that the savings are considerable.

In addition to doing everything possible to avoid layoffs, the company serious about minimizing its unemployment-insurance costs must document its personnel actions. If an employee is terminated for cause, or if an incident occurs that may eventually contribute to such a termination, it should be witnessed and documented. In the case of a voluntary quit, a letter of resignation should be required or a statement explaining the reasons for the quit, signed by the departing employee.

Another important precaution is to check all claims carefully. Does the notice refer to the right George Davis? Check the Social Security number. The company may also be provided with a summary of all claims against its reserve account on an annual or periodic basis. This should be reviewed carefully against personnel records to check employee names, dates of employment, and wage rates. Mistakes can be made by the claimant reporting such information and by the state agency operating the system.

Finally, if a company is notified that its reserve account is going to be charged, it may be advisable to offer the person a job. This assumes that the company can use the help and that it has no particular reason for not reemploying the claimant. If the offer is accepted, it pays the person for working rather than for not working. If it is not accepted, the company can report this information to the state administrative agency and have the claim disqualified.

When it is necessary to lay off or terminate an employee without cause, it is best to inform him or her of the unemployment insurance program (this is usually required by law anyway) and give advice on how to apply for benefits. This may be as simple as telling the employee where to go and explaining that this should not be put off since the waiting period (which varies from zero to ten weeks, depending on the state) usually commences with the application for benefits rather than the loss of employment. It may also be appropriate to inform the employee, and indirectly the other employees, that the company will not contest this claim and that the unemployment compensation is paid for by the employer for the benefit and protection of the employees.

Workers' Compensation

The second major legally mandated benefit is Workers' Compensation. This, too consists of a number of state-run programs that differ widely in their content and administration. They vary much more than unemployment insurance programs, because there are no federal minimum standards and the benefits are more complex. For example, as of 1972, the maximum weekly benefit for *permanent total* disability varied from a low of $49 for 401 weeks in Texas to a high of $112 for an indefinite period in Washington. The maximum weekly benefit for *temporary total* disability ranged from $40 for up to 450 weeks (or a maximum total of $15,000) in Mississippi to $150 for up to 433 weeks (or a maximum total of $65,000) in Arizona. Of course, not all employees qualify for the maximum benefit. Most states provided full coverage of medical costs resulting from employment-related injuries. However, a number of states had time limits and/or dollar limits on such payments.[4] To add to the complexity on the benefit side of the equation is the phenomenon of the *partial permanent* disability. The value of a severed finger depends on which finger it is, on whether the person is right- or left-handed, and on the state in which the accident occurred.

Workers' Compensation is fully paid for by the employer. This is done through the purchase of private insurance, through participation in a state fund, or through self-insurance under conditions allowed by some states. Different states allow different arrangements, and the company usually has a choice as to which method it adopts.

Workers' Compensation is undergoing great change at this time. It had long been recognized that the programs—more so in some states than others—are inadequate. This was affirmed by the National Commission on State Workmen's Compensation Laws in its 1972 report.[5] Since then, numerous changes in the state laws have been, and are continuing to be, made. In 1977, 49 states passed more than 300 laws affecting Workers' Compensation.[6] The result of these and future changes will be to make the programs considerably more costly than in the past. Of course, the cost of the programs will continue to vary from state to state and with the safety record of the employer.

Table 7-2 compares the least and most costly states in regard to Workers' Compensation: Indiana and Oregon. Please note that the data on which this comparison is based are several years old or represent estimates based upon the assumption that certain recommendations were adopted. The data and approximations are presented only for the purpose of illustrating how to evaluate such numbers. In addition, the differences may be explainable by the fact that the states have different industry mixes and, therefore, different accident and severity rates.

With that caution in mind, it appears that Oregon is a significantly more expensive state than Indiana in regard to Workers' Compensation. The dollar figures are substantial. A $125 per year per employee difference cannot be ignored by an effective management. However, whether or not Workers' Compensation costs should play a part in a location decision is debatable. Although the existing programs are often criticized, it is seldom for being overly generous for real injuries and illnesses

TABLE 7-2. A COMPARISON OF WORKERS' COMPENSATION COSTS IN THE STATES OF INDIANA AND OREGON, 1972 AND 1975.

State	Actual % Payroll in 1972	Approx. Cost per Hour in 1972	Approx. Total Cost to Employer in 1972	Estimated % of Payroll in 1975	Approx. Cost per Hour in 1975	Estimated Total Cost to Employer in 1975
Indiana	.385	$0.019	$ 39.52	.521	$0.026	$ 54.08
Oregon	1.450	$0.073	$151.84	1.728	$0.086	$178.88

Note: Calculations assume a work year of 2,080 hours.
Source: Report of the National Commission on State Workmen's Compensation Laws, Washington, D.C.: U.S. Government Printing Office, 1972, p. 145, Table B.2. for columns one and four.

that are employment-related. While contesting fraudulent claims, most employers accept their responsibility for providing a safe workplace and the financial responsibility for those accidents that do occur.

The best way to reduce Workers' Compensation costs is to eliminate the causes of accidents and work-related illness. This costs money—often a lot of money. However, the combined impact of the Occupational Safety and Health Act (OSHA) and the recent and impending modifications in state Workers' Compensation laws have changed the cost-benefit relationship that underlies industrial safety in such a way as to make safety a sound investment, independent of human considerations. Such expenditure would include the purchase of safety-related equipment and supplies, employee training, and an ongoing program of inspection and control.

From a preventive labor relations point of view, too, safety is a sound investment. Industrial safety is a "gut issue." If the employer fails to provide a safe place to work and fair compensation for those accidents that are unavoidable, it is reasonable to expect the employees to do something about it. Other than calling in the OSHA inspectors or quitting, the logical employee response is to form a union. Many would agree that if it takes a union to force an employer to provide a safe work environment, so be it. The nonunion company should be at least as responsible in this area as its unionized counterpart.

Social Security

The Social Security program—or, more formally, Old Age, Survivors, Disability and Health Insurance (OASDHI)—is a complex system of social insurance started in the 1930s and added to over the years. The benefits are financed by equal contributions from employers and employees, and participation is mandatory for covered employment. Although the program covers a wide range, this discussion will focus on retirement income, since that is the most important benefit for most employees. It is also the most important to preventive labor relations.

The Social Security program began as a modest effort to provide an income floor for older persons that could be supplemented with private pensions and personal savings. Until 1972, benefits, and the taxes needed to pay for them, were increased periodically (usually before elections), but otherwise this philosophy remained unchanged. In 1972, in response to the problems caused by several years of high rates of inflation, Congress passed a massive overhaul of the system. Benefit levels were raised 20 percent across the board, and future benefits were "indexed" to the Consumer Price Index. That is, an arrangement was established whereby benefits would rise automatically as the cost of living rose. (Through a faulty formula, benefits actually rose more rapidly than prices. This has since been corrected.)

To pay for these improvements, employer and employee taxes were scheduled to rise steadily throughout the 1970s. This was done by raising both the tax rate and the wage base against which it applies. By 1977, when this arrangement was superseded by a new Social Security law, the maximum yearly contribution had reached 5.85 percent on the first $16,500 of earnings, or $965. As it turned out, this was not high enough to support the benefit levels. Because of the faulty benefit formula and the inflationary recession of 1974, the system experienced increasing benefit levels and decreasing contributions. This was a serious short-run problem. A more serious long-run problem was caused by the fact that people were living longer, and especially by the demographic consequences of the "baby boom" that followed World War II. As the generation born in that period approaches retirement age, it will place an unprecedented strain on the Social Security program and on the economy. This is dramatically demonstrated by the fact that the ratio of working to nonworking Americans has dropped from 4:1 in 1965 to 3.2:1 in 1976. It is expected to drop to 2:1 in the year 2005.[7] Clearly, something had to be done. After lengthy debate on the various alternatives available, Congress passed a new law, which was signed by President Carter in December 1977.[8]

The new law corrected the faulty benefit formula, made various other changes that need not detain us, and greatly increased contributions to the program, as indicated in Table 7-3. It will be noted that both the tax rate and the wage base will increase markedly over the next several years. The tax rate will go from 5.85 percent in 1977 to 7.15 percent in 1987, an increase of 22 percent. The wage base will go from $16,500 in 1977 to $42,000, an increase of 158 percent. The maximum tax paid *separately* by the employer *and* the employee will go from $965 to $3,046 during the same ten-year period. That represents a whopping 216 percent increase! Social Security contributions will cost the high-wage employee and his employer more than $6,000 per year in 1987—three times as much as in 1977. Moreover, *relative* benefit levels, measured as a percentage of the wage base in the year preceding retirement, are scheduled to *decline* considerably. This is portrayed in Table 7-4. Changes of such a

159

TABLE 7-3. SOCIAL SECURITY TAX RATE, WAGE BASE, AND MAXIMUM ANNUAL TAX TO EMPLOYER AND EMPLOYEE, 1977–1987.

Year	Tax Rate	Wage Base*	Maximum Annual Tax	Percent Increase from Previous Year
1977†	5.85%	$16,500	$ 965	—
1978	6.05	17,700	1,071	11
1979	6.13	22,900	1,404	31
1980	6.13	25,900	1,588	11
1981	6.65	29,700	1,975	24
1982	6.70	31,800	2,131	8
1983	6.70	33,900	2,271	7
1984	6.70	36,000	2,412	6
1985	7.05	38,100	2,686	11
1986	7.15	40,200	2,874	7
1987	7.15	42,600	3,046	6

*Wage base fixed by law through 1981. After that, estimated by cost-of-living formula.
†Established under old law.
Source: Derived from "The Payout of the New Social Security Law," *Business Week,* February 20, 1978, p. 116.

magnitude are bound to have important effects on compensation administration and preventive labor relations.

The most disturbing implication of the recent changes involves the growing political clout of the so-called "gray panthers." The older-Americans' lobby is just getting organized but can already claim resounding success. No doubt it will continue to grow in size and effectiveness. And as the people born during the post-war baby boom approach retirement, the lobby's political force may dominate the United States. This could easily translate into still higher Social Security benefits, paid for by those who work and their employers. Whether this is done in the form of payroll taxes or transfers from the general fund affects only its progressivity or regressivity. It will still amount to a massive intergenerational transfer of money.

A more immediate question with respect to the recent development is

TABLE 7-4. MAXIMUM SOCIAL SECURITY RETIREMENT BENEFIT AS A PERCENTAGE OF WAGE BASE, 1978–1987.

Year	Benefit Wage Base*	Maximum Individual Benefit	Percent of Wage Base	Maximum Benefit with Dependent Spouse over 65	Percent of Wage Base
1978	$16,500	$5,610	34%	$ 8,415	51%
1979	17,700	6,195	35	9,293	53
1980	22,900	6,641	29	9,962	44
1981	25,900	7,252	28	10,878	42
1982	29,700	6,831	23	10,247	35
1983	31,800	7,314	23	10,971	35
1984	33,900	7,797	23	11,696	35
1985	36,000	8,280	23	12,420	35
1986	38,100	9,144	24	13,716	36
1987	40,200	9,648	24	14,472	36

*Wage base for year before retirement is used to compute benefits.
Source: Derived from "The Payout of the New Social Security Law," *Business Week,* February 20, 1978, p. 116.

whether or not the present employees will perceive their own contribution and the contribution made by their employer as a good investment. The person now entering the labor force will pay, and will have paid on his behalf by his employers, literally hundreds of thousands of dollars into the Social Security system. While older workers may accept the new taxes as desirable or necessary, it is unlikely that the younger workers will. The younger the employee, the less the perceived value of retirement income. This is partly due to the human trait of not thinking very far ahead and partly an accurate assessment. The present value of a dollar to be received in retirement income or medical benefits 30 years from now is insignificant, even when measured in inflation-proof dollars. Disability benefits are similarly discounted. The probability of an individual employee becoming permanently disabled is low and is probably perceived as being even lower.

The role of the Social Security system has changed in a significant way. It is no longer a modest program to establish a floor upon which private benefit programs may be built in response to the needs of the employer and the employees. Rather, it has become and will remain an important centerpiece in the benefits package.

PREVENTIVE LABOR RELATIONS

One way of viewing the recent and programmed changes is as a further curtailment of managerial discretion in the compensation area. A larger, and increasing, proportion of the compensation dollar has been statutorily shifted from current money wages or other benefits that the employer and the employees may prefer to retirement income. This is a serious matter. Remember, not only will the employer contribute 7.15 percent of covered wages by 1986, the employee will also. This compares to 1.5 percent each in 1950.[9]

One of the effects of the increasing costs of Social Security in the 1980s will be that the higher employee contributions will be seen as canceling out a significant portion of money wage increases. This will be especially so for those high-wage employees whose earnings approach or exceed the wage base. Not only will they be subject to the higher tax rates scheduled to take effect throughout the 1980s, but they will also feel the effect of the increasing wage base.

Just what the employee-relations effect of the higher Social Security bite will be is impossible to say with accuracy. However, it is safe to assume that it will have important ramifications for wage and salary administration. Since relatively highly compensated employees will pay more into the system, it will reduce the slope of the wage structure as measured in take-home pay. On the other hand, the perceived value of the benefits that will derive from the contributions should logically be higher for longer-service and older employees. To the extent that the older long-service employees and the highly compensated employees are the same, this may present no problem. However, if they are not the same, the additional Social Security costs to the employees and the differential perception of their value could influence the acceptability of the wage and salary structure.

A second possible effect stems from the fact that money applied to Social Security cannot be used elsewhere. Assuming that a given level of money wages is necessary to attract and retain the needed quantity and quality of labor and that the amount of money available for employee benefits is fixed, then the additional Social Security costs must be offset with a relative reduction in other benefits. The obvious place to cut would be in the area of other retirement income—the company's private pension plan. In fact, where the private pension plan is coordinated with Social Security benefits, as is commonly the case, such a reduction will occur automatically.[10] Under such an arrangement, increases in the benefit levels of Social Security will automatically result in a partial reduction in

162

the private plan's benefit. This suggests that an employer whose private pension plan is not coordinated with Social Security benefits would be well advised to reexamine the plan.

If it is not feasible to cover the additional Social Security costs from other retirement income, then it will be necessary to do so from other benefits that are not mandated by law. This will be more or less serious from a preventive labor relations perspective, depending on the value such benefits have to the employer and the employees and whether or not these benefits are already established. It is more dangerous to reduce or discontinue an existing benefit than it is to decline to adopt or expand one. The nonunion company considering expanding its benefits package should remember the programmed Social Security cost increases that will take effect throughout the 1980s and probably beyond.

A final observation on the Social Security program is that it is a federal program. Unlike the two other mandated programs examined, unemployment insurance and Workers' Compensation, there are no differences in costs among the states. This means that location is of no importance. A company cannot reduce its Social Security costs by the judicious choice of location and thereby gain a competitive advantage over some of the companies with which it competes. On the other hand, it does not have to worry about its competition getting a better break in this area because it is located in another state.

It is important that a nonunion employer inform the employees that they do have substantial benefits and that such benefits are part of the compensation package. This goes for legally required benefits as well. An employee making $5 per hour in 1980 will have $.31 per hour contributed to the Social Security system on his behalf. When this is added to up to $.17 for unemployment insurance and, say, $.08 for Workers' Compensation, it totals $.56 per hour. This is a hefty sum of money, and the nonunion employer should get as much preventive labor relations value from it as possible.

There are various other state-required employee benefits that are worthy of brief mention. State labor codes (by whatever name) often require coffeebreaks or other nonworking time by restricting the number of hours that may be worked consecutively by all employees or by women. They may also require that the employer grant time off for voting and jury duty, pay for preemployment physicals, tools, and uniforms, pay time and a half for work in excess of eight hours in one day, and the like. Those readers familiar with collective bargaining know that it is common practice to negotiate such provisions into labor agreements along with such federally required measures as reemployment rights for veterans, fair employment practices, and time and a half for work in excess of 40 hours per week. This has the important effect of subjecting disputes over such matters to the negotiated grievance procedure and labor arbitration process, which is usually to everyone's advantage. However, it also works to give the union credit for "winning" such items for the employees. There is nothing wrong with this. It is part of the game of keeping a responsible union and its leadership in business under conditions in which that is the appropriate course of action. It is no less logical that under nonunion conditions, the employer should take credit for such legally mandated benefits by including them in the employee handbook or other communications.

VOLUNTARILY ESTABLISHED EMPLOYEE BENEFITS

Employee benefits voluntarily established by the employer are by far the most important to preventive labor relations. Other than for their internal public-relations value, the government-imposed benefits mentioned are not perceived as "real" benefits by the employee or by the union organizer. Since they have to be provided by all employers, there are no differential effects between union and nonunion employers to the employee. Similarly, there is no difference in cost to the companies beyond that related to location and administrative efficiency. Voluntarily established benefits are a different matter. They are one of the things that a union can claim it gets from its members. They are also what the nonunion employees focus upon (in addition to money wages) when comparing their lot with that of unionized employees.

The more important voluntary benefits are pensions, life insurance, health and welfare plans, and paid time off. The list of less important and less costly items that may also be adopted is long and will be briefly discussed under the rubric of miscellaneous benefits. From a preventive labor relations standpoint, a long list of benefits is not necessary. One authority notes that you do not need more than five to remain nonunion, yet many companies have 25.[11] This sounds reasonable: few employees will incur the costs and risks of unionism to gain jury duty or tuition reimbursement, while they may do so for pensions and medical coverage. On the other hand, many of the lesser "fringe" benefits cost the company little and may have a positive motivational effect on some employees. Just where the line should be drawn for a particular organization is a matter of judgment. The only general guidance that can be offered is the reminder that we are talking about costs and benefits. How much does the benefit cost, and what does the company get for its money? The latter is the more difficult and judgmental question. It should also be remembered that dollars spent on minor fringe benefits cannot be spent elsewhere.

Pensions

One of the more costly voluntary employee benefits is the private pension plan. As indicated in Table 7-5, a significant majority of the employees in the companies reporting to the Bureau of Labor Statistics are covered by private pension plans. However, there are important differences among industries and, in the case of selected services, between plant and office workers. It is safe to assume that virtually all unionized employees are covered by some form of pension plan in addition to Social Security.

Pensions have become more costly to the employer since the passage of the Employee Retirement Income Security Act of 1974 (ERISA). This

TABLE 7-5. PERCENTAGE OF PLANT AND OFFICE WORKERS EMPLOYED IN ESTABLISHMENTS PROVIDING PENSION PLANS AND/OR LIFE INSURANCE.

	All Indus-tries	Manufac-turing	Transporta-tion, Com-munication, and Other Public Utilities	Whole-sale Trade	Retail Trade	Finance, Insurance, and Real Estate	Selected Services
Pension Plans							
Plant	78	85	83	78	70	—	48
Office	85	88	83	78	77	91	68
Life Insurance							
Plant	93	96	99	93	88	—	77
Office	97	98	99	95	91	99	91

Source: U.S. Department of Labor, Bureau of Labor Statistics, *Handbook of Labor Statistics, 1977,* Bulletin 1966, Washington, D.C.: U.S. Government Printing Office, 1977, p. 224, Table 103.

complex law has significantly increased the cost of maintaining a private pension plan by establishing minimum requirements for participation, accrual, vesting, funding, and various other matters. Its regulations and reporting requirements have also added to the administrative expense associated with operating a pension plan. While the protection afforded the long-service employees in companies with pension plans is desirable, the unfortunate effect of such additional expenses has been to force some companies out of providing their employees with pensions and deterring others from establishing them. From a preventive labor relations point of view, this may be dangerous.

Pension programs are highly visible. They lend themselves to easy comparison on a superficial level. If a nonunion company attempts to operate without a respectable pension plan, it provides the union organizer with powerful ammunition, especially if the company employs a large number of older persons. Remember the warning from our discussion on employee selection in Chapter 4: either the benefit package fits the employees or the employees fit the benefits. It is hazardous to operate without a pension plan for any length of time if employees perceive pensions as an important item.

One way of looking at this is as a trade-off between cost and risk. While quantification of either is difficult or impossible, rough approximations can be made for a given situation. In addition, the cost of the program can be lessened in a number of ways. One is to hire a young workforce and accept a high degree of turnover. A second is to make the pension plan contributory. That is, have the employees pay part of the expense of the program. One advantage of this arrangement is that if the employee declines to participate, the employer is not obligated to contribute on his behalf. A third way to avoid some of the cost and administrative expense associated with an in-house plan is to pay the employees an additional sum in the form of money compensation and direct them to an institution offering an Individual Retirement Account plan as allowed by ERISA.

The details of these arrangements, and of pension plans in general, lie beyond this discussion. However, it might be useful to remember that we are still discussing money. The cents-per-hour cost of a defined contribution pension plan may be computed by dividing the employer's monthly contribution by 173 hours. If, for example, the company's monthly contribution is $35 per covered employee, it costs the employer $.20 per hour ($35/173) for those employees participating in the plan. If there are

166

a significant number of employees not participating, then the cents-per-hour cost across the board would be reduced because of the larger base. This example is not unreasonable. In 1974, companies spent an average of $.19 per hour on private pension plans.[12]

Life Insurance

Group life insurance is one of the oldest and most widely offered employee benefits. As Table 7-5 indicates, almost all employers provide some form of coverage to both plant and office employees.

The cost of life insurance varies with the average age of the group, the amount of coverage, the carrier, and such features as additional (usually double) payment for accidental death and dismemberment (ADD). At this writing, group life insurance with ADD can usually be purchased for less than $1 per $1,000 worth of coverage. Thus an employer can provide $5,000 of life insurance ($10,000 for ADD) for about $5 per month per employee. That computes to just under three cents per hour ($.029), or a little more than one half of one percent (.0058), assuming a $5 ASTHE.

Group life insurance is a low-cost benefit. However, from a preventive labor relations point of view, it may be important. While employees may not consciously place a great value on life insurance,[13] it is highly visible and easy to compare from one company to the next. The company without some level of life insurance is inviting a negative comparison from the first union organizer who comes along. Furthermore, should an employee prematurely die or become disabled and the employer not have such coverage, it will raise serious questions in the minds of the employees.

Given its relatively low cost, very wide adoption, and potential importance to some employees, it is unwise for a nonunion employer to operate without a life insurance plan.

Health Insurance

Closely related to life insurance in the minds of many employees, and in the marketplace, is health insurance in its various forms. Table 7-6 shows that some degree of health and welfare coverage is widespread in the United States, although there are important differences among types of coverage offered by different industry groups, and between that provided for office and plant employees. Such differences preclude easy generalization about the cost of health insurance. However, it is safe to assume that it is expensive and will become more expensive in the years ahead.

167

TABLE 7-6. PERCENTAGE OF PLANT AND OFFICE WORKERS EMPLOYED IN ESTABLISHMENTS PROVIDING HEALTH INSURANCE AND SICK LEAVE, 1974.

	All Industries	Manufacturing	Transportation, Communication, and Other Public Utilities	Wholesale Trade	Retail Trade	Finance, Insurance, and Real Estate	Selected Services
Hospitalization							
Plant	95	99	99	97	91	—	79
Office	97	99	99	97	93	98	92
Surgical							
Plant	95	99	99	96	91	—	79
Office	98	99	99	97	93	98	92
Medical							
Plant	90	94	97	93	83	—	73
Office	94	96	98	94	80	97	88
Catastrophe							
Plant	74	72	94	84	74	—	54
Office	93	91	98	90	83	98	89
Sick Leave*							
Plant	83	88	82	85	77	—	56
Office	87	91	93	85	86	84	80

*Sick leave and/or sickness and accident insurance.

Soure: U.S. Department of Labor, Bureau of Labor Statistics, *Handbook of Labor Statistics, 1977,* Bulletin 1966, Washington, D.C.: U.S. Government Printing Office, 1977, p. 224, Table 103.

Table 7-7 shows that in 1974, employers in manufacturing spent $.28 per hour for life, accident, and health insurance. If, for example purposes, we assume that three cents of that was for life and accident insurance, it leaves us with $.25 per hour for health insurance. With a $5 ASTHE, that translates into 5 percent, which makes it a rather expensive benefit. Remember that health care costs have gone up considerably since 1974. Some carriers have raised their rates by as much as 50 percent per year for some customers; 10 percent per year increases are low for the period.[14]

TABLE 7-7. EMPLOYER EXPENDITURES FOR COMPENSATION OF PRODUCTION AND RELATED WORKERS IN MANUFACTURING IN 1974.

	Dollars per Hour (Hours Worked)*		Percent of Straight-Time Pay (ASTHE)
Total Compensation: $5.88			
Pay for time worked	4.52		
Straight-time pay		4.29	
Premium pay		.23	5.4
Paid leave†	.40		9.3
Vacations		.22	5.1
Holidays		.15	3.5
Retirement programs	.48		11.2
Social Security		.27	6.3
Private pensions		.21	4.9
Life insurance and health benefit programs	.37		8.6
Life, accident, and health insurance		.28	6.5
Sick leave		.03	0.7
Workers' Compensation		.07	1.6
Unemployment programs	.08		1.9
Unemployment insurance		.06	1.4
Severance pay and SUB‡		.01	0.2

*Columns do not sum because of rounding and deletion of minor benefit categories.
†Exclusive of sick leave.
‡Supplemental unemployment benefits.
Source: Handbook of Labor Statistics, 1977, p. 237, Table 108.

The spiraling costs of health care have resulted in an important development. In 1973, Congress passed a law designed to encourage the development of health maintenance organizations (HMOs).[15] As modified in 1976, the law requires employers with 25 or more employees living in an area in which an HMO is available to offer the employees an HMO option in place of other health insurance.[16] The company is not required to pay more than it would under its normal health insurance plan. If the HMO is more expensive than the other plan and the employee opts for it, then he must pay the difference. The importance of this legislative development is that, as the costs of the traditional health insurance plans have skyrocketed, HMOs with their emphasis on prevention and early detection have become economically more feasible. While rates for both HMOs and traditional health insurance vary from city to city, they are now running neck and neck nationwide. Over the long run the HMOs seem to have the advantage, since their rates are rising less rapidly than those of the traditional health insurance carriers.[17] It is likely that a health maintenance organization is in the future of all employers of any size.

At present the HMOs and traditional health insurance costs are in the neighborhood of $70 per month per covered employee. That translates into $.40 per hour, or 8 percent, using our standard $5 per hour ASTHE. Thus health insurance is an expensive benefit. However, from a preventive labor relations point of view, it may be a necessary one. Employees favor it over most other benefits.[18] Given its wide availability and perceived importance to the employees, it is dangerous for a nonunion employer to operate without it.

Closely related to health insurance is sick leave or some other program to compensate employees for work time lost due to illness. Table 7-6 shows that some form of sick leave is widespread; Table 7-7 illustrates that it is a relatively inexpensive item ($.03 per hour, or a little more than .5 percent). The cost to a particular company will vary with the number of days per year allowed and the employees' right to accumulate or "cash in" sick days. All in all, sick leave is a highly visible benefit and one that may be worth the relatively modest cost involved.

Pay for Time Off

The final benefit to consider is pay for time not worked. In particular we will focus on vacations and holidays. A certain number of days off per year in the form of vacation and holidays is necessary in all regular employment. At the most basic level, a company simply cannot ask people to work on Christmas without a good reason and additional compensation and/or compensatory time off. Nor can it expect them to work year in and year out. Vacations serve a constructive purpose in both revitalizing the employee and enriching his life. Beyond that, the nonunion employer must be concerned with the comparisons the employees make with other (especially unionized) companies in regard to vacations and holidays.

Vacation time and holidays are interchangeable from a cost standpoint. In rough terms, an additional day of vacation costs as much as an additional holiday. However, the holiday is usually more visible than an additional day of vacation. If the company does not grant Washington's Birthday as a holiday and the companies with whom the employees compare do, the difference is noticeable. If, on the other hand, the company's vacation formula is a little less generous, this is more difficult to discern and less of a problem.

The prevailing pattern in the United States is one or two weeks of vacation after one year of service; three after ten; and four after 15 or 20.[19] The average number of holidays for all industries is 8.4.[20]

In 1974, manufacturing firms spent $0.40 per hour, or 9.3 percent of *actual* ASTHE ($4.29), on paid leave exclusive of sick leave. According to Table 7-7, vacations accounted for $0.22 or 5.1 percent, and holidays for $0.15 or 3.5 percent. This is serious money; however, it should be remembered that a certain level of vacation and holiday time is impossible to avoid. Whereas a nonunion company may be tempted to operate without a pension plan or health insurance, it is unlikely that it would consider having *no* paid time off. Thus, the question is more one of marginal cost than average cost.

The cost of an additional day off in the form of vacation or a holiday may be computed with the following formula (using our usual numbers):

$$\frac{\text{ASTHE} \times 8 \text{ hours}}{2,080} = \frac{\$5 \times 8}{2,080} = \frac{40}{2,080} = \$.019$$

Thus, an additional day off costs just under two cents per hour, or .4 percent. Remember, though, that this is only the simplified direct cost of an additional day off with pay. Unlike most other benefits, paid time off affects production or the normal functioning of the organization. The more important cost may be the loss of revenue from an additional day of production or sales or the expense of having to cover the jobs of vacationing employees in the form of overtime or the maintenance of a larger workforce.

From a preventive labor relations perspective, vacations and holidays are important. They lend themselves to easy comparison. Obviously, three weeks of vacation are better than two and ten holidays better than eight.

Paid holidays are a relatively simple matter, and there is little that the employer can do to reduce their cost. If the companies with which the employees compare have 10 holidays, the nonunion employer might get by with nine, but not eight. The cost of the additional holiday can be reduced by requiring that the employee work the day before and the day after, and/or by making it a "floater," which the employee may take within a certain period of time, on his birthday, or as part of a vacation. When the last approach is adopted, the difference between a holiday and an additional day of vacation all but disappears.

Vacations are somewhat more pliable. It is often possible to get some preventive labor relations value from a vacation improvement that has little or no cost to the company. As an extreme example, if a ten-year-old company adopts a vacation formula that provides five weeks of vacation after 25 years of service, it will have no real cost for the next 15 years, by which time everyone else will probably have it anyway. Further, if the company experiences turnover to the extent that few employees stay that long, this will continue to be a very low-cost item. Similarly, if most employees have been with the company for five or more years, reducing the eligibility for three weeks of vacations from five years to three years may prove to be relatively cheap.

A growing practice is to compute vacation eligibility on the basis of so many hours of vacation for a given period of time. This allows the company to adjust its vacation formula in increments of less than one week, which may be an important administrative convenience. It also serves to lessen the contrast between a more generous unionized employer and the nonunion firm.

Miscellaneous Voluntary Benefits

The list of other possible discretionary employee benefits is almost endless. Benefits in addition to those mentioned earlier are probably not necessary for remaining nonunion. As mentioned, no one joins a union for tuition reimbursement. On the other hand, such benefits may be relatively low-cost or even give the company a positive return on its investment. Many employers have discovered in recent years that maternity leave is not that bad. Why lose a trained and dependable employee because she needs three months off to have a baby? The same reasoning applies to leaves of absence for other legitimate reasons. In many situations, allowing such leaves may cost the employer nothing, yet such benefits may be of great importance to some employees. Such items are usually included in labor agreements. There is usually no reason for a nonunion employer not to be as responsive to employees' needs as a unionized company.

Jury duty pay is another item that may prove to be inexpensive to the company but of considerable importance to the employee who happens to be called. Such a policy can be made more economical by paying only for those hours actually served on days when the employee was scheduled to work (plus a reasonable amount of travel time) or by starting payment on the second day and allowing the employee to use a floating holiday for the first day. The cautious employer may also want to exclude service on a grand jury.

Tuition reimbursement may also be worth the relatively small cost involved. This would be especially so if there is an inexpensive tax-supported university nearby and the company pays on a sliding scale based on the grade received (full amount for an A, 75 percent for a B, and so forth). The more important cost of encouraging employees to go to school may appear in the form of additional scheduling problems and more turnover and absenteeism.

BENEFITS REQUIRED BY THE NATURE OR LOCATION OF THE WORK

Various benefits are often required by the nature of the work or the location at which it is performed. Included in this category would be uniforms or special clothing provided by the employer; tools and equipment; transportation; parking; breaks and wash-up time in addition to what is mandated by law; meals; eating facilities; and medical services. It may also be necessary to provide shift-differential premiums to encourage employees to work less desirable hours. Certain premiums may also be necessary to motivate employees to perform unpleasant or hazardous work. Without overdoing it, the employer can often present such items as benefits and thereby gain a degree of motivational and preventive labor relations value. Looking at such matters in the negative, *not* providing them may be perceived as a serious cause for complaint by some employees if it is known or claimed that the union can obtain such things for them.

CONCLUSION

No matter how the arithmetic is done, the importance of benefits to preventive labor relations is great. Table 7-8 collects and summarizes the various costs from the examples developed in this chapter. They total to $1.58 per hour or, using our standard $5 per hour ASTHE, 31.6 percent. Although the examples are only estimates drawn from various sources and different years, none of them is unrealistic for a company operating in the United States in 1980. Similarly, the cents-per-hour and percentage totals are well within the range of reasonability.

Table 7-9 portrays the increase of money wages and benefits, using various measures for selected years between 1968 and 1974. During this period, total compensation increased by 59.3 percent and wages and salaries by 52.1 percent while supplements to wages and salaries (bene-

TABLE 7-8. SUMMARY OF BENEFIT-COST ESTIMATES USED IN CHAPTER 7.

Program	Estimated Cost per Hour	Estimated Cost in Percent of $5 Average Straight-Time Hourly Earnings
Social Security	$0.31	6.2
Unemployment insurance	.17	3.4
Workers' Compensation	.08	1.6
Private pension plan	.19	3.8
Life insurance	.03	0.6
Medical insurance	.40	8.0
Sick leave	.03	0.6
Vacations	.22	4.4
Holidays	.15	3.0
Total	$1.58	31.6

Note: All numbers are estimates and offered for expository purposes only.
Source: Derived from examples developed in Chapter 7.

TABLE 7-9. PERCENTAGE OF COMPENSATION PAID IN FRINGE BENEFITS, 1968, 1970, 1972, AND 1974.

Year	Total Compensation	Wages and Salaries (Gross Pay-roll)	Supplements to Wages and Salaries	Supplements as a Percentage of: Total Compensation	Supplements as a Percentage of: Wages and Salaries	Straight-Time Pay (ASTHE)*	Total Compensation Minus ASTHE	Difference as a Percent of ASTHE
1968	$3.69	$3.26	$0.43	11.7	13.2	$2.86	$0.83	29.0
1970	4.24	3.70	0.53	12.5	14.3	3.23	1.01	31.3
1972	4.86	4.18	0.68	14.0	16.3	3.64	1.22	33.5
1974	5.88	4.96	0.92	15.6	18.5	4.29	1.59	37.1
Percent Difference 1968–1974	59.3	52.1	114.1	—	—	50.0	75.9	—

*Work hours.

Source: Derived from U.S. Department of Labor, Bureau of Labor Statistics, *Handbook of Labor Statistics, 1977,* Bulletin 1966, Washington, D.C.: U.S. Government Printing Office, 1977, p. 237, Table 108.

fits) went up 114.1 percent. The difference reflects the growing importance of nonmonetary compensation relative to money wages. There is no reason to expect this trend to reverse or even slow down. In fact, as the programmed increases in the Social Security tax, additional Workers' Compensation costs, and the expenses associated with ERISA take effect during the 1980s, and as high rates of inflation and a progressive tax structure reduce the value of increases in money wage rates, the disproportionate growth in nonmonetary compensation will continue. The non-union employer who ignores or is unresponsive to this development is courting a union problem. To cast this in more positive terms, the company intent upon remaining union-free must pay particular attention to the nonmonetary components of its compensation program. This is not to suggest that other elements of employee relations or personnel administration should receive less attention—they remain as important as ever and must continue to be handled in an effective manner. However, there is no employment area with relevance to preventive labor relations that is experiencing as rapid and important a change as is nonmonetary compensation.

NOTES

1. U.S. Department of Labor, Employment and Training Administration, Unemployment Insurance Service, "Significant Provisions of State Unemployment Insurance Laws, January 3, 1977."

2. "How Your Tax Dollars Support Strikes," *Nation's Business,* March 1973, pp. 21–25.

3. There are various state and federal programs that extend the duration of benefits when the unemployment rate goes above certain levels. The employer's account is usually not charged for such benefits, and they are therefore not included in our calculations.

4. Robert J. Paul, "Workers' Compensation—An Adequate Employee Benefit?" *Academy of Management Review,* October 1976, pp. 118–119, Table 1.

5. *Report of the National Commission on State Workmen's Compensation Laws,* Washington, D.C.: U.S. Government Printing Office, 1972.

6. For a summary of these changes, see Amy S. Hribal, "Workers' Compensation Laws—Significant Enactments in 1977," *Monthly Labor Review,* December 1977, pp. 25–33.

7. "Social Security: What Next?" *Business Week,* January 19, 1976, p. 37.

8. PL 95–216, "Congress Clears Social Security Tax Increase," *1977 Congressional Quarterly Almanac,* 161–162.

9. Dan M. McGill, *Fundamentals of Private Pensions,* 3rd ed., Homewood, Ill.: Richard D. Irwin, 1975, p. 13.

10.   A typical benefit formula in a private pension plan will specify the monthly benefit as, say, years of credited service times a certain dollar factor minus a proportion of Social Security benefits (often one-half, which is proportionate to the employer's contribution).

11.   Charles L. Hughes, as reported by Thomas M. Rohan, "Would a Union Look Good to Your Workers?" *Industrial World,* January 26, 1976, p. 37.

12.   U.S. Department of Labor, Bureau of Labor Statistics, *Handbook of Labor Statistics, 1977,* Washington, D.C.: U.S. Government Printing Office, 1977, p. 237, Table 108. Based on an hourly rate of $5.40 in 1974 for all hours worked.

13.   William F. Glueck, *Personnel: A Diagnostic Approach,* Dallas: Business Publications, 1978, p. 496.

14.   *Business Week,* May 17, 1976, pp. 144–146; May 30, 1977, pp. 74–76.

15.   PL 93–222, *1973 Congressional Quarterly Almanac,* 499.

16.   PL 94–460, *1976 Congressional Quarterly Almanac,* 546.

17.   *Business Week,* May 30, 1977, p. 74.

18.   Glueck, op. cit., p. 495.

19.   *Handbook of Labor Statistics, 1977,* p. 230, Table 105.

20.   Ibid., p. 231, Table 106.

8

THE UNION
ORGANIZING DRIVE

It is important for the company intent upon remaining nonunion not to ignore the possibility of a union organizing drive, regardless of how heavily it invests in the other dimensions of union prevention. It is best to assume that someday, for some reason, a union will appear on the scene and put the company and its preventive labor relations program to the test. While most organizations would rather avoid such encounters, the opportunity to learn from the experience and make improvements where called for should not be ignored. There is no better test of the effectiveness of the program.

The organizing drive and the company's response to it should be considered an integral part of the preventive labor relations program. It is almost never the beginning of the union problem, nor is it the end. The fact that a presumably rational labor organization either responded to an invitation from the employees or for some other reason chose the company as an organizing target suggests that the employer was already vulnerable and that mistakes had already been made. Furthermore, the successful or unsuccessful completion of a representational proceeding may only be the beginning. As will be discussed, there is a good chance that the union will be back a year later if it loses. If it wins, the company will have an important decision to make in regard to whether to learn to live with the union or continue the fight.

It is dangerous and potentially expensive for a company to rely upon thwarting union drives as a way of remaining nonunion, especially if the overall preventive labor relations program is less than adequate. It should always be remembered that the important work of preventive labor relations is done before the union appears on the scene. If it is done effectively, the union may never show up and the subject matter of the present chapter never called upon. However, thousands of organizing drives do occur every year, and it is important that everybody involved in employee relations in a nonunion firm be knowledgeable about the subject.

THE LABOR MOVEMENT

The labor movement in the United States is a massive and complex set of organizations that all but defies generalization. As of 1975, it consisted of 210 separate organizations, 173 of which were classified by the Bureau of Labor Statistics as unions and 37 as professional and state employee associations.[1] For an employer faced with an unwanted organizing drive the distinction between union and employee association is unimportant. One hundred and eight of these organizations were affiliated with the American Federation of Labor–Congress of Industrial Organizations (AFL–CIO), which is an organization of organizations. That is, individuals do not usually belong to the AFL–CIO but to the separate national and international unions. The member's relationship to the AFL–CIO is through the national or international union, usually through membership in a local or some other subdivision.

In North America an international union is one that has locals in Canada. The distinction is not significant unless the company does business on both side of the border. However, the fact that many U.S.-based unions have sizable Canadian operations should be kept in mind when examining union membership data.

In 1976 there were 24 million members of U.S.-based unions and employee associations in the United States and Canada, 22.5 million of whom were in the United States. In relative terms, 23.2 percent of the total labor force and 28.3 percent of the employees in nonagricultural establishments belonged to unions and associations. Since the 1950s, union membership has declined steadily as a percentage of the labor force.[2] Those gains that have been made in absolute terms have been concentrated in the public sector and have been more than offset by losses in other areas and by an expanding labor force.

Individual unions vary from the huge International Brotherhood of Teamsters, Chauffeurs, Warehousemen, and Helpers of America (which is not affiliated with the AFL–CIO) with its 2 million members, 805 locals, and complex structure, to the Italian Actors Union with 75 members and no locals.[3] Not surprisingly, the bulk of the members and most of the organizing activity are centered in the 52 unions and five employee associations reporting 100,000 or more members.[4] For preventive labor relations purposes, they are the American labor movement. Few employers have to worry about the Italian Actors Union or the many other small organizations on the fringe, which are of mainly historical interest. Almost all effective union organization is done by a handful of unions that tend to specialize in given industries, areas, and/or markets. In most cases, the nonunion employer only has to worry about two or three unions that have an interest in organizing the employees in a given plant. It is probable that the number of union organizations will continue to decline in the years ahead as the less important ones merge or pass out of existence. With the passage of various laws and executive orders allowing and encouraging collective bargaining by government employees, the public sector will be the main growth area for unions during the 1980s.

National and international unions are usually made up of a large number of local union organizations, which operate within their assigned jurisdiction with more or less autonomy (depending on the union and the subject matter) under a charter granted by the national organization. Between the national and the local there is usually some form of intermediate structure made up of district councils, joint councils, conferences, or whatever. The allocation of functions among the units and levels varies from one union to another and reflects the functional activities of the organization.

Organizing, for example, may be initiated and conducted at the national, intermediate, or local level, depending on the traditions of the union and the size and geographical dispersion of the target. Indeed, it may even involve a number of national unions operating in concert and coordinating their efforts through one of the departments of the AFL–CIO. Having said this, it is important to recognize that most union organizing is done at the local level. There may be help from the national or intermediate body in the form of legal and technical advice and/or printed campaign material; however, organizing usually remains in local hands. There are a number of important exceptions to this observation. Some unions do not have locals, and by definition organizing is a function of the national body. This form of organization is found in relatively small unions and in the maritime industry. A second important exception is commonly found where a company in an industry dominated by industrial-type unions opens up a new plant. Under such circumstances, the responsibility to organize the new facility may fall upon the international representative who services the territory. When the plant is organized, a new local is chartered to represent the employee-members. A third exception occurs when the logical bargaining unit is too large and/or geographically spread out to be effectively handled by a local union. These conditions are not mutually exclusive.

The fact that most, though not all, union organizing activity is initiated at the local level has important implications for preventive labor relations. One is that the union organizer is seldom a stranger in town who gets off the bus and starts fishing around for basic information. Such information is usually already in the union's files or provided by the employees who extended the invitation to the union in the first place. Similarly, the union organizer is already familiar with the state or local laws and ordinances that may affect picketing or other aspects of the organizing campaign.

A more important implication of the local emphasis of union organizing involves the timing. If the union sends a team of organizers into a Southern textile town, the chances that they will catch the employer in an especially vulnerable position are close to random. If, on the other hand, the union is already established in the community, it will wait for an opportune time to mount its drive. This will usually be signaled by an invitation from one or more employees, who will then serve as the union's inside organizing committee. In addition, a local union operating in its own territory is not subject to the time constraints that are often a serious problem for out-of-town organizers. It costs money to maintain an organizing effort in a strange location. In addition to the usual expenses associated with the organizing drive, the living and entertainment expenses of the union personnel must be covered. Thus, if no results appear in a relatively short period of time, the union is inclined to cut its losses by either calling off the campaign or going for a premature election. The local union organizer, on the other hand, has few additional expenses. He lives at home and integrates the organizing activity with other union business. Moreover, the local union can afford to wait indefinitely for the right time to initiate the active part of the campaign.

The local nature of most union organizing campaigns corresponds to the relatively small size of the bargaining unit involved in the great majority of NLRB-conducted elections. Local union organizing efforts would be at a disadvantage in an attempt to unionize a large and geographically dispersed unit. But in view of the fact that large and spread-out bargaining units are inherently difficult to unionize, the logical level for a union to assign organizing responsibility is at the bottom.

THE ORGANIZING DECISION

It has often been observed that unions seldom go looking for companies to organize. This may have occurred in the past, and may occur under unusual circumstances today, such as when a union is attempting to consolidate its control over a market or area. However, under such a haphazard approach, the union's chances of success are low and its costs high. Similarly, the tactic of sending a professional organizer to apply for a job in the proposed target firm is almost never used. The chances of being hired for a job that would allow the person to operate undetected as an inside organizer are prohibitively low. It may take months or years to develop the knowledge, respect, and trust necessary for effective inside organizing. The much more common hiring mistake is to bring in too many people with an inclination to join unions or individuals who, for one reason or another, are pro-union.

The most prevalent pattern of union organizing is for one or more employees who are unhappy about some aspect of their employment to approach the union with an "invitation" to organize the plant. Explicit or implicit in the invitation is an offer to work for the cause and serve as inside organizers for the union. The union's response to the invitation depends on how promising the situation appears.

The degree of commitment on the part of the union is an important element in the campaign, since it indicates how generously the union will spend its time and money on that particular plant. Unions seldom turn potential members away unless a fellow AFL–CIO affiliate already has an "established collective bargaining relationship" with their employer or unless their work is beyond the union's claimed jurisdiction (in which case the employees will be referred to a union that would be more interested). However, the response can vary from lukewarm interest to an immediate, well-run, and well-financed campaign. The difference is of great importance to the employer involved.

As developed earlier, successful unions are run in a rational and businesslike way. The factors that influence the degree of enthusiasm with which a labor organization responds to an invitation from a group of employees logically include:

The number of potential dues payers involved.
The estimated cost of the organizing drive.
The estimated chances of success.
The estimated cost of "servicing" the bargaining unit or local once it is organized.
The strategic importance of the proposed unit to the union's other collective-bargaining relationships and/or organizing ambitions.
Other demands on the union's organizing budget and staff time.

At the margin, questions of "principle," such as the need of the employees in question for representation, may come into play—but only at the margin. A union leadership that operates too much on principle, as opposed to the practical matters mentioned, will find itself faced with a poor organizing record and criticism from the membership and opposition leaders.

An example is in order. If it costs a local union $1,000 to organize 10 employees who will then pay $100 per year in union dues, it will take the union at least a year to get its money back. Actually, it will take much longer, since it costs the union something to negotiate contracts and handle grievances and other matters for the new members. In addition, a sizable piece of the dues will be remitted to the national union in the form of per capita (the amount per member that the union forwards to the national union, to intermediate bodies, and to the AFL–CIO). Thus the local union may really have a payback period of many years. Naturally, if an alternative organizing opportunity with the same probability of success but with a larger number of potential members for the same or a lower cost presents itself, the union will direct its serious efforts toward that target. Similarly, if the numbers were the same but one opportunity was perceived as having a higher probability of success, the union would concentrate its scarce resources in that area. Of course, all this assumes rational decision making and a finite amount of time and money within the union. It would be difficult to challenge either assumption.

I am not suggesting that union leaders sit around discussing their organizing efforts in such rational and marginalist terms, any more than do employers when deciding whether or not to move into a new market. Most decisions are made in a "seat of the pants" way that has the same effect. The "market" enforces the right decisions. If the union leaders (managers) make too many wrong decisions, they or the union (company) pass from the scene.

In summary, it is important to understand that union organizers do not randomly appear at the plant gate or on the company payroll. They are called in by the employees in response to real or imagined complaints. That is why effective personnel administration, as covered in Chapters 4 through 7, is so important to preventive labor relations. The strength of the union's response to such an invitation will be a function of the numbers involved and the perceived probability of success. That is why the material treated in Chapter 2 (avoiding and deterring unions) and in Chapter 3 (bargaining units) is important. Note again the interrelationship between the various elements of an overall preventive labor relations program.

HOW UNIONS GAIN RECOGNITION

The purpose of the union organizing drive is to gain recognition from the employer as the bargaining agent and exclusive representative of the employees in the unit. When management "recognizes" the union, it acknowledges the union as the representative of the employees and, in effect, agrees to bargain with it. Recognition under the National Labor Relations Act, and under almost all other situations in the United States, is "exclusive." That is, the labor organization chosen by a majority of the employees in the bargaining unit has the sole right (and duty) to represent *all* the employees in the unit. Management has a statutory duty to bargain with the union holding such exclusive recognition. It may not negotiate with another organization on behalf of the employees in that unit. Nor may it bargain *individually* with the employees involved in regard to wages, hours, and working conditions if the union objects.[5]

A union may gain recognition from an employer in a number of ways. One is through the employer's *voluntarily* recognizing the union on the basis of proof of its majority status. This almost always takes the form of signed "authorization cards" (sometimes called "pledge cards"). In many cases the recognition is truly voluntary in that the employer willingly accepts the union's claim and documentation of a majority. There are whole industries in which the company would not think of attempting to operate nonunion. In most situations, however, the employer's "voluntary" recognition is the reluctant acceptance of the fact that unionization is inevitable, either because the union has an overwhelming majority of the employees signed up or because it would be impossible to do business in the industry or area without the union's approval.

A second, but related, way in which the union may obtain recognition is to *bluff* the employer into granting it. It is not unheard of for a union organizer to demand recognition when he does not have a majority of the employees signed up. In fact, he may not have any of them signed up. It works like this: someone goes into business or opens up a branch in a new area or market and is soon paid a visit by the business agent of a local union, who claims to represent the employees involved because they fall within his union's jurisdiction. A gullible employer may accept the claim at face value and grant recognition. Of course, part of the bluff may be that if recognition is not forthcoming, the union will impose certain direct or indirect sanctions. Another approach is for the union representative to explain that if the company signs with this union, it will get a better contract than if some other union organizes the employees. This may even be true for the first year or two. But beyond that, everything is negotiable. Of course, if the union representative agrees to a long-term substandard contract in exchange for concessions from the employer—perhaps going beyond the mere granting of recognition—it is called a "sweetheart contract" and is illegal. This amounts to selling out the employees, and it is assumed that no responsible employer would engage in such activity.

Under no circumstances should a nonunion employer voluntarily recognize a union, either with or without proof of majority status. No union has an automatic right to represent a group of employees without an election or some other official proceeding.

A third way in which a union may win recognitiion is to *trap* the employer into witnessing its majority status. This is done by getting the employer to count the signed authorization cards, have them counted by a third party, or in some other way ascertain that the union does, indeed, represent a majority of the employees in the unit. Should management officially witness proof of the union's majority, it has a legal duty to bargain with that union. Moreover, it will have given away its claim to a "good faith doubt" of the union's majority status or of the validity of authorization cards as a true expression of employee intent. Should management make this mistake, the NLRB may decline to conduct an election, since the union has already demonstrated its majority to the employer. This complex and serious matter will be more fully discussed in Chapter 10.

The fourth way in which a union may gain recognition is through an *NLRB-conducted election* This is the official mechanism about which we have the most information. It is also the only way in which a union may be recognized that gives the employees a thoughtful secret-ballot choice away from the influence of the union organizer and pro-union fellow employees. If the union wins the election, it is "certified" by the NLRB as the exclusive representative of the employees in the bargaining unit. The employer then has a duty to bargain with and recognize the union.

A fifth method by which a union may win recognition is through a *bargaining order*. Since 1969, if the union at some point has demonstrated its majority status but subsequently loses the election and the employer is found to have committed serious unfair labor practices, the NLRB may order the company to bargain with the union.

A sixth way for the union to force recognition is for it to call its supporters out on strike or engage in some other legally protected concerted activity (picketing). If the union does not petition for an election within 30 days, the employer may ask the NLRB to conduct an expedited election without the usual requirement of a 30 percent show of interest (to be discussed). This throws the matter into the formal NLRB election procedures. If the union loses the election, its picketing may be enjoined and the strike becomes nonprotected activity. If the union wins, it is the same as if it had won a regular NLRB-conducted election. Another scenario is that the picketing or other job action so hurts business that the employer "voluntarily" recognizes the union to put an end to the affair. If a substantial majority of the employees are really out on strike and the plant is shut down, this may be the appropriate thing to do. However, if the disruption is caused by a number of employees in a relatively small unit within the company who, because of their strategic position, can shut down the operation, the granting of recognition may be a mistake. It would be better to go to the Board and get a ruling on the appropriate bargaining unit before taking action. It may be that the long-run advantages of nonunion operation will outweigh the short-run cost of the strike or picketing.

There are a few other ways in which a union may gain the right to represent certain employees, such as through a unit-clarification proceeding. They are unimportant for our purposes and will not be examined. Throughout most of our subsequent discussion we will assume that the employer will not be bluffed or trapped into granting voluntary recognition and that the union will end up petitioning the NLRB for an election. This is the normal course of events when the company knows what it is doing and wishes to remain nonunion.

A final note on recognition: once the employer has negotiated a labor agreement with a union, that agreement will contain a "recognition clause." This is usually a short paragraph stating that the employer recognizes the union involved as the exclusive representative of certain specified employees. The main purpose of the recognition clause is to define the bargaining unit. This is an important matter in situations in which the unit was not defined during an NLRB-conducted election, or where the parties have changed the unit by mutual agreement since the union was certified.

INSIDE CADRE AND OUTSIDE ORGANIZER

Assuming the union responds to the invitation, its first step is to establish a small group of inside union organizers if one does not already exist. In most cases, the employees who supported or approved of approaching the union will serve this function. However, it may be necessary to expand the group in one direction or another in order for it to be representative.[6] For instance, if a department or other organizational unit is not represented within the probable bargaining unit, it will be necessary to bring one or more persons onto the team from that area. If there are no representatives from an important employee group—women, older persons, ethnic groups—it may be necessary to expand in that direction. And if there are individuals who, because of their leadership abilities or social position in the workplace, could be instrumental in forming opinions, it may be important to get them involved as well. Leaving important groups unrepresented or important individuals out of the inside group is dangerous. Not only does it deny the union their support and effort; it may also establish points within the plant that can develop into centers of opposition to the union, either pro-company or pro some other union.

187

On the other hand, there may be some risk in expanding the inside organizing team prematurely. The greater the number of people involved or approached, the more difficult it is to hide the fact that an organizing drive is in progress. Since the employer will eventually become aware of the problem, this is really a question of timing. If the employer identifies the drive early, the union will usually expedite its organizing to limit the company's opportunity to mount an effective countercampaign before opinions are formed by a majority of the employees. In most cases, the best assumption for the union to operate under is that the employer will detect the union drive at an early date by means to be developed in Chapter 9.

One or more members of the inside cadre will remain in communication with the local union officials or staff members (business agent, organizer, field representative, international or conference representative, or whatever), whom we shall call the "outside organizer." The relationship between the outside organizer and the inside cadre is interesting. The outside organizer provides those on the inside with legal and technical advice on what to do and when to do it. He also provides authorization cards, campaign literature, and moral support and engages in' some outside organizing activities: leafleting, picketing, home visits, media releases, and representation at NLRB or other administrative proceedings. The inside cadre provides the outside organizer with access to the other employees and needed information. The access, direct or indirect, allows the union to spread its message and obtain signatures on the all-important authorization cards. The information takes the form of feedback on how the campaign is going and what countermoves the company is making. This is important for the union in making its decision on when to demand recognition or petition for an election. The inside cadre also provides information on the layout of the plant, occupational relationships, and the various other factors needed to make an intelligent bargainining unit decision.

Another important function of the outside union organizer is to keep the inside group under control. This may be difficult. The problem to the union can take several forms. The inside organizers may make claims or engage in activities that constitute union unfair labor practices and thus jeopardize an otherwise successful union campaign. Or they may proceed too fast or too slowly with their organizing activities and throw the union's timing off. Or, worst of all, they may conclude that they would be better served by some other union (or unions) or decide to establish an independent union.[7] Such developments can most easily occur when there is a leadership split within the inside cadre. It is important, from the union's point of view, that the natural leaders within the plant be identified, brought onto the union team, and supported. This is no mean feat, and the ability to do it well separates the effective from the ineffective outside organizer.

AUTHORIZATION CARDS AND THE SHOWING OF INTEREST

The procedural mechanics of union organizing are simple. The labor organization establishes proof that it represents a majority of the employees in an appropriate bargaining unit and then either demands recognition from the employer or petitions the National Labor Relations Board for a representation election.

Proof of majority status to the employer and/or showing of interest to the NLRB is almost always done with authorization cards. These are documents upon which the employees apply for membership in the union, authorize the union to represent them, and/or petition for a representation election. Cards that only request that an election be conducted have also been held to be valid when they clearly state that the purpose of the election is to certify the union.[8]

To be accepted by the NLRB, cards must be dated and must be "current." However, the Board's definition of current depends to some extent on the surrounding circumstances. It has held in one case that cards over a year old were valid, while in another case cards signed only three months earlier, but before a state-conducted election, were not.[9]

Once signed, the cards speak for themselves. The NLRB does not inquire into, and will not accept testimony on, the employee's state of mind or reasons for signing an authorization card.[10] Thus a card signed on a whim, under duress, or when the employee was roaring drunk is acceptable. No doubt many authorization cards are signed other than as thoughtful expressions of a desire for union representation.

The NLRB requires that a union petitioning for an election demonstrate that it speaks for a "substantial number" (30 percent) of the employees in the proposed unit as of the date of the petition or during the pay period immediately preceding its filing. When the unit found appropriate by the NLRB is different from that sought by the union, the 30 percent showing of interest must be demonstrated in the new unit as of the date of the hearing.[11] Notice the power of the bargaining unit weapon in this context. If a union organizes the employees within what it considers the appropriate bargaining unit and the employer can convince the NLRB that that unit is inappropriate, the union's campaign may end then and there. Note also the value of limiting the union's access to information that will let it accurately gauge the appropriate unit.

Should an additional union wish to enter the election as an intervenor, it must *usually* demonstrate a 10 percent showing of interest within the same unit.[12] If, however, it is seeking to represent the employees in a different unit from that proposed by the petitioner, it must demonstrate a 30 percent showing of interest in its proposed unit. Thus the showing of interest must relate to the bargining unit sought.

It is interesting to note that when two or more unions are involved in an NLRB-conducted election, the chances of a union victory increase dramatically. In 1977, unions won 44.2 percent of all single-union representation elections but over 75 percent of all elections in which two or more unions were involved.[13] This suggests that when two or more unions are present, their competition generates more information and, thus, more employee interest. It is probably also the case that some nonunion employees who would vote for the company in a single-union election end up voting for the union they dislike the least in a multiple-union election. For example, an employee who would rather remain nonunion may vote for the Machinists in order to avoid becoming a Teamster. If the choice was ''Machinists'' or ''no union,'' he would vote for the latter.

On the other hand, the higher percentage of union wins in multiple-union elections may be due only to an additional union coming in for the kill in a sure union victory. If a new paper mill or auto assembly plant is built on the West Coast, there is almost no chance of it remaining nonunion for any length of time. The companies recognize this fact and direct their labor relations efforts at ending up with something they can live with. Under such circumstances, a second or third union may enter the election as an intervenor seeking to represent all or a portion of the employees involved. The cost to the union of such a move is low, since it involves little or no real organizing. While its chances of winning may also be low, they are at least positive.

Given the opportunity, the employer should attempt to thwart the efforts of an intervening union. It is better to go to an election facing one union than two or three. The data do not support the theory, held by unions as well as management, that employees will find interunion squabbling distasteful or confusing and end up voting for the company.[14]

A caveat is in order. The percentage figures cited earlier in this section involve only those elections in which a choice was made. If a multiple-union election results in none of the choices on the ballot receiving a majority of the votes cast, the NLRB declares the election "inconclusive" and conducts a "runoff" election between the top two choices of the employees.[15] Thus a representation proceeding that begins as a multiple-union election may conclude and be reported as a single-union election. This suggests that, under some circumstances, a divide-and-conquer approach may be effective and the employer should do the opposite of what was recommended here.

It should not be thought that, because of the ambiguity or complexity of the data, this is not an important decision. The employer is often in a position to help or hinder the chances of an intervening union. Of course, this is especially so if the company voluntarily recognizes the other union on the basis of cards. But even when the matter goes to an election, the employer can affect the second union's chances of winning by how expeditiously it responds to the requirements of the procedures. Furthermore, the position the company takes in regard to the bargaining unit decision is critical in a case in which two or more unions are contending for different unit decisions. Remember the high degree of control that the employer has in this area.

The 30 percent and 10 percent showing-of-interest numbers are not in the Act. Rather, they have been adopted by the National Labor Relations Board as an interpretation of public policy. Questions regarding a union's showing of interest are administrative matters and, as such, may not be challenged or litigated by the parties. Similarly, the need to demonstrate such an interest may not be waived by the parties.[16]

It is most unusual for a union to petition the NLRB for an election with a bare 30 percent of the employees signed up. About the only time this happens is when the union has given up on the unit and is playing a "long shot" or is using the election as a way of disengaging from the affair. Under such circumstances, the employer may be better off having the election and getting it over with than disputing the union's showing of interest. It is better to demonstrate the union's lack of support through a formal election than through an administrative or legal technicality. In addition, if a valid election is held, the NLRB may not hold another in the same unit for the next 12 months.[17]

The more common situation is for the union to have at least a majority of the employees signed up before it files a petition.[18] In fact, it has been reported that unions like to have at least 60 to 70 percent of the employees committed, since it is expected that some will change their mind or fail to vote.[19]

There is another reason for the union not to go to the NLRB until it has a majority. Should the union at some time in the proceeding demonstrate that it does represent a majority of the employees in the unit—and should the employer subsequently commit serious unfair labor practices—the NLRB may order the company to bargain with the union even though the employer won the election.[20] The Board's authority to use this remedy was first upheld in 1969.[21] Since then, it has evolved considerably. In 1977, a bargaining order was issued in a case in which the union never demonstrated a majority; what the NLRB did was to add to the pro-union ballots the signed cards of those employees who did not vote or whose votes were challenged.[22] This development and its implications will be examined more fully in Chapter 12.

UNION ORGANIZING TACTICS

This section will examine various aspects of union organizing. Its purpose is to familiarize the reader with some of the tactics and details of union organizing and to serve as a base for a subsequent discussion on the company's response.

Timing

The specifics of organizing drives vary with the peculiarities of the situation. However, one consideration in all campaigns is timing. It is important to the union that its efforts peak at the time of the election.[23] Should the union campaign peak out too early, it will start to lose support due to a loss of interest or because of the management countercampaign. In a close election this could mean the difference between a union win and a union loss. Alternatively, if the union peaks too early, it will have to spend time and money protecting its majority against such attrition. On the other hand, if the union's efforts have not yet reached their full extent at the time of the election, it may also lose.

The union has some control over the situation, because it is the party that starts the clock running by demanding recognition or petitioning the NLRB for an election. It also has control over when to start its initial organizing efforts and the rate at which it expends organizing staff time and other resources. However, this control is by no means perfect, and timing is one of the main problems of the union organizer.

Anything the employer can do to throw the union's timing off will work to the company's advantage either by costing the union votes or by increasing the cost of the campaign. While it may be appropriate for the company to seek an early election that would be premature from the union's point of view, this is unusual. Given the facts that the union initiates the formal procedure and that the union could probably find some way of postponing the election, it is unlikely that seeking an early election will work to the advantage of the company. The more important way to throw a union's timing off is for the company to delay the election for as long as is necessary.

There are various ways in which the company can delay the representation decision. One of the most important and easiest is not to grant voluntary recognition to a union's demand on the basis of authorization cards. Another is to contest the appropriateness of the union's proposed bargaining unit. Of course, the company will often want to do this for reasons unconnected with timing; however, if it takes several months to resolve the bargaining unit question, it may work to the advantage of the employer, even if the union ends up with the unit that it initially proposed. Once the formal proceedings have started, the attorneys have little trouble extending them in one way or another. Examples include an electronics firm that sent its industrial-relations manager out of the country for five months as a stalling tactic and a large bank that extended the bargaining unit proceedings for 13 months. In the latter case, the union won its preferred unit, but by the time the elections were held (in two small branch banks) it had long since lost its majority by attrition.

Employer delay in representation cases has been roundly criticized by organized labor and others as unfair to employees and against the spirit of the law. There is enough justification in this charge to generate considerable support. Indeed, one of the elements in the proposed (but unsuccessful) Labor Law Reform Bill of 1978 [24] was the adoption of statutory time limits designed to thwart such employer tactics. Given the fact that delay is often helpful not only to throw the union's timing off but also to give the employer an opportunity to take corrective action and respond to the union's charges, such time limits could present problems.

Delay will be examined from a somewhat different perspective in our discussion of the employer campaign in Chapter 11.

Inside Organizing

Most effective union organizing is done inside the workplace by employees. Much of it takes place long before the formal campaign begins. In fact, the existence of a sizable number of already committed union supporters is often a precondition for a union to get serious about an organizing campaign. In most situations it is almost impossible for an outside organizer to operate successfully without such inside support. This has been developed earlier, as has the relationship between the outside organizer and the inside cadre. We have also discussed a number of things the employer can do to hamper inside organizing activity (see Chapter 2). Beyond that, there are few generalizations that can be made about inside organizing. It is informal and can occur at any time or place. The form it takes depends on the interpersonal relationships in the work group. Further, there is little the employer can do about inside organizing beyond adopting no-solicitation rules and other devices designed to restrict access to nonunion employees. Once the organizing drive is under way, these restrictions have relatively little impact. If the union already has a large number of supporters in the plant, it will have little difficulty communicating with the remaining employees. Indeed, the employees have a right to receive such information; to prohibit it, even if this were possible, raises legal and ethical questions. The important role of such restrictions is to deter the outside organizer, to make it more difficult for a small minority of union supporters to operate within the plant, and to slow down the organizing drive so that the company can detect it and mount an effective counterunion campaign.

The fact that there is little the employer can do to deter inside organizing in no way detracts from its importance. Most employees who end up voting for the union make their decision before the active campaign begins. The main function of the card-signing drive and the active campaign is to reinforce existing pro-union attitudes. While a few employees may be convinced to vote one way or the other by the parties during the active campaign, there are seldom enough of them to make a difference in the outcome of the election.[25] This suggests that the real union proselytizing takes place early and through the efforts of the inside union organizers. It also reinforces our central theme that the employer's main preventive labor relations efforts must take place early and must be based on sound programs of personnel administration and compensation.

Leafleting

The distribution of union leaflets or "throw sheets" is associated with the initiation of union organizing in the minds of many. However, it is most unusual for a union to appear suddenly at the plant gate or office door and start passing out leaflets to kick off an organizing campaign. By the time this happens, the union will almost always have considerable employee support and an inside cadre in operation. Further, a decision to "go public" or "surface" will have been made. This may have been caused by the fact that the union has discovered that the employer has detected the union's organizing activities, in which case there is no reason to continue with a "silent campaign."

It has been observed that if the union distributes leaflets, it probably does not have a majority at that time.[26] This may be the case, but there are other reasons for a union to engage in leafleting. One is to extend its influence to departments or other organizational units in which it currently does not have support. While leaflets in themselves may not convince anyone to change his voting intentions, they are an effective way to communicate with employees in other departments who may join the inside group.

Leafleting may serve other purposes as well. One is that the distribution of one or more leaflets is strong proof that the employer knows that an organizing drive is in progress. This may be helpful in proving that the reason the company took certain personnel actions was to quell union interest, since the company could not claim that it had no knowledge of the campaign. Of course, the union could do the same thing with a certified letter or a witnessed personal visit to the company's office. Many unions have a policy of officially notifying the target company at an early date that a drive is in progress so as to strengthen its position in future unfair labor practice proceedings.[27]

Another legalistic purpose of union leaflets is to trap the employer into committing an unfair labor practice.[28] For example, the union may contend that the company has no choice but to continue to do business in that community, whether or not the union is elected. The employer may be tempted to reply to the effect that this is not true and that it is considering closing the plant and having the work done in Mexico or Taiwan. The company has just issued a threat of reprisal and thrown away its Section 8(c) (employer free speech) protection.

Union leaflets must be handled with care. In particular, they should never be answered without advice of counsel. In most cases it is better not to answer them at all, for answering them places the company on the defensive and allows the union to control the substance of the debate. There are exceptions, of course. One is when the union has zeroed in on a real issue that the company cannot safely ignore. For instance, should the union and the employees be especially concerned with pensions or the quality of supervision, the company's silence on the subject may communicate that it has no intention to correct an existing problem that has been forcibly brought to its attention. If this is not the case, the fact should be communicated to the employees. However, such a communication must be handled with caution so as not to read as a "promise of benefit." Again, advice of counsel is essential.

Another situation in which the employer may wish to respond to union literature is when the union emphasizes the wrong issues. One of the common mistakes of union organizers is to base a campaign on "false issues" that may have been provided to the union by a small number of discontented employees.[29] Should the company discover this, it will want to set the record straight, though perhaps not too early. It may be better to let the union continue its campaign with the wrong issues and then respond shortly before the election rather than give the union this feedback in time to use it.

There are three features of effective union leafleting that deserve mention. First, union leaflets usually come in a series. There will typically be several leaflets distributed to the employees over a period of time, each of which presents a part of the overall message. Each leaflet may build on the ones before it and lead into the ones that follow. Further, this printed matter has probably been provided to the local by the international union or been modified from other campaigns in which the union has been involved. This suggests that the better union-printed material has been tested over time and may be generally effective. However, it is also possible that the message does not fit the facts of the current situation, in which case the company has an opportunity to capitalize on inaccuracies. Union leaflets should be collected and studied by management for such opportunities. But remember, advice of counsel must be sought before responding.

196

A second important feature of effective union campaign literature is that it is simple, easy to read, and usually designed to convey a single message quickly and with little effort on the part of the reader. While format and content may vary with the educational level of the employees and the stage of the campaign, the union usually errs on the side of simplicity. A person walking into the plant at seven in the morning is not going to read three paragraphs of single-spaced nine-point type discussing the philosophy of trade unionism in North America. But a simple message, presented in large easy-to-read print, perhaps with the aid of a picture, cartoon, or symbol, will be read and absorbed. One union source soundly suggests that an effective union leaflet should have "eye appeal," a concise idea presented in simple, vigorous language, and a suggested course of action.[30]

The simplicity theme is especially important during early stages of the campaign. During this period the union's purpose is to arouse interest on the part of those who are not already committed. If the cost of reading the union message is too great in terms of time and effort, the nonunion or uncommitted employee will not read it. On the other hand, if all it takes is a glance to find out what the union has to say, and if that glance leaves an impression or a question in the employee's mind, the leaflet has done its job. As the campaign progresses, the union's printed material may become more wordy and more detailed in an attempt to convince the more thoughtfully uncommitted. A second purpose of the more lengthy union communication may be to provide the union supporters with information to use in the course of their inside organizing.

A third interesting feature of union communications is that they are almost always in good taste, reasonably accurate, and not presented as a personal attack on management.[31] Unions have learned through the years that they do not need to overstate their case and/or engage in smear tactics to gain the support of those who would vote union anyway, and they realize that such measures tend to offend others. In addition, there may be legal problems associated with overstatement and personal attacks that are best avoided. It has been observed that when a union resorts to personal attacks on management, it is a sign that it is in trouble.[32] Thus the content of union leaflets is usually tasteful and factual, with an emphasis on what the union has accomplished. Management communication to the employees during an organizing drive should be just as tasteful, factual, and accomplishment-oriented.

Meetings

Another union tactic is the organizational meeting. This is not to be confused with the usual union business meeting, which is part of the governing mechanism of the local union. Rather, the organizational meeting is a social affair designed to transmit information and impressions to uncommitted workers and to reinforce the loyalty and dedication of those who already support the union. Organizational meetings range from low-key affairs held in someone's home to fairly lavish events in a rented hall with free refreshments and other inducements designed to generate attendance. An extension of the organizational meeting concept is the "rally," which usually takes place late in the campaign (if at all) in a highly visible location.

Most of the attendees at the union's organizational meeting will be employees who are already committed to the union. However, some uncommitted or pro-company employees may also attend out of curiosity or for the free beer. The important communication content of the meeting will be directed at them and will mainly take the form of friendly and informal conversations between the union staff or union supporters and the "shoppers."

A correlation and probable causal relationship has been shown between attendance at union meetings, familiarity with the issues of the campaign, and vote switching in favor of the union.[33] This suggests that the union organizational meeting is a fairly important communication tool.

A related purpose of the organizational meeting is to impress upon the attendees, and indirectly upon those employees who do not attend, that the union represents a significant proportion of the workforce, and thereby to create a "bandwagon effect." Of course, if the meeting is a flop, the opposite impression may be projected and the union could lose support. It is therefore important to the union that the organizational meeting be well attended or, at least, appear to be well attended.

Since attendance is voluntary and on the employees' own time, the meeting must be scheduled when it least conflicts with other demands on the time of the employees. It should not conflict with Monday-night football, a bowling league, or some other popular activity. If the employees involved start work at 6 or 7 AM, it will have to be scheduled early in the evening or on the weekend. If the employees' homes are clustered at some distance from the plant, it may be necessary to locate the meeting as close to their homes as possible. On the other hand, if they commute to the plant from all directions, it will be best to hold the meeting near the plant during lunch hour or shortly after the employees get out of work. Remember our discussion in Chapter 2 on staggering lunch and quitting times. If the target plant operates on two or three shifts, the union will have to schedule more than one affair or time the meeting so that it spans the change of shift.

Obviously, when and where to schedule a union organizational meeting is a delicate decision. If the organizer fails to take any of the above considerations into account, the meeting may be poorly attended and do more harm than good. Imagine the impact on the organizing drive at a plant with 100 employees when only ten of them show up at a well-publicized meeting. Of course, an effective union organizer will not let this happen. The meeting will be held at a convenient time and appropriate location or not at all. It will be attended by a number of non-employees—either union staffers or union members from other plants—to give the appearance of a large attendance. Moreover, the meeting will be held in a room that is a little too small for the expected crowd. A meeting attended by 50 people in a room designed to comfortably hold 40 looks more successful than if held in a room designed to hold 300. The same meeting in an auditorium would be a disaster.

Home Visits

A sometimes-used organizing tactic is the home visit. However, it is not as popular as is often thought. Home visits are an expensive organizing technique. Unless the employees live close to each other, a great deal of time can be spent driving from one home to another. Further, the union representative must schedule the visit at a time that is convenient for the whole family. This usually requires limiting home calls to the period between 7 and 10 AM. Further, the conversation cannot be limited to union matters and must usually include other members of the family.[34] All this has the tendency of embroiling the union representative in irrelevant conversation with the wrong people. Even worse, the spouse may be keenly interested in the impact of a strike or the other costs of unionization on the income of the family's prime breadwinner. Fielding such questions on a one-on-one basis with someone unfamiliar with unionism can be time-consuming—yet they must be answered or the home visit will have been dysfunctional.

All this means that only a few effective home visits can be conducted

199

in an evening. The outside organizer's way of coping with this limitation is to be selective in their use. There is no point in wasting home visits on employees who will probably vote for the union anyway or on employees who are so pro-company that they will in any case not vote union. It is the middle group of uncommitted employees, especially those who would be flattered by the personal attention or receptive to the organizer's rational arguments for whom this device is most suited. This suggests that home calls will be reserved for late in the campaign, by which time the union will have pretty good information on who the uncommitted voters are. Should the union already have a substantial majority, home visits may not be used at all.

A second way in which the union can reduce the cost of home visits to the outside union organizer is to assign the task to already committed pro-union employees. This will probably reduce the impact of the visit, both in terms of personal attention and the quality of the debate. However, the loss may be more than made up by the larger number of home calls allowed.

Of great aid to the union in conducting a program of home visits is an early and accurate mailing list. Not only do such lists facilitate the mailing of campaign literature to employees' homes, but they also allow a systematic approach to home calls. A ready-made list saves the union a great deal of time constructing such information from the memories of union supporters and phone books. Remember the advice against allowing Christmas card lists and similar material in Chapter 2. As will be discussed, the union must eventually be given a list of the names and addresses of the employees. However, there is no point in providing this information any earlier than necessary.

Telephone Organizing

A somewhat less effective but more economical organizing tool is the telephone. An organizer can make a large number of phone calls in the time it takes to make a single home visit. Moreover, he talks directly to the employee involved, and there is less need for the social chitchat that is inevitable in a home call. If he should happen to call at an inopportune time or when the employee is out, he can call back later.

Of course, telephone organizing and home visits are not mutually exclusive. One function of the telephone call can be to gauge the appropriateness of a home visit. If the organizer decerns from the telephone

200

conversation that the employee is already pro-union or firmly pro-company, he can limit the call to presenting his pitch and offering to answer questions that the employee may have. If, on the other hand, the employee is undecided, the organizer may follow up with a home visit or some other personal contact.

In addition to its low cost and flexibility, telephone organizing has the advantage of allowing the union to take an informal poll of its strength. This can be done early in the campaign and repeated as often as necessary for those employees who remain uncommitted. Such information is valuable to the union in helping it decide when to petition for an election, when to stall, and when and where to invest more time and effort in the campaign. Needless to say, anything the employer can do to restrict the union's easy access to a list of home telephone numbers should be done. In particular, lists of phone numbers used for call-in purposes in many work organizations should be available only to supervisors.

The Media Campaign

In some organizing campaigns, public opinion is an important factor. An extreme example would be the grape and lettuce boycotts by the United Farm Workers during the early 1970s. The use of symbols and pageantry, the alliances with established interest groups and public figures, and the working of the media by Cesar Chavez and his mentors was masterful. However, this was the extreme. Few employment relationships of the 1980s lend themselves to such drama. The more common situation in the private sector is that the employer may suffer some loss of business and community goodwill as a result of the image of the organizing drive projected in the press. This can be important if the employer is highly visible and sells a product or service to the public that can be purchased elsewhere or done without. In the public sector, the pressure may be more direct and be perpetrated through the perceptions of the political decision makers involved.

A secondary purpose of a media campaign that should not be overlooked is to influence the employees of the target company. On one level, the media serve as a convenient way for the union to communicate with the employees. This may be especially important when the bargaining unit is large and/or geographically dispersed and the employer has been effective in restricting the union's access to more direct contact. On another level, the image of the dispute portrayed by the press may have an effect on the employees' perception of the union and thereby on the vote. Such an impression may also operate indirectly through the employee's family and friends.

One of the jobs of the outside union organizer is to issue news releases when appropriate.[35] If the dispute is small and of no general importance, the media may not consider it newsworthy. Given that time is critical in this subject matter, news of organizing drives does not make good "filler" that the paper will publish eventually even if it is not of great public interest. If, however, the employer is important and subject to consumer pressure, and if the organizer has a flair for public relations, there may begin to appear in the local press a series of news items about the organizing drive. In the absence of picketing or violence, such stories are seldom the result of the investigatory efforts of the newspaper's staff. Rather, they are sent in as news releases by the union or are the result of an invited interview. Naturally, they tend to tell the story from the point of view of the party providing the information.

Media releases by the union present the nonunion company with a public-relations dilemma. Should it respond to the union's stories and charges? Should the company attempt to preempt the field by issuing its side of the story first? Or should it simply maintain a dignified silence? There is no general answer. Rather, the company's response will hinge upon the importance of public opinion to its market position, the nature of the community within which it operates, and other factors specific to the situation. It should be recognized, however, that this is an important decision that must not be ignored. It should be made early, deliberately, and with advice of the company's public-relations staff if one exists. In addition, nothing should be released that has not been approved by counsel. It is too easy for a company official to include an illegal threat or promise in a news release or interview. It is also important that the company not project itself as being paternalistic or patronizing in relation to the employees.

Indirect Pressure

A related source of pressure may come from other employers or from prominent members of the community. Of course, direct union pressure on a customer or supplier to stop doing business with the target company would constitute an illegal secondary boycott.[36] The pressure will seldom be that direct. It is more likely to come in the form of a casual and friendly piece of advice to the effect that resisting the union is futile or not the right thing to do. A Teamsters organizing manual contains the intriguing remark that "a simple telephone call from an associate may help to make the firm's officials receptive to having the employees organized."[37]

A recent union organizing tactic of ominous proportion is to threaten to withdraw union-controlled funds from a particular bank that is the target of an organizing campaign.[38] Given the large sums of money controlled by labor–management pension and benefit plans, this may not be an idle threat. While this matter is of most immediate interest to the largely nonunion banking industry, its ramifications are broader. Only a small number of such abuses of union power have become public; however, there is no way of knowing the number of more discreet suggestions that have been made by depositors to banks or lenders to borrowers. There are many situations in which remaining nonunion requires taking a strike or withstanding a period of reduced revenue due to picketing or a consumer boycott. At such times a bank may be especially vulnerable to a suggestion from an important customer, or a borrower from a creditor. In fact, the suggestion may not be needed. The response to a request for an extension on the due date of a loan or account payment may be enough.

Most employers are supportive of other employers with union problems, and the actions mentioned are the exception rather than the rule. However, the nonunion employer should not be surprised if indirect pressure comes from unusual sources during an organizing drive. The best defense is to have a firmly established and widely communicated policy in favor of remaining nonunion. Further, it is best for a nonunion employer not to become overly dependent on one supplier, customer, or source of credit. As in so many instances, this sound preventive labor relations advice is a good business practice in its own right.

Picketing

The final organizing tactic to be examined in this chapter is picketing. Although this activity is usually associated with collective-bargaining-related strikes by unionized employees, it is sometimes an important part of an organizing drive. In this context, picketing takes two main forms: organizational picketing and informational picketing. The important distinction is in the law that applies rather than in who does the picketing and what its real objective is.

Organizational picketing is controlled by Section 8(b)(7) of the National Labor Relations Act, as amended.[39] This section makes it a union unfair labor practice to picket or threaten to picket if the purpose of the action is to force the employer to recognize or bargain with a union or force the employees to accept a union as their representative where:

1. Another union has been lawfully recognized under the Act and a question of representation may not be appropriately raised under Section 9(c) of the Act (which governs representation elections).
2. A valid election has been held in the unit within the past 12 months.
3. The union engaging in the picketing does not petition for an election within 30 days of the commencement of the picketing.

Should such a petition be filed by employees claiming that the employer refuses to recognize their majority representative or that the union presently certified or recognized is no longer their majority representative, or should the employer file a so-called RM petition after a union has demanded recognition, the NLRB will conduct an expedited election. Under such conditions it is not necessary to demonstrate the usual 30 percent showing of interest.

If the union continues to picket for more than the allowed 30 days without filing a petition for an election, the company may petition for an election itself and/or file unfair-labor-practice charges against the union for unlawful picketing. It is usually recommended that an employer confronted with this decision not petition for an election. Under the NLRB's procedures the unlawful-picketing charges will be dismissed while the expedited election is processed.[40] If, on the other hand, the employer only files unfair-labor-practice charges that are found to be true in an expedited investigation, the Board will ask a Federal District Court for appropriate injunctive relief under Section 10(1) of the Act.[41] The resulting injunction or temporary restraining order will usually put a quick end to the picketing.

Under most circumstances, filing unlawful-picketing charges rather than petitioning for an election is good advice to the employer confronted with organizational picketing. But as usual, there are exceptions that should at least be considered. If the union continues to picket without petitioning for an election, this suggests that it does not have a majority of the employees signed up and may not even have the 30 percent showing of interest necessary to get an election. It may also mean that the union recognizes that it has no hope of getting a majority in the probable bargaining unit and that its only chance to gain recognition is to force it from the employer by shutting down that part of the company's operation where it does have some strength. Under such circumstances, it may be to the employer's advantage to file an RM petition and get the election over with. Such an election may demonstrate the union's weak position to all concerned and thus be more effective than catching the union on what the employees may perceive to be a technicality. By seeking an election the employer will be in a position to speak for the employees' right to make up their own minds. If the union is truly in a weak position, it may withdraw from the election rather than suffer a humiliating defeat. This will leave the employer in a very strong position.

There are two other advantages of seeking an election. One is that if a valid election is held, another election cannot be conducted for the next 12 months and the union cannot picket during that period.[42] This, in effect, gives the employer about ten months to take whatever action is necessary while the company is not in a "critical period" and, thus, under suspicion. If the picketing is enjoined but the organizing drive continues, the situation is less clear. Also, if the union is soundly trounced in an election, it is less likely to hang around for a year before it has another chance.

The second advantage of going for an early election is that it gives the company an opportunity to have the appropriate bargaining unit determined. Not only is organizational picketing a strong indication that the union does not presently represent a substantial number of the employees in the probable bargaining unit, it also suggests that the union does not represent enough employees in *any* unit that is likely to be found appropriate by the NLRB.

Obviously, the decision of whether to file unlawful-picketing charges or to seek an election is an important one. It does not lend itself to easy generalization. The most that can be said is that it must be made in light of the facts of the situation and with advice of counsel.

The second form of picketing with relevance for union organizing and for preventive labor relations is informational or publicity picketing. There is an important proviso in Section 8(b)(7) that exempts such picketing from the *de facto* requirement that a union may not picket for organizational purposes for more than 30 days without petitioning for an election. The wording is important:

> Provided further, that nothing in this subparagraph (C) shall be construed to prohibit any picketing or other publicity for the purpose of truthfully advising the public (including customers) that an employer does not employ members of, or have a contract with, a labor organization, unless an effect of such picketing is to induce any individual employed by any other person . . . not to pick up, deliver or transport any goods or not to perform any services.[43]

The practical effect of this is that unions may engage in informational picketing indefinitely so long as it does not have the effect of interrupting deliveries and the like. This is a compromise solution to the conflict between the sanctity of the freedom-of-speech provisions of the Constitution and the realities of labor relations.

Some unions make significant use of informational picketing as an organizing tool. In particular, the Culinary Workers or Hotel and Restaurant Employees and Bartenders International Union (AFL–CIO) have used it extensively. The usual arrangement is for the union to hire people to picket target establishments during peak hours. The picket signs are carefully worded to explain to the public that this is a nonunion establishment and/or that it does not pay union scale. The pickets (perhaps only one) will be instructed not to misinform anyone who asks about the nature of the picketing and not to interrupt any pickups or deliveries. In fact, if a friendly Teamster should volunteer not to cross the line, the picket will probably insist that he do his job. Otherwise the *effect* of the picketing will have changed, and it will have become unlawful.

Of course, the intent of the picketing is to inform union members and other pro-union potential customers that the target establishment is not a good place to eat because it is nonunion. Doubtless, it also deters others who assume that the employees of the restaurant are on strike or that crossing the line may entail some hazard or unpleasantness. Very few people stop to study the wording on the picket sign or appreciate the distinction between informational and economic picketing.

As mentioned, informational picketing can continue indefinitely, with no requirement for the union to petition for an election and no right of the employer to petition for an election or to file charges of unlawful picketing. This is what makes it such a problem to the nonunion employer who deals directly with the public in a relatively pro-union area. A single picket (who is not even an employee of the target firm!) can turn away a lot of business. And the affair can turn into a drawn-out contest to be won by the party whose resources last the longest.

Informational picketing by nonemployees lends itself to one of the worst abuses allowed in the labor law of the United States. By its nature, such picketing is most effective against the marginal employer who cannot withstand a lengthy reduction in revenue. However, it is often this very employer who also cannot afford the additional labor costs associated with unionization. Too frequently the result is that the employer goes out of business and the employees end up losing their jobs.

The nonunion employer has three defenses against informational picketing. The first is to post counter signs informing the public that there is no strike in progress and that the pickets are not employees of the establishment (assuming that this is the case). If this information can be effectively communicated to the public, the impact of the picketing will be greatly reduced. Most people, including many union members, find the concept of such picketing by nonemployees objectionable and are inclined to cross such picket lines. Since the employer controls the premises, there is usually no difficulty in finding a place to mount a tasteful and effective sign informing the public of the truth.

The second defense is to take advantage of anything that weakens the informational protection of the picketing. The wording on the picket signs should be studied by management and counsel for accuracy. Remember: the public must be "truthfully" advised. In addition, the company should keep careful records of all pickups, deliveries, and other services rendered by the employees of other companies, as well as any incidents that occur between the pickets and such employees.[44] If it can be demonstrated that the picketing has had the effect of substantially interrupting such activities, the nature of the picketing will have changed and it may no longer be exempted from the requirements of Section 8(b)(7).

Third, state law and/or local ordinance may in some cases bear upon picketing. Indeed, the logical targets for an informational-picketing campaign will often fall below the NLRB's jurisdictional standards and, therefore, be primarily covered by state or local law. Notwithstanding this, it will sometimes be the case that pickets must register as solicitors or some such thing, and that the employer, with the aid of counsel, can harass a union engaged in informational picketing. Given the fact that such picketing, when done by nonemployees, is to a great extent a matter of harassing the company until it capitulates, such reciprocation is quite in order. On a somewhat more sophisticated level, the employer's harassment may be viewed as a way of increasing the cost of informational picketing to the union, which is also within bounds.

A final consideration regarding either informational or organizational picketing involves the question of where the pickets may picket. In many situations the employer's place of business and its physical layout will be such that no question on this subject will arise. In others, such as in the case of shopping centers and other retail establishments with large parking lots and facilities located away from the main road, the union may have difficulty effectively picketing the establishment without raising the question of trespass. This matter is too complex and too much subject to change to allow safe generalization. However, the possibility of restricting the area in which the union may engage in informing the public should at least be explored with counsel.

NOTES

1. U.S. Department of Labor, Bureau of Labor Statistics, *Directory of National Unions and Employee Associations, 1975*, Bulletin 1937, Washington, D.C.: U.S. Government Printing Office, 1977, p. 1. Hereinafter, *Directory of National Unions*.

2. U.S. Department of Labor, Bureau of Labor Statistics, *News*, "Labor Union and Employee Association Membership, 1976," released Labor Day Weekend, 1978 (undated), p. 1, Table 1; p. 2, Table 2; p. 5, Table 5.

3. *Directory of National Unions*, pp. 22, 46.

4. Ibid., p. 65, Table 9.

5. Employees do have the right to present grievances individually, provided their resolution does not conflict with the collective-bargaining agreement and provided the union has a right to be present during any such grievance meeting.

6. Eastern Conference of Teamsters, *Manual for Union Organizers* (revised 1970), Bethesda, Md.: Eastern Conference of Teamsters, 1974, p. 22. Hereinafter, Teamsters, *Manual for Union Organizers*.

7. An independent union in this context is one that is not affiliated with one of the national or international unions. Their membership is usually limited to a single plant or company. However, they should not be confused with the term "company union." The latter implies company domination, which is illegal in the United States.

8. Office of the General Counsel, National Labor Relations Board, *An Outline of Law and Procedure in Representation Cases*, Washington, D.C.: U.S. Government Printing Office, 1974, p. 40. Hereinafter, NLRB, *An Outline of Law and Procedure*.

9. Ibid., p. 43.

10. Ibid., p. 42; Robert Lewis, "The Law and Strategy of Dealing with Union Organizing Campaigns," *Labor Law Journal*, January 1974, p. 45.

11. NLRB, *An Outline of Law and Procedure*, p. 46.

12. Ibid., p. 45. However, another source reports that an intervenor may get on the ballot with the showing of only one signed card; Teamsters, *Manual for Union Organizers*, p. 34.

13. 42 NLRB Annual Report 294, Table 13 (1977).

208

14. Teamsters, *Manual for Union Organizers,* p. 27.

15. NLRB, *An Outline of Law and Procedure,* p. 278; 42 NLRB Annual Report 296, Table 13, fn. 2 (1977).

16. NLRB, *An Outline of Law and Procedure,* p. 39.

17. National Labor Relations Act, Section 9(c)(3).

18. Julius G. Getman, Stephen B. Goldberg, and Jeanne B. Herman, *Union Representation Elections: Law and Reality,* New York: Russell Sage Foundation, 1976, p. 102.

19. Thomas M. Rohan, "Would a Union Look Good to Your Workers?" *Industrial World,* January 26, 1976, pp. 39–40; J. W. Lawson II, *How to Meet the Challenge of the Union Organizer,* Chicago: The Dartnell Corporation, 1973, p. 66.

20. Getman, Goldberg, and Herman, op. cit., p. 135, fn. 10.

21. 395 US 575, 603 (1969).

22. 42 NLRB Annual Report 94–95 (1977) discussing Pinter Bros., 227 NLRB No. 123.

23. Teamsters, *Manual for Union Organizers,* p. 27.

24. Message from the president of the United States: "Proposals to Make Laws Governing Labor-Management Relations Work More Efficiently, Quickly, and Equitably," H. Doc. No. 95–186, Congressional Record (July 18, 1977), pp. H. 7257–58. Discussed at *Proposed Amendments to the National Labor Relations Act,* Washington, D.C.: American Enterprise Institute, February 23, 1978, pp. 24–26.

25. Getman, Goldberg, and Herman, op. cit., pp. 107 and 142.

26. Lawson, op. cit., p. 59.

27. Getman, Goldberg, and Herman, op. cit., p. 135.

28. Lawson, op. cit., p. 60.

29. Rohan, op. cit., p. 41.

30. Teamsters, *Manual for Union Organizers,* p. 24.

31. Ibid., pp. 24 and 27; Lawson, op. cit., p. 38.

32. Lawson, op. cit., p. 169.

33. Getman, Goldberg, and Herman, op. cit., p. 105.

34. Teamsters, op. cit., p. 23.

35. Ibid., p. 23.

36. National Labor Relations Act, Section 8(b)(4)(B).

37. Teamsters, op. cit., p. 23.

38. *Business Week,* February 26, 1979, pp. 47–48; April 23, 1979, p. 46.

39. National Labor Relations Act, 8(b)(7).

40. I. Herbert Rothenberg and Steven B. Silverman, *Labor Unions—How to Avert Them, Beat Them, Out-Negotiate Them, Live with Them, Unload Them,* Elkins Park, Pa.: Management Relations, Inc., 1973, p. 185.

41. National Labor Relations Act, Section 10(1).

42. Ibid., Sections 8(7)(b) and 9(e)(2).

43. Ibid., Section 8(b)(7)(C). A similar protection of informational picketing is found in Section 8(b)(4) of the Act.

44. Rothenberg and Silverman, op. cit., p. 184.

9

THE DETECTION
OF UNION ACTIVITY

The importance of early detection of and appropriate response to union organizing activity cannot be overstated. Employee attitudes and positions on unionization are quite stable and, once articulated in the form of a signed authorization card, resistant to change. Further, those card signers who do switch in favor of the company do not seem to do so in response to the employer's countercampaign.[1] This observation reaffirms the main thesis of this book: the important work of preventive labor relations takes place before the active campaign begins. It also suggests that any advanced warning that an active campaign is in progress may be of considerable value to the employer. If the first the company knows of the union drive is that the union has demanded recognition or petitioned for an election on the basis of a substantial majority of signed cards, it may be too late to avoid unionization. This is not uncommon. Getman, Goldberg, and Herman found that in 10 out of the 18 elections in which such a determination could be made, *all* cards had been signed before the em-

210

ployer was aware that a drive was in progress. In 4 others, 50 to 75 percent of the cards were signed before the employer was aware of the problem.[2]

It is difficult to counter such "silent campaigns."[3] By definition, they are hidden from the employer. On the other hand, once the company has been officially notified that a petition for an election has been filed, the so-called "critical period" has begun and the employer's ability to respond to the problem is greatly curtailed. Anything the company does in the way of changing compensation or conditions of employment between the filing of the petition and the election is likely to be viewed as illegal interference with the employees' rights. In some organizing situations the union will make it a point to formally notify the employer at an early date that a drive is in progress so as to better support subsequent unfair-labor-practice charges.[4] Given the expanded use in recent years of bargaining orders in cases in which the union loses the election, this has become an extremely serious matter.

If the union drive is detected before the petition for an election is filed or before the company *officially* learns of the union's presence in some other way, the company gains two advantages. One is that it can unilaterally initiate changes in the employment relationship that would be suspect if done at a later date. The other is that it can plan and mount a counterunion campaign in time to do some good.

SPOTTING POTENTIAL UNION ACTIVITY

Given the importance of the period between the initiation of union activity and the filing of a petition for an election, it is essential that the company establish a system to detect the existence or increase likelihood of a union problem. Most of our attention will be focused on those things that can be done within the organization: employee attitude surveys, indirect indicators of employee dissatisfaction, and reports by supervisory personnel. Before turning to such internal and company-specific matters, however, three more remote sensing devices that are external to the business organization will be introduced: management gossip, the union press, and the *NLRB Election Report.*

Whether or not a particular company is likely to receive the serious attentions of a labor organization is to some extent a function of how actively unions are organizing in the company's industry and/or geographical area. For instance, whether or not the Teamsters or the Office Workers are actively organizing banks in the Pacific Northwest is of considerable importance to the chances of a particular bank in Seattle or Portland having a union problem. If the company is in a priority industry or area of one or more effective labor organizations, it should logically invest more in its preventive labor relations efforts. If the company finds that the level of union organizing in its industry or region is low, it may decide to ease off a bit or invest in other areas of management concern. Although there is no way to fine-tune the level of preventive labor relations that a company needs, it is always better to have too much than not enough. Management should not lose sight of the fact that remaining nonunion is an objective that competes for resources with other important objectives of the firm.

The usual way to stay apprised of industry and area labor problems is to "keep one's ear to the ground." Informal and semiformal communication with other managers, sales representatives, and attorneys is an excellent and often reliable source of information. One function of the professional luncheon or the trade association meeting is to exhange such information. A related source is trade or professional publications. For example, *Banking,* the main trade publication of the banking industry, regularly carries industry-specific labor news. By staying tuned in to such readily available sources, management can remain fairly knowledgeable about who is organizing where and with what degree of success.

A second source of information on union organizing is the labor press. All important national and international unions publish newspapers, as do many of their local and intermediate bodies. The AFL–CIO and its state and local organizations also publish various journals and newspapers. These publications are internal communications between the union leadership and the members and contain a heavy dose of what might be characterized as propaganda. This usually includes information on recent, current, and planned organizing activities, with emphasis on union victories. The nonunion company should assign a manager the task of subscribing to and reading such union publications regularly. For example, someone in a nonunion bank or other financial institution operating in Oakland, California, should read *White Collar,* the "house organ" of the Office and Professional Employees International Union (OPEIU); the *29'er,* the paper of the main OPEIU local in the area; and the *East Bay Labor Journal,* the local AFL–CIO publication. Unions generally allow nonmembers

212

to subscribe to their publications. In addition, these publications are often available at university and local libraries.

Finally, the best independent source of union election information is the *NLRB Election Report,* a monthly publication (with semiannual summaries) issued by the National Labor Relations Board. Copies may be obtained free of charge from Division of Information, NLRB, Washington, D.C. 20570, and are available in many university libraries and those public libraries designated as government document repositories.

Figure 9-1 reproduces a page from the December 1978 *NLRB Election Report* for illustrative purposes. It shows the details of all NLRB-conducted elections closed during that month. Elections are listed by the union involved—first those won by the union, and then those lost. Other information provided includes the city and state of the election, an industry code number (48 represents communications; 80, health services; 39, miscellaneous manufacturing; and so on), type of unit (C represents craft; W, office, clerical, and other white-collar workers), type of election (S represents stipulated; C, consent; R, Regional Director ordered), the size of the unit, and the number of votes cast for and against the union. The code numbers and abbreviations are explained in the front of the report.

Observe how this can be used. An interested manager can quickly zero in on those labor organizations of interest and get a detailed month-by-month survey of most of their organizing activity nationwide. The state column can be scanned to identify those unions that are particularly active in the area of interest, and a quick check of the industry-code column will reveal how much organizing is being done in the company's industry and by whom. Finally, information on the size of the bargaining units and the closeness of the vote is provided in a way that allows the reader to extract information on the industry and/or area of interest.

Various other things can be extracted from different parts of the *Election Report,* but they need not detain us here. It is enough to point out that this is a goldmine of information that can provide the nonunion company with accurate and timely data on which unions are organizing where and with what degree of success. The *NLRB Election Report,* when used in conjunction with the other external sources of information mentioned, can often give the company an important early warning of a change in its probabilities of being chosen as an organizing target. The logical effect of such a warning should be to increase the company's in-house monitoring

FIGURE 9-1. SAMPLE PAGE FROM NLRB ELECTION REPORT.

NATIONAL LABOR RELATIONS BOARD

RESULTS OF SINGLE-UNION ELECTIONS REPORT
AFL-CIO AFFILIATES

FOR CASES CLOSED: DECEMBER 1978

UNION / EMPLOYER(S)	CITY - STATE		CASE NO.	INDUSTRY CODE	UNIT	TYPE ELECTION	NO. ELIGIBLE EMPLOYEES IN UNIT	VALID VOTES FOR	AGAINST
OFFICE EMPLS									166-WON
*TELEPROMPER CORP	SEATTLE	WAS	19-RM-01538	48	W	S	28	18	10
LAFAYETTE MANOR NURSING HOME	LEXINGTON	MO	17-RM-08637	80	R	S	72	38	28
EATON CORP	KENOSHA	WIS	30-RC-03496	39	W	S	183	110	61
GROUP HEALTH INC	CORAL GABLES	FLA	12-RC-05581	63	W	S	276	154	102
OFFICE EMPLS									166-LOST
*DOCTORS HOSPITAL	SAN LEANDRO	CAL	32-RD-00132	80	N	S	12	0	9
CHILDRENS HOME SOCIETY	BAKERSFIELD	CAL	31-RC-04365	80	W	S	18	5	12
FORD MOTOR CO	ROMEO	MIC	07-RC-15086	50	C	S	211	70	132
OIL CHEM. & ATOMIC WKRS									422-WON
CITIES SERVICE CO	DALLAS	TEX	28-RC-33542	29	A	R	23	17	6
OIL CHEM. & ATOMIC WKRS									422-LOST
*WITCO CHEMICAL CORP	BRADFORD	PA	06-RD-00633	29	P	S	7	1	6
BEE COATEFLIM CO	CHICAGO	ILL	13-RC-14822	30	A	R	21	10	11
ARMAK CO	PASADENA	TEX	23-RC-04694	28	A	S	27	9	18
KUTZ UNION GATHERING CO	KUTZ CANYON	N M	28-RC-03566	49	A	S	38	9	28
MIDWEST PIPE COATING INC	SCHFRERVILLE	IND	13-RC-14932	34	A	R	60	7	48
BEE CHEMICAL CO	CHICAGO	ILL	13-RC-14884	27	A	S	89	27	62
SOUTHERN UNION CO	KUTZ CANYON	N M	28-RC-03567	49	A	S	105	28	72
PAINTERS									171-WON
SETTLES GLASS CO	WEYMOUTH	MAS	01-RC-16010	52	C	S	4	3	0
GRAPHIC EXHIBITS INC	ST PAUL	MIN	16-RC-12130	26	A	C	5	4	0
FOTO MARK INC	MENDOTA HGTS	MIN	16-RC-11938	17	A	C	22	10	9

Source: National Labor Relations Board, *NLRB Election Report*, Cases Closed December 1978 (May 25, 1979), p. 13 reproduced.

efforts. By far the most important mechanisms for detecting union activity operate within the business organization.

Employee Attitude Surveys

Many companies, either on their own or with the aid of a consultant, conduct periodic surveys of their workforce to gauge the level of employee satisfaction. This usually takes the form of a confidential questionnaire administered to all employees or to a sample of the workforce at regular intervals. The survey instrument may be mailed to the employees' homes or, more typically, distributed at the workplace. Either way, for the survey to be effective, it must be returned or collected in a manner that guarantees anonymity to the respondent.

Surveys vary from powerful and sophisticated instruments designed to measure a wide range of direct and indirect indicators of employee attitude on unionization and related matters to simple homegrown varieties. For example, Dr. Charles L. Hughes and his associates at the Center for Values Research, Inc., promote the use of their Attitude Survey Analysis program, which comes in a handy instruction manual complete with five audio casettes, a sample questionnaire, and other material.[5] The questionnaire consists of ten identification items and 20 substantive questions to which the respondent indicates agreement or disagreement. The survey is administered by management personnel in a meeting room on the employer's premises to a relatively large number of employees at a time. The completed questionnaires and certain code sheets are then sent to the Hughes organization in Dallas, where they are scored and analyzed by a computer. A number of very useful reports are sent to the employer, along with a discussion, taped on an audio cassette, of the statistical results, possible problem areas, and recommendations.

None of the 20 questions is directly related to unions. However, six of them are used to compute an industrial-relations index that may predict labor trouble. The first time the survey is used, these data are compared to external norms. After that, they are also compared to various internal norms generated from earlier surveys.

Upon receipt of the results of the survey, it is recommended that management conduct one or more meetings with an appointed or randomly selected (not elected) employee committee to discuss problem areas and recommend solutions.

This is a sophisticated and impressive product. When used properly it goes beyond the mere identification of union interest and can contribute to the firm's organizational development in the larger sense. It is also somewhat expensive. In 1979 the minimum fee was $1,250 for the first year and $1,600 for the second, with the cost per employee decreasing with the number surveyed. For example, it would cost an organization with 336 employees $3,340 in the first year and $4,330 in the second ($9.94 and $12.89 per employee respectively). A company with 622 employees would pay $4,852 in the first year and $6,222 in the second ($7.80 and $10.00 per employee respectively).

Whether or not this is too expensive is a matter of judgment and will depend to some extent on the value to management of continued nonunion operation and the importance of an early warning of union interest as part of the company's preventive labor relations program. It has been observed that Hughes's survey is "supersensitive" and can give an employer three or four months advance warning of union activity.[6] Additional information on this program may be obtained from: Center for Values Research, Inc., Keystone Park, 13773 North Central Expressway, Suite 1401, Dallas, Texas 75243.

Of course, there are other programs available. J. W. Lawson has published as part of a comprehensive package an Employer Vulnerability Audit, a Supervisory Opinion Audit, and an Employee Opinion Survey. They are designed to measure what their titles suggest.[7] The Employee Opinion Survey contains 54 questions on ten subjects: hours and pay, status and recognition, communications, job security, working conditions, co-workers, personnel policy and practice, supervision, the company, and "about the survey."[8]

If a company cannot afford or is not inclined to invest in one of the more sophistocated "canned" programs, it may find that it can gain some of the same benefits from a "homegrown" survey. This can vary from a high-powered instrument developed over time by company personnel that is as effective as anything on the market to a simple "quick and dirty" questionnaire with few pretensions. The latter approach may be of special interest to a small business with limited resources.

A simple ten-question survey form, such as that shown in Figure 9-2, administered to all or a sample of the workforce once a year, will give the company usable feedback on employee attitudes at a modest cost. A mean and standard deviation or some other simple statistic can be computed and recorded for each question every time the survey is administered. In addition, an overall point score or average can be computed and recorded for each department and for the whole plant to provide a ready

216

FIGURE 9-2. SAMPLE HOMEGROWN EMPLOYEE ATTITUDE SURVEY.

Please circle the number that best describes your feelings. Do not sign your name. Your answers are strictly anonymous.

1. *How do you feel about your present job?*
   Bad   1   2   3   4   5   Good

2. *How does this company compare with other companies with which you have worked or are familiar as a place to work?*
   Worse   1   2   3   4   5   Better

3. *How do wages and salaries at this company compare with those at other companies with which you are familiar?*
   Unfavorably   1   2   3   4   5   Favorably

4. *How do benefits (pensions, health insurance, etc.) at this company compare with those of other companies with which you are familiar?*
   Unfavorably   1   2   3   4   5   Favorably

5. *How fairly is your job paid compared with other jobs in the plant or company?*
   Unfairly   1   2   3   4   5   Fairly

6. *How would you describe the person to whom you report?*
   Bad   Good
   Supervisor   1   2   3   4   5   Supervisor

7. *How would you describe the shop rules and their interpretation and enforcement at this company?*
   Unfair and   Fair and
   Unreasonable   1   2   3   4   5   Reasonable

8. *In general, has management been responsive to the needs of the employees?*
   No   1   2   3   4   5   Yes

9. *In general, how do you feel about your long-run future at this company?*
   Not Good   1   2   3   4   5   Good

10. *Would you recommend this company as a good place to work on a long-term career basis to a friend or relative?*
    No   1   2   3   4   5   Yes

index of the climate of the unit. An alternate approach to developing one's own survey instrument is to adopt a sophisticated and tested survey found in the behavioral literature, such as the Cornell Job Description Index (JDI).[9]

The numbers generated by a survey are of little value in the absence of a statistical base with which to compare them. One of the important features of the Hughes survey discussed earlier is that it provides such an external statistical base. However, once a company has administered its own survey a number of times and has gotten the "bugs" worked out of it, it will have its own base. If responses to a particular question change significantly, it is reasonable to infer that employee attitude in that area has also changed.

A word of caution: homegrown surveys are far from precise instruments that detect subtle changes in employee morale and allow the company to fine-tune its personnel policies and practices. Some response variation is inevitable owing to the selection of different samples (especially if the sample sizes are relatively small), the weather, the time of year, the state of the economy, and normal fluctuations in employee morale. If, however, the changes are substantial, sudden, and unexplained, they should be considered as important indications that something *may* be wrong. While such indications may not warrant making immediate changes or taking specific action, they at least call for a closer look and continued attention.

A second caution is that in the absence of reliable external norms the important information generated by such an instrument is the significant changes in employee response, not their absolute level. An average answer of 2.5 may be just as good as a 3.5, provided it is consistent with past readings. However, if the 2.5 or 3.5 represents a decline from a usually higher reading, it may be an important warning.

A third caution is that such surveys should not be used as a way of evaluating the effectiveness of supervisers. Employees and supervisors should know that this is not the purpose of the questionnaire. Otherwise, the employees may use the opportunity to reward or punish supervisors, and the supervisors may adjust their behavior accordingly. This will not only reduce the usefulness of the survey but detract from the effectiveness of supervision.

A strong case can be made for starting an employee survey program early, before the advent of union activity. If the normal state of affairs is considered to be the absence of serious union organizing, then it is important to establish the statistical base with which to contrast future changes. If the normal state has already been destroyed, there is no internal way to measure effective change. Also, the longer the period over which the survey is used, the more valid will be the comparisons.

Second, the main value of such a survey is to function as an *early* warning system. Since one of the main causes of union interest among employees is real and legitimate complaints about the company's personnel or compensation policies, one of the appropriate responses to union interest is to make real changes. It is important that information on employee discontent be gathered in time to be used to advantage. Even if the complaints are not based on facts, the employer needs time to set the record straight. Once a drive is well advanced and a majority of the employees have become convinced that a union is the only way to make the company respond, it is of little value to discover that the employees are dissatisfied with an aspect of their compensation or working conditions. It is also important from a tactical preventive labor relations perspective that early signs of trouble be received. The more time the employer has to plan and execute its counterunion campaign, the more effective it will be.

Finally, should an employer wait until the organizing drive has reached the "critical period," surveying employees may constitute objectionable activity or an unfair labor practice.[10] While the circumstances under which the NLRB would arrive at such a finding do not lend themselves to easy generalization, an employer with an ongoing survey program that is not specifically union-oriented is probably safe. As usual, advice of counsel should be sought.

Indirect Indicators

Employee interest in and receptivity to unionism are not independent of other aspects of the employment relationship. Of course, among some employees the desirability of union representation may be an article of faith because of upbringing, ideological orientation, or personal experience. Most, however, view union representation as a way to respond to on-the-job problems.

If interest in unionization is one response to on-the-job problems and frustrations, it will presumably correlate with other such responses. How do employees respond to employment-related dissatisfaction? They quit, stay home, come in late, complain, or take it out on someone or something else (co-workers, supervisors, customers, the product or equipment). Of course, they also join unions. All are normal responses to frustration, and no work organization is ever completely without them. However, if there is a causal relationship between on-the-job dissatisfaction and the response, we would expect to find that the intensity of the responses changes with the amount of dissatisfaction and frustration. Therefore, if a significant change in the level of such activity is observed, it may represent an early warning of potential union activity.

The behavior mentioned is measured in most work organizations in the form of turnover ratios, absenteeism and tardiness data, summaries of disciplinary or administrative actions, production and quality control records, and customer complaints. Most, if not all, of these data are generated for purposes not connected with preventive labor relations. It is a simple and inexpensive step to have them reviewed periodically by the manager responsible for maintaining the firm's nonunion status.

Turnover, attendance, and production data particularly lend themselves to such review. For example, should monthly or quarterly turnover statistics suddenly be 10 or 15 percent above what they were in the same period last year or some other accepted norm, it would suggest that a closer examination is required. One would naturally begin with external variables such as a tighter labor market or a new higher-wage employer entering the area. In the absence of such a finding, the increased turnover may be taken as an indication that something is wrong.

It should never be assumed that, since the discontented employees are the ones who are leaving, the problem will take care of itself. Those who replace them, and those who do not leave because they are "locked in" due to longevity, benefit accrual, or lack of other prospects, may respond in other, more damaging ways. Of course, turnover should usually be minimized on its own account. Not only are there substantial costs associated with the continual hiring and training of new employees, but there are risks as well. For every new hire there is a certain probability that the company has acquired a potential union activist. While this probability can be reduced by careful screening and other techniques discussed earlier, it can never be eliminated. To the extent that relatively long-service employees are replaced by new and less well tested recruits, the risk from this source is usually increased.

An important exception to this occurs when the employer must accept or prefers to accept a high degree of turnover as a matter of necessity or policy. If that is the case, the employees may develop a short-run view of their present employment and its problems that may work to deter unionization.

Should absenteeism, production, or other factors substantially change without ready explanation, they may be an early indication of a deeper problem, especially if they all change in conjunction with a change in the turnover rate.

The interpretation and the implications of such information are highly company-specific. There are few generalizations that can be offered. However, with time, a person in a central position who is sensitive to the preventive labor relations objectives of the company can develop a feel for the data. Such a person must also be aware and knowledgeable of what is happening in the community within which the plant or company operates. For example, in Seattle the turnover of every employer is influenced by whether Boeing Aircraft is hiring or laying off. There are similar economic facts that must be considered in other locations when assessing turnover data. Absenteeism data can be similarly influenced by an outbreak of the flu, inclement weather, or the opening of deer season. Production and quality control figures can be influenced by poor input materials, equipment problems, and changes in turnover and absentee rates.

With such cautions in mind, management can often infer from unexplained changes in already available information that something is happening. This in itself should prompt further inquiry. In the absence of other indication, such changes will seldom mean that a union drive is in progress. What it may mean, however, is that there is enough employee dissatisfaction to manifest itself in one or more of the usual outlets for such feelings. Given the high degree of substitution between withdrawing from a work-related problem in the form of quitting and remaining off the job (physically or mentally) and attempting to correct the problem by inviting a union into the plant, such indications should be taken seriously by any nonunion company.

Another common response to on-the-job problems is to complain. If the company is not already doing so, it should take steps to facilitate employee complaints. That is not to say that complaining should be encouraged for its own sake, but those complaints that do emerge should be reviewed from a preventive labor relations perspective. In addition, for employee relations reasons, complaints should almost always be answered in the form of corrective action or an explanation.

Employee complaints may be facilitated in a number of ways. One is the old-fashioned suggestion box. While this time-honored institution is often made light of, its preventive labor relations value should not be ignored. It is a convenient and effective way for employees to communicate with management (anonymously if desired) without having to go through a supervisor, who may be the source of the problem.

A second way to facilitate upward employee communication is to establish a nonunion employee grievance procedure. In addition to its other virtues (discussed in Chapter 5), such an arrangement can be an excellent source of information. Both the number and the type of grievances submitted should be evaluated for their preventive labor relations implications. In addition, less formal complaints to supervision—which may best be thought of as first-step grievances—should be communicated to management and evaluated in the same way.

The exit interview is an especially rich source of feedback on employee attitudes and of direct union information. The employee who is terminating voluntarily is doing so for a reason. What is it? This is important information in its own right; it may also have preventive labor relations value when placed in context. In addition, the exiting employee is in a position to be frank with the interviewer and may want to set the record straight or make a final contribution to the company. The employee is also no longer subject to the peer pressure of the work group that may operate to restrict direct upward communication on sensitive subjects such as unionism. All this suggests that the exit interview in the hands of a manager aware of the company's preventive labor relations needs can be an important element in the early detection system.

When the several indirect indicators of employee satisfaction identified (and perhaps others that the reader can think of) are evaluated for their preventive labor relations content, a pattern may emerge that contains a message about union or potential union activity. Note that this evaluation is not a substitute for or in any way inconsistent with the use of external information or an employee attitude survey. Nor is it a substitute for or inconsistent with the most reliable union-detection device of all—the supervisor.

Reporting by Supervisory Personnel

Without question, the best source of information on union activity is first-line supervision. It is unlikely that anything as important and involved as a serious union organizing effort can get started without the supervisor in the unit knowing or at least suspecting it. Supervisors are usually in a position to identify a union drive long before it gets under way. The problem is not that the supervisors are unaware of what is going on but that they think it is none of their business or that a union victory may be to the advantage of supervisory personnel.

It is important that supervisors identify with the company on this and on all other matters. It is unfair and potentially disastrous for management not to let supervisors know what is expected of them in the area of union activity. This involves communicating the essential fact that, by definition, supervisors are not "employees" and do not have the protection of the National Labor Relations Act. The employer has a legal and ethical right to demand their complete loyalty in regard to labor relations. The role of supervisors in preventive labor relations is central and cannot be left in doubt.

Three things must be present for supervision to operate as an effective early-detection system of union activity. Supervisors must know what activities to look for; they must understand that reporting such activities is important and does not detract from their position; and they must know how to report early signs of union activity. All this material should be treated as an integral part of supervisory training. It should also be contained in supervisors' standing instructions and repeated often. In addition to reminding supervisors of their responsibility in this area, such repetition will serve to impress upon them the seriousness with which the company considers the subject.

1. *What to look for.* Knowing what to look for is an important requirement. Obviously, if employees start wearing union buttons and union propaganda appears on bulletin boards, union activity is in progress. By then, of course, the union campaign may be so advanced that there is nothing the company can do about it. Much more valuable is the early sign, the overheard comment, the slip of the tongue, or the pattern of unusual activity and attitude that suggests that something is taking place. Any manager can walk through the plant and spot union buttons and posters. But only the first-line supervisor is in a position to monitor the day-in-and-day-out communications of the work group. Indeed, even if the supervisor has been promoted out of that work group, he may still be an integral part of such activity.

It is difficult to generalize about early signs of union activity. Many nonunion companies live with a certain level of union interest among their employees. The important question under such circumstances is the degree and intensity rather than how to spot initial signs. In other situations the plant or company may be free of serious union interest; in that

223

case, the program of detection should focus on subtle signs that are easily overlooked.

Figure 9-3 presents a list of possible indicators of union activity. It is derived from a document in use in a large West Coast bank and is similar to material that has been published elsewhere.[11] Some of the items may seem trivial or even ludicrous. However, they do serve as examples of employee behavior that could be important. They also serve to impress upon the supervisor that the company takes any such indications of union activity, however slight, as serious matters worth reporting.

2. *Self-interest.* The second needed condition for an effective supervisory reporting system is that the supervisor must not be placed in a position that conflicts with his own self-interest. He must not be blamed for the presence of union activity in the organizational unit involved, for this will place him in the position of having to inform on himself. The inevitable outcome of such an arrangement is that important signs will be overlooked (consciously or unconsciously) or their upward communication will be suppressed. It must be made clear to everyone that union activity is almost never anyone's "fault."

Supervisors should also know that the reporting of apparently trivial and probably unimportant signs of possible or potential union activity is encouraged, expected, and taken seriously. This is important. An inquiry from a customer as to whether or not the tellers at a branch bank are unionized may be harmless. However, should such an inquiry be made at

FIGURE 9-3. COMMON SIGNS OF UNION ACTIVITY.

1. *Changes in Employee Behavior:*
   a. Become silent in the presence of supervisors and managers.
   b. Meet and talk in unusual locations and/or with employees from different departments or job levels.
   c. Begin leaving the premises for lunch in unusual numbers.
   d. Avoid being seen with supervisors.
   e. Show unusual interest in compensation, personnel, or other company policies.
   f. Become belligerent toward supervisors in the course of everyday conversations.
   g. Start using unusual terms in the course of everyday conversation ("management" in place of "the company").

224

2. *Communications Changes:*
   a. Supervisors are no longer privy to the jokes and rumors of the work group.
   b. The grapevine shuts down.
   c. The number of employee complaints either increases or decreases markedly.
   d. Complaints are made by a delegation or by an individual on behalf of a group.

3. *Work Group Changes:*
   a. The quantity and quality of output of the group becomes more homogeneous; the work of better employees declines while that of poorer employees improves.
   b. Some high-status persons in the work group suffer a loss in status. Some formerly low-status persons suddenly become popular.
   c. Some employees direct gibes at others who are known to be pro-company about their loyalty to the employer or their work.

4. *Strangers:*
   a. Appear on or near the plant or even in work areas.
   b. Customers or others not in the employ of the company show undue interest in the operations or policies of the company.

5. *Direct Signs:*
   a. Union literature is distributed within the work group or left at a convenient location (lunchroom, rest room).
   b. Union posters appear on bulletin boards.
   c. Union or anticompany graffiti appear in rest rooms or elsewhere.
   d. Some employees begin wearing union buttons or other insignia.
   e. Comments are made directly to the supervisor or within hearing to the effect that a union is needed or inevitable.
   f. Employees are seen passing out authorization cards.
   g. A labor agreement from another company is found or seen being passed from one employee to another.

half a dozen branches within a short period of time, it may herald the beginning of a serious organizing effort by a union. Think of the opportunity that would be lost to the company if the supervisors or branch managers involved concluded that such casual events were not worth passing along! Yet that is exactly what is likely to happen if they are not encouraged to report such incidents. It is *sure* to happen if such reports are perceived as an admission that supervision or local management cannot handle its own problems or as a case of "crying wolf."

There should be a reward system designed to encourage such supervisory reporting. When the reports prove to be valid indicators of early union activity, those making the identification should be rewarded either monetarily or otherwise. If "punishment" (negative reward) is involved at all, it should be directed at discouraging failure to report relevant information rather than discouraging overreporting of possible union activity.

3. *How to report.* The third requirement for an effective supervisory union-spotting system is that the supervisors know what, when, where, and how to report. The "what" is easy: everything. When in doubt, report it. The "when" is even easier: immediately. Few things should take precedence over reporting an indication of union activity in a non-union firm. Given the fact that management's discretion is serverely limited once the critical period begins, a few days more or less advanced warning can be important to the outcome of an election.

The "where" and "how" are a little more difficult and will vary with the organizational structure, geographical dispersion, and formality of the company. A common arrangement is for supervisors to report any unusual event immediately to plant management in person or by phone and for plant management to report to regional or corporate management—also immediately, also by phone. This should be followed by a confidential confirming memo describing the incident (date, time, place, persons involved, and action taken). Similarly, the party receiving such a telephone communication should reduce it to a file memo. Written descriptions may be important at a later date to reconstruct and evaluate what has occurred or to identify a possible pattern from seemingly innocuous events and statements. Such memoranda also reduce the chances of someone "dropping the ball." Imagine a number of phone reports being received by the appropriate authority shortly before he goes on vacation or leaves the company. In the absence of proper documentation, the fill-in or replacement that takes over would be unaware that a problem was developing, and valuable time may be lost.

Figure 9-4 is drawn from the standing instructions of the same bank as Figure 9-3. While the specifics will vary from company to company, the principle does not. Indications of union activity should be reported immediately and fully to a designated manager or office. If the supervisor does not know that such information is important, or if he has to spend time inquiring about what to do with it, chances are that an indication of early union activity will never reach the person with the authority and responsibility for evaluation and response.

Another approach to drawing upon the unique position of the supervisors is to have them evaluate how their subordinates would probably vote in a representation election should one occur "today." One way

FIGURE 9-4. REPORTING INSTRUCTIONS IN THE EVENT SIGNS OF UNION ACTIVITY ARE OBSERVED.

1. *What to Report:*

   a. Any obvious signs of union activity.
   b. Any changes in employee behavior that may indicate union activity.
   c. Any inquiries from customers or others about company operations or policies.
   Err on the side of caution. If it might be important, it *is* important.

2. *When to Report:*

   Immediately.

3. *How to Report:*

   a. Supervisors will report any signs of union activity to plant management immediately in person or by telephone.
   b. Plant management will communicate supervisor reports or other indications of union activity to the office of the Vice President—Employee Relations immediately by telephone. This will be followed by a detailed written report of the incident within three work days.

of doing this is to have supervisors divide the members of the work group into three categories: pro-union, pro-company, and uncommitted.[12] While such supervisory polls are usually associated with an active campaign or an impending election, there is no reason why they cannot be conducted periodically as part of an ongoing preventive labor relations program.

As with employee attitude surveys, the important information to be derived from such polls centers on change, especially unexplained change, in the values reported. This suggests that, as with attitude surveys, supervisory polls should be initiated early and conducted over time so that management can develop a base against which to compare new readings.

A refinement of this instrument might be to have the supervisor evaluate each employee on a numerical (say 1-to-5) scale. The number 1 could indicate "pro-union" and 5 "pro-company," with 3 indicating uncommitted or undetermined. The numerical total, mean, and/or measure of variance may then be computed and recorded. Of course, such evaluations are subject to considerable rater bias. This is not a problem. The subjectivity of the supervisory staff is an important element in the climate of the plant or company. Provided it is fairly constant, it will not influence the relative values of the reports. If the states of mind of the supervisors change, they will probably change in the same direction as those of the employees being assessed. This will tend to heighten or emphasize changes in the poll. If, on the other hand, the changed values are entirely due to changes in the outlook of supervision, independent of that of the employees whom they supervise, this too calls for further study.

Rater error is also not a serious problem in a supervisory poll. Of course, it will be present and may be considerable. But assuming it is true or unsystematic error, it will be random and will cancel out in a population of any size.

It follows that the supervisors' evaluation of employees' probable position in regard to unions can be a powerful early detection device if properly used. This is especially so if the polls are started early enough to be used as a base for making comparisons. This does not mean that supervisory polls alone are an infallible method of spotting union activity. However, when used in conjunction with one or more of the other methods discussed, they can provide important additional insight into the labor relations climate of the workplace.

WHAT NOT TO DO

A loud warning must be sounded in regard to management's efforts to detect actual or potential union activity. While supervisors and managers may listen to or receive any communication regarding unions that is *voluntarily* offered by employees, there are legal implications and constraints whenever the company seeks it out. In general, the employer should not question, interrogate, or directly poll the employees in regard to unions without advice of counsel. And that advice will usually be, "Don't do it."

In general, it is not a good idea to remind nonunion employees that unions exist or that they are a concern to management—and directly questioning them on the subject does just that. The reminder may cause some employees to wonder whether or not unions may be appropriate for them. Further, if management displays concern about unionization, beyond a firm policy statement to the effect that the company intends to remain nonunion, it may give the impression that it is more vulnerable than the employees may otherwise think. If the employees need a union to get management to address legitimate complaints or if the company really is vulnerable, the employees will know it anyway. The reminder will only serve to confirm their conclusions and suspicions. If this is not the case, then the reminder may confuse and mislead some of them. If, on the other hand, the company maintains a posture that communicates that the employees do not need a union and that a union would have little chance of winning an election, the employees will probably adjust their thoughts and actions accordingly.

It should not be thought that employee interrogation serves as a deterrent to union activity. In most situations the employees involved do not realize that interrogation has taken place, even when the NLRB has found that such employer activity constitutes an unfair labor practice. Further, most pro-union employees simply assume that the employer knows about their union activities.[13] It follows that interrogation has little, if any, effect on union attitude or employee voting behavior.

The main reason for not engaging in employee interrogation is that it can easily constitute illegal activity. The general rule is that the employer (including supervision) cannot safely engage in employee questioning unless certain safeguards are observed. For interrogation in general, these are the so-called Blue Flash standards:[14]

1. The purpose of the interrogation must be legitimate.
2. The purpose must be communicated to the employees.
3. The employees must be given assurances against reprisals.
4. The overall background must be free of antiunion hostility and unfair labor practices.

Further, if the interrogation is systematic or may be characterized as "polling," the so-called Strucksness safeguards require that it be done by secret ballot, and its purpose can only be to determine the validity of the union's claim to majority status.[15] The Board has also observed that taking a poll while a petition for an election is pending (during the critical period) serves no purpose that would not better be served by the election itself. Given the extreme constraints on employee interrogation and the legal consequences of doing it inappropriately, it follows that the prudent nonunion employer should avoid its use.

While the Strucksness safeguards appear to be concerned with a formal secret-ballot poll, it is best to assume that they also restrict the less formal but closely related matter of employee questioning. Managers and supervisors cannot question employees about their union activities with safety under almost any circumstances. In fact, it is not a good idea for management or supervision even to discuss unionization with potential bargaining unit personnel on a casual basis unless the management spokesman is well versed in the legal intricacies involved. Such a discussion will almost always require that management state its position in regard to unions. It is only a short step between such an expression and a "threat" or "promise" that may later be construed as illegal activity that could jeopardize an otherwise successful counterunion campaign

Finally, should the employer discover through a poll or through employee interrogation that the union represents a majority of the employees, it will be difficult or impossible to maintain a "good-faith doubt" about the union's claim to a majority or the validity of signed authorization cards. Think of the predicament of an employer who, in the course of doing a little investigation, discovers that 90 percent of the personnel polled or questioned favor the union. If this was done in an overt way that was known to the employees and/or the union involved, the company may have just granted the union de facto recognition or created proof of the union's majority, which may serve to support an eventual bargaining order.

While this is a simplification of a complex legal area, and employee polling or questioning may be recommended by attorneys under some circumstances, the best advice for the operating manager or supervisor is never to poll or interrogate employees on union matters without specific advice from counsel. Such activity can do little good, but a good deal of harm. Besides, the more subtle or less obtrusive ways of measuring union activity developed earlier in this section will provide enough information for most of management's needs.

None of this is to suggest that managers or supervisors cannot listen to or otherwise receive information about unions or union activity *voluntarily* provided by employees. The supervisor can listen to anything on the subject and, of course, pass it along to management. As mentioned, it is essential that such information be passed along. However, the company cannot reward or promise rewards for such voluntary information or other antiunion activity.[16] That would change the nature of the communication.

NOTES

1. Julius G. Getman, Stephen B. Goldberg, and Jeanne B. Herman, *Union Representation Elections: Law and Reality,* New York: Russell Sage Foundation, 1976, pp. 135, 149.
2. Ibid., p. 135.
3. J. W. Lawson II, *How to Meet the Challenge of the Union Organizer,* Chicago: The Dartnell Corporation, 1973, p. 40.
4. Getman, Goldberg, and Herman, op. cit., p. 135.
5. *Attitude Survey Analysis: Audio Casette Program,* Dallas, Texas: Center for Values Research, Inc., 1979.
6. Thomas M. Rohan, "Would a Union Look Good to Your Workers?" *Industrial World,* January 26, 1976, p. 37; Phillis Payne, "Consultants Who Coach the Violators," *American Federalist,* September 1977, p. 25.
7. Lawson, op. cit., pp. 93–97.
8. Ibid., p. 100.
9. Patricia Cain Smith, "The Development of a Method of Measuring Job Satisfaction: The Cornell Studies," in Edwin A. Fleishman, *Studies in Personnel and Industrial Psychology,* Homewood, Ill.: The Dorsey Press, 1967, pp. 343–350.
10. Office of the General Counsel, National Labor Relations Board, *An Outline of Law and Procedure in Representation Cases,* Washington, D.C.: U.S. Government Printing Office, 1974, pp. 307–308; Rohan, op. cit., p. 37.
11. Similar material may be found in M. Scott Myers, *Managing Without Unions,* Reading, Mass.: Addison-Wesley, 1976, pp. 138–139; Lawson, op.

cit., pp. 54–55; and James Wilson, "Thoughts on Union Avoidance," *Personnel Administrator,* June 1977, p. 15.

12. Myers, op. cit., p. 126.

13. Getman, Goldberg, and Herman, op. cit., pp. 127–128.

14. Blue Flash Express, Inc., 1098 NLRB 591, 593–94 (1954).

15. Strucksness Construction Co., Inc., 165 NLRB 1062, 1063 (1967); discussed at Getman, Goldberg, and Herman, 10, fn. 50; and NLRB, *An Outline of Law and Procedure,* p. 306.

16. Myers, op. cit., p. 137.

10

EMPLOYER RESPONSE

The purpose of maintaining a union detection system is to spot organizing activity in time to do something about it. There are two reasons why early detection is essential. One is that it is easier to combat a union drive when it is still a small problem confined to a part of the company than when it becomes more extensive. In fact, once the problem gets beyond a certain magnitude, there may be little that the employer can do to counter it. If 80 or 90 percent of the employees are convinced that they need a union, it may be impossible for the company to turn the situation around in time to win the election.

The second reason involves the "critical period," which starts with the filing of the petition with the NLRB by the union and ends with the election. Anything the employer does or says during this period that destroys the "laboratory conditions" deemed necessary for a representation election may support objections to the election and result in an employer victory being set aside. It is important to remember that there is a difference between unfair-labor-practice charges and objections. Under the General Shoe doctrine [1] adopted by the Board in 1948, employer conduct that renders a free employee choice improbable will warrant setting aside an election even though that conduct may not constitute an unfair labor practice. [2] It is also important to remember that Section 8(c), the employer free-speech provision, applies only to unfair labor practices and not to representational matters. An employer statement that may be perfectly legal before the critical period could have serious consequences if made while an election is pending.

Another consequence of the union's filing its petition is that once this is done and the company is notified, management officially knows that a union drive is in progress. Such knowledge is important in proving intent in some unfair-labor-practice matters. Remember that some unions have a practice of notifying the employer when they start an organizing campaign so as to better support such charges and perhaps obtain a bargaining order should they lose the elections. [3] The chances of having a successful election invalidated or of being found to have committed an unfair labor practice are considerably greater once the company is officially aware of the union drive. It follows that any unofficial advance warning that a union drive is in progress or about to start is of considerable value, since it allows the company to respond to the problem without the constraints that exist during the critical period.

What is the best employer response when organizing activity is discovered? There is no general answer to this question. The appropriate response will depend on various factors, including the duration and extent of union activity, its location within the organization, the structure of the company, the causes of employee interest in union representation, the sophistication of the union involved, and the level and effectiveness of existing preventive labor relations efforts. Each case will have to be decided on its own merits. However, a few general observations can be offered.

1. *Don't overreact.* Few work organizations of any size are ever totally without some union interest on the part of some employees. Naturally, the level of that interest will go up and down over time in response to many things. Management must be careful not to exacerbate a small problem which may work itself out by engaging in activity that supports the claim that a union is needed. An example is where management or supervision responds to the discovery of union activity by firing the union adherents or in some way discriminates against them for their indiscretion. In addition to being dysfunctional, such actions are illegal.

The best thing to do when union activity is discovered or when its level increases is to (1) report it to the appropriate authority, (2) get competent legal counsel if it is not already available, and (3) ask a few questions. How long has this been going on? How strong is the union? Why are the employees interested or more interested in union representation? Are their complaints justified? What can be done about them? Are we prepared for the next step? How much help do we need? The answers to such questions will usually be obvious. If not, then additional information is needed. The most important objective of the company at this time is to avoid engaging in unfair labor practices or other activity that may support the union's objections to an otherwise successful election. Nothing should be done until there is enough information and labor relations expertise available to do it right.

2. *Fragment or isolate the problem.* It is sometimes found that the detected union activity is confined to a particular organizational unit—one department, an individual store or branch, a particular employee group. If this is the case, it may be appropriate for the company either to fragment or isolate the problem. For example, if the finishing department is the center of union interest, one approach for the company to take is to transfer the personnel involved to other duties and locations in order to break up the union's organization. If the numbers are small and the rest of the plant is safely nonunion, this may be an effective response. The danger in this approach is that the union supporters may now be spread throughout the plant or company and be in a position to continue their organizing efforts on a grander scale.

A second approach is for the company to isolate the center of union activity and then wear it down by attrition. Particular attention must be paid to the transfer of employees out of the unit and into other parts of the company. Interaction between the employees in the affected unit and others should be minimized. This may involve some rearrangement of the usual work flow or communications process. The company may also want to review the effectiveness of supervision and be especially sensitive to employee complaints or other problems in the affected unit. Meanwhile, hiring and promotion decisions must be carefully reviewed from a preventive labor relations perspective. Whether or not additional turnover of personnel should be generated within the unit is a difficult question. In addition to conflicting with the company's responsiveness to employee problems, the actions needed to induce the additional turnover may constitute unfair labor practices. There are also important ethical considerations involved. Finally, the company must be careful not to carry its strategy of isolation so far as to create a separate bargaining unit where one is not wanted.

3. *Review the bargaining unit.* The subject of bargaining units and their importance in preventive labor relations was examined in Chapter 3. Ideally, the company will already be organized in such a way as to take full advantage of the bargaining unit decision. However, upon detection of union activity, this matter should be reviewed. It may be found that there are peculiarities in the situation that should be taken advantage of before the union petitions for an election. Or it may be found that things have changed since the first thinking on the bargaining unit was done and some updating is needed. Moreover, the best bargaining unit arrangement for preventive labor relations purposes may have been deemed inappropriate or prohibitively expensive from an operational point of view. However, with an organizing drive in progress, the cost-benefit relationships may have changed. A higher degree of cross-training, interchange of personnel, and so on may now be appropriate, given the increased probability of a representation election. If so, changes should be made early.

4. *Address the cause of the problem.* The possibility that the employees might be right in their conclusion that they need union representation should not be overlooked. If union activity appears in a nonunion company or plant, there is a reason. If the cause of union interest is real or imagined complaints with the employment relationship, the logical employer response is to examine and correct such problems. It may be thought that the company cannot afford the wages and benefits needed to keep the union out. This leads to the question: Will it be better able to afford them six months later with the aid of a union?

It is important that the company identify the true cause of employee dissatisfaction. Solving problems that do not exist may do more harm than good. This is especially so if only a small number of vocal employees view the condition as a serious problem. Such actions usually cost money that cannot be used where it is really needed. Further, they may lull management into thinking that it has been responsive while, in fact, it has not.

RESPONDING TO A DEMAND FOR UNION RECOGNITION

Recognition, it will be remembered, is the act whereby the employer accepts the union as the representative of the employees and acquires a legal obligation to bargain with it. It may be granted voluntarily on the basis of proof of the union's majority position without going through an NLRB election. It may also be granted accidentally.

One of the more critical incidents in the life of a nonunion business organization occurs when it is presented with a demand for union recognition. Such a demand is almost always based on authorization cards signed by a majority of the employees in the proposed unit. It is important that the company, in the person of the manager or supervisor involved, correctly handle such a demand. To do otherwise can result in accidentally granting recognition to the union. Should the manager or supervisor count the cards or otherwise authenticate the union's majority and then make a statement or engage in conduct that constitutes explicit or implicit recognition, it will be most difficult to withdraw that recognition at a later date.[4]

The company is not required to grant recognition on the basis of cards and may insist that the union seek an election from the National Labor Relations Board. However, should management ascertain the union's majority status on the basis of cards and have independent knowledge of that majority from having questioned or polled the employees, it has a duty to bargain with the union. For all practical purposes, it has just recognized the union.

If the union at some point demonstrates a majority position and the company subsequently engages in unfair labor practices that have the effect of destroying that majority, the NLRB may order the employer to bargain with the union even if the union loses the election. While the union can demonstrate its majority simply by going to the NLRB and presenting its cards with its petition, there is no point in the company helping the union in this. Further, it may be that the union has a bare majority and fears that if it went for an election it would not win because of nonvoting and attrition.

The company's objective in responding to a demand for recognition should be to maintain its good-faith doubt about the union's majority status and the validity of the authorization cards. It should also question the appropriateness of the bargaining unit proposed.

The employer's good-faith doubt hinges upon maintaining a demonstrable ignorance of the union's majority and avoiding unfair labor practices or other objectionable conduct. Under no circumstances should management place itself in the position of authenticating the union's majority. The company may generally claim a good-faith doubt when:

1.   It has not engaged in unfair labor practices designed to dissipate the union's majority.

2.   It has not engaged in conduct indicating undue delay or a rejection of the concept of collective bargaining.

3.   There is no other evidence indicating its bad faith.[5]

A union may demand recognition in a number of ways, at any time or place, and from any reasonable representative of the employer. Of course, a company with an effective preventive labor relations program will not be caught by surprise. If union activity is in progress, management will know about it long before a meaningful demand for recognition can be made. All managers and supervisors will have been familiarized with the various ways in which a demand may be presented and with the proper response. They will be discussed in turn.

Responding to Personal Visits

Perhaps the most common way in which unions present employers with demands for recognition is for the union organizer and/or a delegation of employees to approach management directly.

The demand may or may not be accompanied by an offer to present signed authorization cards as proof of the union's majority status either directly to the employer or to a mutually agreed-upon third party. The first thing a manager or supervisor confronted with this situation should do is get one or more witnesses, preferably another manager. It is probable that the union will have at least two people present. The employer representative involved must not count the cards or agree to let a third party count them. Indeed, the employer should refuse to handle, touch, or in any way take possession of the cards. Rather, management should state that it has a good-faith doubt in the union's claim to a majority, in authorization cards as a valid indication of employee intent, and in the appropriateness of the proposed bargaining unit. The union representative should be advised to seek an election from the National Labor Relations Board.

Should the union organizer attempt to leave the authorization cards, management should decline to accept them and insist that the organizer take them with him. Should they be left in the plant or office anyway, the personnel involved must immediately place the *unexamined* cards in an envelope and seal it.[6] The incident should then be recorded in individual memos stating that the cards were sealed in the envelope without being examined at that particular time, date, place, and so on, along with any other information that may be relevant. Company personnel should not offer opinions as to whether or not the union had a majority of the employees signed up.

Immediately upon termination of the encounter, the managers involved should call (not write) the appropriate company personnel and/or counsel. This is important. It must not be put off until the next day or until it is more convenient. Employee relations management or counsel will want to get a detailed and accurate description of all that took place before memories dim. Also, the company may have need for the additional time between the presentation of the demand and the filing of the petition to prepare its strategy.

One way to reduce the chances of having management caught by surprise by a union organizer is to have secretaries, receptionists, and plant guards require all visitors to identify themselves before being admitted.[7]

Responding to Telephone Demands for Recognition

A second way in which a union may demand recognition is by telephone. This is similar to the personal visit, except for the absence of authorization cards. The telephone demand is at least as likely to catch the employer by surprise and result in some sort of mistake. While there is no possibility of inadvertently counting cards over the phone, there are other hazards. One is the temptation not to take the matter seriously. This may result in the recipient of the call failing to get a witness to the conversation and/or failing to report the incident and reduce it to writing. It should be assumed that the union spokesman has at least one person listening in and may even be taping the conversation. Failure to take the matter seriously may even result in the manager simply hanging up on the caller or engaging in a little colorful rhetoric. This is not the best way to handle the situation.

The appropriate response to a telephone demand is to inform the caller politely that the request should be put in writing and addressed to the manager who is responsible for such matters. The receiver of the call should not agree to have the company call back or otherwise communicate with the union by a certain date or in a particular way.[8] It should be made clear that the company is not granting recognition at this time. It is important that the situation not be left ambiguous enough for the union to claim tacit recognition.

Of course, all this should be witnessed by at least one other manager or secretary on an extension line. Upon completion of the conversation, employee relations management and/or counsel should be called and the situation reduced to writing by all concerned. These statements should be signed and dated. This is important. It is possible that administrative proceedings or litigation concerning the event will take place many months later. Not only do people forget the particulars of such events, but they leave the employ of the company and may move out of the area. It is a good idea to document everything that takes place in regard to union matters. A detailed chronology of events will be helpful in briefing counsel or corporate management at a later date. It is also helpful in identifying patterns in a multilocation company and in evaluating management's performance once the affair is over.

Responding to Letters

Another common way for a union to demand recognition is to send a registered or certified letter to the employer. Such letters are of two types: those that do not contain authorization cards or other proof of the union's majority, and those that do.

If the demand is in the form of a simple letter, it should be directed to the appropriate manager or to the company's attorney as soon as possible. Such a letter will typically state that the union represents a majority of the employees involved, demands recognition from the employer, and offers to meet with the company to negotiate a labor agreement. It is important that the letter be answered so as not to allow the union to claim that it has implied or tacit recognition.[9] The response should contain an expression of the employer's good-faith doubt and refer the union to the National Labor Relations Board. Whenever reasonable it should also question the appropriateness of the proposed bargaining unit.[10]

If the letter is accompanied by authorization cards or other proof of the union's majority, it presents another problem. Remember, if the company is to maintain a good-faith doubt, it should not ascertain the union's majority. This pertains whether the cards are received in person in the presence of union witnesses or through the mail. Management personnel may have to attest under oath that they really did have a good-faith doubt.

A demand accompanied by cards will almost certainly come by registered or certified mail with the return address of the union evident. If such an envelope is received from a union, it is likely to be a demand for recognition. The best course of action is to send the *unopened* envelope directly to the employee relations department or to counsel.[11]

When such a letter is opened—either on purpose or inadvertently—certain precautions must be taken. The authorization cards or other proof must not be counted or examined under any circumstances. Rather, they should be immediately sealed in another envelope in the presence of witnesses. The personnel present should then write and sign statements describing the incident, with particular attention to the fact that the cards were not counted.[12] The cards should then either be returned to the union or retained to be turned over to the NLRB at a later date at the discretion of counsel. The accompanying letter should be answered the same way as a letter containing no authorization cards.

Note the importance of training secretaries likely to receive such communications on the appropriate way to handle them. Particular attention should be paid to the secretarial and clerical staff in the office of the top manager and in the personnel and labor relations departments. They should be informed on how to identify a probable demand for recognition, what to do with the unopened letter, and what to do in the event the envelope is accidentally opened.[13]

Responding to Employees' Demands for Recognition

Another way in which the employer may grant recognition is directly to the employees. One or a group of employees may approach management with signed authorization cards and formally demand recognition. If that occurs, management should handle the situation just as if a union organizer were present. The more likely event is that one or more employees will come forward to complain or discuss a matter on behalf of the other members of the work group. While the legality of such informal or semiformal dealings is less clear than a formal demand for recognition from a union, it is possible for the company accidentally to recognize the individual or delegation as the legal representative of the employees. In addition, allowing a particular individual or group to operate on behalf of the other employees may establish traditions and expectations that are better avoided in a nonunion firm. It is only a short step from such informal arrangements to formal union representation. And should the employees become dissatisfied with the informal arrangements, it is only natural for them to think of strengthening them rather than reverting to handling their own employment-related problems. Also, the existence and operation of such an informal representational arrangement may someday be important to a bargaining unit determination.

The correct response for a supervisor or manager confronted by an individual or delegation claiming to speak on behalf of the other employees is to refuse to discuss the matter on those terms.[14] None of this is to suggest that supervisors should not discuss and resolve employee complaints with the employees who step forward. Of course they should. But it should be made clear that they are speaking only for themselves and not for any or all of their co-workers.

It should be remembered that a delegation of employees approaching management to demand recognition, present a grievance, or do anything else related to the employment relationship is "concerted activity" and, as such, protected under Section 7 of the National Labor Relations Act. Section 8(a)(1) makes it an unfair labor practice for the employer "to interfere with, restrain, or coerce employees in the exercise of the rights guaranteed in Section 7." It goes without saying that management should be careful in how it handles employee delegations.

NLRB Petition

A common and important way in which a union may present its demand is to file a petition for an election directly with the National Labor Relations Board. Although the Act indicates that the employer must have declined to recognize the union before an election may be held,[15] the Board has in a long series of cases nullified this provision. Today the filing of a petition itself constitutes a demand for recognition.[16]

When this route is taken, the union will present its showing of interest (authorization cards) directly to the staff of the NLRB rather than to the employer. This will be followed by a communication from the NLRB to the employer requesting certain information (to be discussed). By this time the company is in the critical period, and its main concern should be to avoid committing unfair labor practices. There is little that can be done wrong in regard to the demand for recognition itself. It is too late for that. However, any and all personnel actions that the company takes as well as anything it says will be suspect and should be carefully reviewed by counsel. Remember, the employer's good-faith doubt must be supported by an absence of unfair labor practices designed to destroy the union's majority and by an absence of undue delay.

The message that emerges from this discussion is that managers and supervisors (and relevant secretaries) must be familiar with the various ways in which a demand for recognition may be made and must know how to respond appropriately. The risks in this area are too great to assume that the people involved will automatically do the right thing. It is too easy for someone to get caught by surprise and accidentally recognize a union, destroy the company's claim to a good-faith doubt, commit unfair labor practices, or in some other way ruin an otherwise effective preventive labor relations program. It should be assumed that sooner or later a manager or supervisor will be confronted with a demand for recognition. The question is not "if" but "when" the demand is made. It follows that material on this subject should be included in supervisory and management training programs and that it be viewed as an important part of the company's preventive labor relations program.

INITIAL RESPONSE TO THE NLRB

If attorneys have not yet been brought into the picture, a notification from the National Labor Relations Board will change that. Once the union has filed its petition and the critical period has begun, things are too sensitive and technical to be left in the hands of laymen. In fact, if general or corporate counsel has been used up to this point, it may be advisable to get specialized legal assistance from a firm that concentrates on labor law.

Shortly after the union files its petition and presents its showing of interest, the NLRB will send a form letter to the employer asking for certain information, including commerce data and a list of the names and job classifications of the employees in the proposed unit (see Figure 10-1). Other interested parties are also informed. In addition to the petitioner and the immediate employer, interested parties may include the owner of a leased department in a store, any union or individual listed on the petition as having an interest in the matter, or any union that in one of several other ways has established an interest in the matter.[17] The employer is also informed that a list of names and addresses of the employees eligible to vote must be provided within seven days following the agreement or direction of an election. This second, so-called Excelsior list is in addition to the first proposed-unit list.[18]

The purpose of the commerce data is for the Regional Director to determine whether or not the NLRB has jurisdiction. A finding on jurisdiction is necessary in every case, whether or not any of the parties contest it.[19] Jurisdiction will be asserted if the employer is in interstate commerce, is not excepted for some statutory reason, and meets any one of the Board's dollar jurisdictional standards (see Chapter 2). It is usually appropriate for the company to respond to the request for commerce data. If it does not, the Board will assert jurisdiction anyway.

Throughout most of our discussion we have conveniently assumed that

FIGURE 10-1. LETTER FROM NLRB TO THE EMPLOYER, SENT AFTER THE FILING OF A PETITION.

Re:

Case No.

Gentlemen:

We have a petition docketed as above requesting this Agency to conduct an election among certain of your employees. Please post the copy of the petition where your employees will see it.

Attention is called to your right to be represented by counsel or other representative in any proceeding before the National Labor Relations Board. In the event you choose to have a representative appear on your behalf, please have completed, "Notice of Appearance" Form NLRB-4701 or "Notice of Designation of Representative as Agent for Service of Documents" Form NLRB-4813 and forward one promptly to this office. Failing to recieve one of these Notices, we will assume that you do not choose to be so represented.

To help us determine whether the Board has jurisdiction in this matter, will you please, at your earliest convenience, submit to this office one copy of the enclosed Commerce Data froms.

So that we may ascertain whether the petition is supported by 30% of the employees in the unit, please submit as soon as possible a list of the names of all employees within the described unit, with their respective job classifications, prepared from your most recent payroll. If there is a current or recently expired collective bargaining agreement covering any of the employees described in the petition, please enclose a copy; also advise whether there are other unions claiming an interest in representing these employees.

If a question concerning representation affecting commerce exists, the parties may execute an agreement for an election to be supervised by this office. We have tentatively assigned a date of _____ for a hearing to be conducted in this matter should the investigation disclose issues which cannot be otherwise resolved. In such a case, a formal notice of hearing will be issued.

It has been our experience that by the time a petition such as this one has been filed employees have questions about what is going on and what may happen. At this point in the handling of this case, we of course do not know what disposition will be made of the petition, but experience tells us that an explanation of rights, responsibilities, and Board procedures can be helpful to your employees. The Board believes that employees should have readily available information abour their rights and the proper conduct of employee representation elections. At the same time employers and unions should be appraised of their responsibilities to refrain from conduct which would impede employees' freedom of choice.

Accordingly, you are requested to post the enclosed Notice to Employees in conspicuous places in areas where employees such as those described in the enclosed peitition work. Copies of this Notice are being made available to the labor organization(s) involved.

In the event an election is agreed to or directed in this case, the Board requires that a list of names and addresses of all the eligible voters be filed by the Employer with the undersigned, who will in turn make it available to all parties to the case. The list must be furnished to the undersigned within 7 days of the direction of or agreement to election. I am advising you now of this requirement so that you will have ample time to prepare for the eventuality that such a list may become necessary.

Investigation of this matter has been assigned to the staff members named below. If you have any questions, do not hesitate to communicate with this Board Agent.

Your cooperation in this matter will be appreciated.

Very truly yours,

Michael A. Taylor
Regional Director

Enclosures

Case assigned to: Agent's Telephone number:

---

the employer is subject to the National Labor Relations Act. This was done to avoid the considerable complications of treating topical material under different laws. Most private-sector employers of any size do fall under the NLRA. However, the possibility of avoiding the usually more liberal (from a union point of view) federal legislation should not be overlooked. Under certain circumstances this can be important. (See Chapter 2 for a more detailed discussion of this topic.)

The NLRB's initial request for a list of the names of the employees in the proposed unit should usually not be granted. In contrast to the mandated Excelsior list, which will be discussed, this list is not legally required of the employer. There are two reasons why the employer should not provide the proposed-unit list. One is that it may suggest acquiescence to the unit proposed by the union. The other is that the union just might receive a copy of the proposed-unit list long before the legally required Excelsior list is submitted.[20] This can be of considerable value to the union and should be avoided.

Finally, the employer should not agree to what is called a "consent agreement election" and sometimes not even to a "stipulation for certification upon consent election." The details of elections will be discussed later. Here it is enough to note that if the employer enters into a *consent* agreement election, it will take place quickly, since the important questions surrounding the representation proceeding are agreed upon by the parties beforehand and any disputes arising out of the campaign or the election are determined locally by the regional director. In the case of a *stipulated* election, the balloting may also take place at a fairly early date if the parties so choose, but questions and disputes may be brought to the NLRB in Washington, which guarantees considerable delay.[21] It is seldom to the employer's advantage to have an early election.

NOTES

1. General Shoe Corporation, 77 NLRB 124.
2. Office of the General Counsel, National Labor Relations Board, *An Outline of Law and Procedure in Representation Cases,* Washington, D.C.: U.S. Government Printing Office, 1974, p. 319. Hereinafter, NLRB, *An Outline of Law and Procedure.*
3. Julius G. Getman, Stephen B. Goldberg, and Jeanne B. Herman, *Union Representation Elections: Law and Reality,* New York: Russell Sage Foundation, 1976, p. 135.
4. 43 NLRB Annual Report 23–24 (1978).
5. J. W. Lawson II, *How to Meet the Challenge of the Union Organizer,* Chicago: The Dartnell Corporation, 1973, p. 138, citing Aaron Brothers of California, 62 LRRM 1160 (1966).
6. M. Scott Myers, *Managing Without Unions,* Reading, Mass.: Addison-Wesley, 1976, p. 131.
7. Lawson, op. cit., p. 66.
8. Myers, op. cit., p. 131.
9. "Employer Pitfalls in Unionization Drives," *CPA Journal,* August 1977, p. 69.
10. Lawson, op. cit., pp. 130–132.
11. I have never heard or read of it being done, but another approach would be to refuse to accept delivery of such a letter. However, counsel should be consulted before doing any innovating in this area.
12. Myers, op. cit., p. 130.
13. Ibid.

14. Ibid., p. 132.
15. National Labor Relations Act, Section 9(c)(1).
16. NLRB, *An Outline of Law and Procedure,* p. 59.
17. Ibid., pp. 31–32.
18. Ibid., p. 32.
19. Ibid., p. 2.
20. I was informed of this by a union attorney. It has been denied by an NLRB staff member.
21. NLRB, *An Outline of Law and Procedure,* p. 33.

11

THE COMPANY CAMPAIGN

The company campaign usually begins when the union files a petition and continues until the election. It is conceivable that the company campaign could start with the union's demand for recognition, or even earlier; and in practice, companies often postpone their active counterunion efforts until a few weeks before the election so as to peak at the right time. This may be especially important when the employer uses delay as a tactic. For expositional purposes, however, we will assume that the employer campaign and the critical period are coextensive. Remember, anything the employer does during this time is suspect and may result in the setting aside of an employer-won election or even in an NLRB bargaining order.

EMPLOYER OBJECTIVES

The immediate objective of the employer's counterunion campaign usually is to win the election. However, the union drive is not the beginning, nor is it usually the end, of the problem. Correspondingly, the company campaign is only one element in an ongoing preventive labor relations program, the ultimate objective of which is to remain nonunion. Winning the election may be necessary for the attainment of that objective, but it is by no means sufficient. In other words, the immediate objective of the company campaign should not be confused with the ultimate goal of remaining nonunion indefinitely. This suggests that the employer should approach the campaign with a number of more specific and longer-run objectives in addition to the goal of winning the election. These will include:

Avoiding having a successful election set aside or replaced by an NLRB bargaining order.
Deterring the union from seeking a second or subsequent election a year later, as allowed by law.
Ending up with a situation that will allow the company to continue to prosper.

Attaining all these objectives may be more difficult than simply winning the election. Indeed, there may be conditions under which some of them are mutually exclusive. It must be kept in mind, however, that winning an election only to have it set aside by the NLRB or reversed by an order to bargain with the defeated union is not much of a victory. Winning an election in such a way as to ensure that the union will win a second election after having learned from its mistakes is not much better. It may even be better to have lost such an election and gotten on with the business of building a workable relationship with the union. Likewise, winning in such a way as to leave the company's relationships with its employees, customers, and community in shambles may be worse than losing.

How does a business organization confronted with a union drive and an impending representation election achieve the objectives listed? At the minimum, the company must wage its campaign within the law. That is, all management and supervisory actions and statements must be within the letter and spirit of the National Labor Relations Act or other relevant statute.

Beyond winning the election, the employer should also *defeat* the union. These two results are not necessarily the same thing. If the company responds to the union drive in such a way as to convince the employees who voted for the company or against a particular union that they really do need a union to protect them, or handles itself after the election in such a way as to make them regret not having voted union, the victory may be a brief one. The company should never lose sight of the fact that—win or lose—it will have to continue to live with the employees when the battle is over.[1] The ideal outcome is to have the union and the idea that the employees need union representation fairly and soundly defeated. If the employer wins by scaring employees out of voting for the union or in some way that appears to be underhanded, it may result in employees' long-run feelings that they have been treated unfairly. Also, if the employer "wins" on the basis of a legal technicality, such as a jurisdictional or bargaining unit determination, it should explain the matter and its position to the employees. Winning the contest under either set of conditions may leave the employees with the thought that what they need is a stronger union than the one they had.

Another outcome that should be avoided, if possible, is a company victory that leaves the union encouraged. This can happen when the vote is close enough to give the impression that the union did well considering its expenditure and that it has a good chance of winning a second election at a modest additional cost. By the end of the election the company should have impressed the union with the fact that management will fight it all the way. Of course, the pro-union employees will continue to support the union or, at least, the concept of collective bargaining; however, the degree of interest that the union leadership has in a rematch will be influenced by its perceived chances of winning. Its decision to remain active or withdraw will be based on the same factors as the initial decision to choose the company as a target or respond to an invitation from the employees, with two important qualifications. One is that the union will have an investment in the situation. The other is that the union will have more and better information than when it started.

It should be expected that the union will not give up the field unless it is convinced that victory is unlikely. Many organizing costs are "start-up" in nature: learning about the company, developing the inside cadre, obtaining a mailing list, and so on. Similarly, some of the risk is also one-time in nature. Once the legal jurisdiction and the appropriate bargaining unit have been established, the union can be relatively certain that its efforts will not be wiped out by a legal maneuver.

It follows that the employer should endeavor to convey to the decision makers in the union that the cost (risk) of a second campaign will be at least as great as in the first. Of course, the impact of this communication will be influenced by the closeness of the vote. If the vote is close, and the bargaining unit size worth the investment, the union will not be scared away, regardless of the employer's dedication to remaining nonunion. On the other hand, if the company won by a comfortable margin, the message conveyed by the employer's preventive labor relations efforts will reinforce the significance of the loss.

A final thought on longer-run objectives is that the company should learn from its experience. Management should emerge from the campaign and election with a better understanding of how to deter and combat unionization. The fact that an organizing attempt was mounted suggests that something was wrong. The employees had reason to believe that they needed union representation, and/or a labor organization thought that there was a good chance of winning. The company should do everything possible to ensure that this does not happen again. The issues, positions, and statements that emerged during the campaign, as well as the company's response and overall preventive labor relations posture, should be evaluated. If the employees have legitimate complaints, they should be addressed. If the complaints are fancied, employee communications should be given more attention. If management or supervision made mistakes during the campaign, this should be taken into account in future training programs.

The best approach is to view the whole affair as a test of the system. As in many areas of business, control procedures should be established that allow the company to audit its performance so as to improve in the future. The evaluation should be positive and constructive, not recriminative. The emphasis should be on how well *we* did and how *we* can do better next time, not on who goofed or who is to blame. When it is found that a manager or supervisor did something right, credit should be given.

All this may sound a bit too easy. While it is not my purpose to promote pessimism, management must be realistic about what to expect from the active counterunion campaign. The important work of preventive labor relations should take place early and build over the years. The company cannot ignore the material covered in the earlier chapters of this book and rely on knocking down a union drive at the last minute with an effective barrage of public relations and legal maneuvers. That is fire fighting, not prevention.

REASONABLE EXPECTATIONS

What can the employer realistically expect from the company campaign? The answer depends on the situation. It has been found that intent is the best predictor of vote and that employee attitudes prior to the advent of the campaign create a "strong and stable predisposition" that explains 81 percent of the vote. Thus, as in political elections, most people decide how they will vote before the campaign begins and do not change in response to campaign rhetoric.[2]

It has also been shown that 33 percent of nonunion employees in general (exclusive of managers and the self-employed) and 39 percent of blue-collar workers would vote union if given the opportunity.[3] It appears that in most companies an organizing union is almost guaranteed a respectable number of union supporters and card signers who are quite immune to the employer's counterunion campaign. Part of that immunity is due to the fact that both pro-union and pro-company employees are selective in their intake of campaign information and discount information that conflicts with their established beliefs. This is important. For a company (or union) campaign to influence the voting behavior of those employees already committed, it must convince them that their prior position was wrong. Yet neither pro-union nor pro-company employees pay much attention to campaign communication with which they disagree.[4] Thus rational argument will have little effect on that part of the workforce already committed.

It should also not be thought that the employer can scare or bribe already committed employees out of voting for the union. Contrary to popular belief, employees are not usually responsive to employer threats and promises. Most of the employees who would be influenced by employer intimidation are scared off before the campaign begins, while those that remain committed to the union interpret such actions as evidence that the union is needed more than ever. Likewise, promises of benefit offered during the campaign are taken as unreliable by pro-union workers.[5] It follows that heavy-handed tactics can do little good and a great deal of harm and should be avoided.

The subject is not as hopeless as the preceding discussion may suggest. If a third of the nonunion workforce is inclined to vote union, the other two-thirds is presumably not. If union supporters are distributed more or less evenly among companies, the nonunion employer has an important general advantage. But of course they are not evenly distributed.

Some lines of work attract and retain employees who are likely to support a union, or they require conditions that make them more prone to unionization. Others do the opposite. Further, the knowledgeable company can improve the predisposition of its workforce by careful selection, prudent location decisions, and other preventive labor relations policies developed earlier. Thus, in addition to the general numerical advantage, the well-run nonunion firm has a considerable specific advantage.

The usual state of affairs in a contested election is that the employees are divided into three groups: those committed to the union who have signed cards, those who are either pro-company or antiunion but have declined to sign, and those who are uncommitted or undecided and may or may not have signed authorization cards. The pro-union group is relatively stable and not easily influenced by the company campaign. For all practical purposes, these employees can be written off. In regard to the others, the company campaign performs two important functions. One is to reinforce the position and attitudes of those employees who already support the company. This takes the form of offsetting union information and attention and providing information to help them debate the issues with the union supporters and thereby influence those employees who are still uncommitted. The second purpose is to convince uncommitted employees that they should vote with the company. This is best done by reinforcing currently held positive attitudes toward the company or negative attitudes toward unions.[6] Thus the tactical objective of the company campaign is to protect and support the base of pro-company advocates and directly or indirectly convince the middle group of uncommitted employees that they should side with the employer.

ORGANIZING THE COMPANY CAMPAIGN

The Campaign Manager

At the beginning of any project, a decision must be made as to who is to have the authority and responsibility to get the job done. A counterunion campaign is no exception. In a large nonunion company the decision may already have been made in the assignment of the preventive labor relations function to a manager or other professional. This is what one would expect to find in a large nongrocery retail chain. Under such conditions, an active organizing campaign at some location may be a common occurrence to be handled by corporate staff as part of its regular duties. In a small or medium-size firm, or in a large firm that has not had much experience with unions, the matter may be more difficult. In-house employee relations staff may never have encountered an organizing drive and may not be knowledgeable about the applicable law and techniques. If that is the case, it may be necessary to obtain help from a consultant and/or labor attorney.

Almost all business organizations maintain a relationship with a law firm. Even if this firm does not do labor work in general or representation election work in particular, it will be a good source of information on who does. But be careful. Check out the firm or firms recommended with other companies which they have served. Go with a firm that has a proven track record and the resources and expertise to do the job. Remember, labor law is specialized and the situation is critical. Avoid the generalist or the new hand who will have to research basic questions when a quick response is needed or, worse, may have to guess because the situation does not allow time for research. Also avoid the university professor or untried consultant who would like to learn and earn at the company's expense. Remember, the company will have to pay for and live with his mistakes.

Shopping for effective outside help takes time. Ideally, it should be done in advance and the person or firm chosen should help develop the company's overall preventive labor relations program. If this has not been done, help should be sought at the first sign of trouble. This highlights the importance of an early-warning system. If union activity is detected, the company should not wait until a petition has been filed or a demand received before seeking help. By then, so many mistakes may have been made that the situation is irretrievable.

However it is arranged, one individual should have the authority for the conduct of the campaign. Even if the company employs a trusted attorney or consultant, ultimate control should be with a manager with enough know-how to operate as a liaison and evaluate the performance of the "hired gun," and enough authority and stature to mobilize the resources of the organization when needed. These requirements usually preclude plant-level personnel management, the chief executive officer, and most line managers, who cannot disengage from their usual functions and/or do not have the needed expertise. The alternatives usually boil down to a senior staff manager in personnel, labor relations, or law, or someone with considerable stature and broad experience on a project management basis. The individual placed in command should report to the CEO and must have the full support of top management as well as adequate resources and staff.

254

Once it has been decided who will run the company campaign, it is necessary to define that person's duties. It must be understood that the campaign manager is the only company official with the authority to meet and talk with the union representatives.[7] Other managers and supervisors must be instructed not to communicate directly with anyone representing a union. It is too easy to say or do something illegal. All managers and supervisors should be instructed to report anything even remotely connected to the campaign directly to the campaign manager immediately and by telephone.[8] This will involve dispensing with the usual reporting procedures for union-related matters for the duration of the campaign. Of course, the person to whom the manager or supervisor usually reports should be kept informed, and the campaign manager should work through normal channels insofar as that does not detract from the efficiency of the campaign.

Thus the campaign manager will be the focal point of the organization for as long as the active campaign continues. Other managers should support and defer to him on all campaign and employee-related matters. To avoid confusion and legal difficulties, there must be no conflicting decisions and information coming from different sources within the organization.

Supervisors

The other element directly involved in the counterunion campaign is supervisory personnel. The campaign manager will have to work closely with first-line supervision. If the supervisors have been well chosen and well trained and understand and accept their responsibilities to the company during an organizing drive, they will be a strong asset. If they are less qualified or committed, they may present difficulties. There are two ways of dealing with such a problem. One is to conduct a campaign that depends on the supervisors as little as possible. That is, communication will be directly from management to the employees, as far as possible.[9] This will have the effect of bypassing and isolating the supervisors. Care and tact must be used. If an offended supervisory force tacitly throws its weight behind the union, it can be serious. Although the company can legally discharge or otherwise discipline a supervisor for such disloyalty, it may be hard to detect, and by the time it is discovered that such activities were going on, the damage will have been done.

The second way to respond to such a supervisory problem is to engage in some quick and intensive training designed to upgrade supervisors' skills and information and to explain their legal and ethical duties during the campaign. These two approaches are not mutually exclusive. Direct communication from management to the employees is an important part of most campaigns, and some supervisory training will be necessary in every organizing drive to update and reinforce the supervisors' command of the subject matter.

A related problem may occur when the supervisors are part of the reason the employees want a union. If the employees' complaint is the quality or some other aspect of supervision, it may be difficult or counterproductive to use the supervisors to communicate the company's position. If that is the case, management will have to base its campaign on direct communication to the employees. Further, if the complaints are justified, it will be necessary to address the issue during the campaign. This will have to be handled with care so as not to offend the supervisors involved or create expectations that may be hard to live with after the campaign.

The company will have to make an early decision on the extent to which it will base its campaign on the supervisors. This is an important decision and should be made objectively. Assuming that management can count on the supervisory personnel—which will almost always be the case—they should be considered an important and integral part of the company campaign from the beginning. Remember, supervisors can commit unfair labor practices and other indiscretions on behalf of the employer. In the eyes of most employees they *are* the company and are influential in shaping attitudes toward the company. The employees will go to the supervisor for information on and clarification of the company's position during the campaign. Because of their legal role and because they are a natural source of information to the employees, the supervisors must not only know what they can and cannot say but also understand the employer's position on the various issues in the campaign.

One of the services often provided by a consultant during an organizing drive is supervisory training, either in person or indirectly through management personnel. A firm not using the services of an outside consultant should conduct training sessions on its own. Such training may be facilitated by the use of two excellent and readily available printed sources. One is a concise checklist distributed by the Industrial Relations Department of the National Association of Manufacturers, titled ''Some Dos and Don'ts for Supervisors.'' The other is a pamphlet titled *The Supervisor's Handbook on Maintaining Non-Union Status,* which may be obtained at bulk rates from Executive Enterprises Publications Co., Inc.,

10 Columbus Circle, New York, N.Y. 10019. A firm expecting union trouble may be wise to order a supply of these or other similar publications in advance. Alternatively, anyone familiar with the area of labor relations could write a supervisory fact sheet that would do the same job while being more specific to the company. This, too, should be done in advance. Once the campaign begins, the personnel who would logically handle this job will be busy with other things. In fact, it may be a good idea to develop such material and incorporate it into the company's regular supervisory training program, whether or not a union problem is present.

Even if no additional training is required, management will have to conduct regular supervisor meetings throughout the campaign. It is essential that supervisors know what is going on. The supervisor will be expected to explain management's position on the issues of the campaign and must never be placed in a position of being unable to answer a question or, worse, giving the wrong answer. The supervisors should see campaign literature before it is distributed.[10] Even better, if time permits, rough copy of company campaign material should be presented to the supervisors before it is printed. Their feedback may be helpful in testing both the content of the communication and the way in which it is presented. If the company's position is not clear to supervisors, the employees will have trouble as well. Moreover, the supervisors will probably ask the same questions as the personnel in the bargaining unit. It is better to have such questions asked in a supervisor conference than on the shop floor before an appropriate response has been developed. The supervisors may also be in a position to detect an insincere or patronizing tone in the company communication or an inconsistency or other flaw in management's logic, as viewed by the employees, that may otherwise have been missed. Finally, bringing supervisors into some of the operational decision making of the campaign will be beneficial to their morale. It will change the campaign material in their eyes from the "company's position" to "our position." Given the central importance of the supervisory staff to most campaigns, this is not an unimportant matter.

"Vote No" Employee Committee

Another subject to be touched upon under the heading of management organization is the "vote no" employee committee. This is a delicate subject, because any management involvement in creating or encouraging such a committee is illegal and because the line between providing infor-

257

mation to interested employees and encouragement does not lend itself to safe generalization. If management is operating without the help of professionals experienced with such committees, it is best to refrain from any activity in this area.

One of the advantages of a vote-no committee is that its members are not agents of the employer and can therefore engage in conduct that would constitute unfair labor practices or other objectionable activity if done by managers or supervisors. For example, the company may not use home visits as part of its campaign; but there is no restriction on employee members of a vote-no committee visiting other employees in their homes to discuss the upcoming election. There are also no restrictions on the same employees speculating on the possible negative consequences of a union victory or future benefits from the employer should the union lose, or saying any number of other things that would be illegal if said by the employer.

Again, caution is urged. This is a touchy matter that must not be attempted by an unexperienced management. If management encouragement is present, the legal status of the actions and statements of the vote-no committee members may change. Of course, if such committees emerge on their own, the employer would have no reason to discourage them.

Once it is determined who will manage the company's campaign, it is generally advisable for the company to take the offensive.[11] The union should not be allowed to control either the timing or the issues of the campaign. These matters will be discussed in the next section. Here it is enough to note that the company must avoid being placed in a position of merely responding to the union's attacks.

A final observation worth mentioning before getting into the details of the company campaign is that there are no "haymakers" in a counterunion campaign.[12] It is unlikely that the employer will find an issue that will suddenly turn a substantial amount of union support into company support. In most cases the company will have to direct its attention at the relatively small number of uncommitted employees who will go in one direction or the other for any number of reasons, and in maintaining and strengthening the existing pro-company support. Thus, while the best defense may be an offense, it is the offense of trench warfare rather than the dramatic cavalry charge that counts in the end.

TIME AND TIMING

As noted, the union initiates the organizing drive and, by presenting its demand or filing its petition, the active campaign. This is a potential advantage to the union. An employer may find a union at the gate during the only period of strained relations with its employees in 20 years. The problem may be temporary and due to business conditions or a necessary organizational change, or the company may be in the process of correcting it. Yet the union may be able to use the existing employee dissatisfaction to advantage. Given this, the employer will often find it helpful to change the timing of the campaign. This will usually take the form of delay.

Delay, as mentioned earlier, works to the advantage of the company. Not only does it throw the union's timetable off, but it has been found that between 1962 and 1977 the average drop in union victories was 2.5 percent per month of delay.[13] This is an important piece of information. Viewed in light of Getman, Goldberg, and Herman's finding that the average drop from the card signing to the election was only 4 percent whereas the drop in the 5 most successful employer campaigns averaged 35 percent,[14] it suggests that one of the employer's main strategies is to wear down the union's majority over time. Part of the attrition in union support is undoubtedly natural, as some card signers reconsider or discover the costs and benefits of unionization. Some may be due to the employees becoming discouraged as the election is postponed.[15] And some may be due to the replacement of union supporters by more carefully selected nonunion employees as a result of normal turnover.

As developed in our discussion of the union campaign, one of the objectives—and one of the main difficulties—of the union organizer is to have his campaign peak just before the election. The company should be equally concerned with the timing of its campaign. In the case of the company, the question is when to initiate the *active* campaign, and, of course, it has complete control over this decision. It is quite appropriate for the employer to remain silent until it is ready to respond to the union problem in an organized and well thought-out fashion. This is one of the employer's important advantages.

One authority recommends starting the active employer campaign three to four weeks before the election.[16] This is not unreasonable; however, it should be recognized that there is a trade-off between the length of the campaign and its intensity. A judgment will have to be made as to the amount of information that will be necessary to offset the union's efforts, and then a second judgment as to the number of employer speeches, personal contacts, and written communications needed, and their proper sequencing and spacing. Generally, a relatively short campaign (in the neighborhood of three or four weeks) is reasonable. If it is shorter, the company may find that it does not have enough time to get all of its information out without bombarding the employees with excessive communication that does not allow enough time for discussion and absorption. A company campaign that lasts too long may move too slowly to retain interest and have its various elements complement each other. This is a common problem in union campaigns and somewhat of an advantage to the employer. After organizing for several months, the union will have used up its material. By the time the election is about to take place, the employees will already have heard all that the union has to say. The employer's message, on the other hand, will be fresh and, if presented right, of greater interest. Another reason for keeping the active campaign relatively short is to minimize the union's opportunity to respond to the employer's positions and statements.

The timing of the employer's campaign relates to the election date, not the beginning of the organizing drive. It is important to know when the election will take place. Of course, the parties will know the date of the election several weeks in advance once it is scheduled by the NLRB, but the more relevant information concerns the month in which the election will be held, not the day.

As a practical matter, the union controls the initiation of the organizing drive and the beginning of the critical period, but the company controls the end. This is done by delaying the election until the employer is ready and, often, until the union has lost some of its support by attrition.

The most powerful delaying tactic has become almost institutionalized. It is simply to decline to agree to an "agreement for consent election" (consent agreement) in which the regional director of the NLRB rules upon objections and the election takes place fairly quickly. Should the employer refuse to sign a consent agreement, the election will be held under one of the other formats, usually a "stipulation for certification upon consent election" (stipulation) in which the regional director of the NLRB may order hearings but the parties have the right of appeal to the NLRB in Washington.[17] This means that it will take longer for the NLRB to hold the election should the company wish to postpone it until it is better prepared. When the company has competent legal counsel, there is little chance of agreeing to a consent election when it is inappropriate. It's more likely to happen to a small or unsophisticated company that attempts to weather a union drive without help or with the help of its general counsel.

A related method of delay is to refuse to stipulate to anything. The company may dispute the jurisdiction of the NLRB, that the union is a labor organization, or that the proposed bargaining unit is appropriate.[18] The bargaining unit issue is often a legitimate area of disagreement between the parties and especially lends itself to lengthy debate.

The combination of refusing to agree to the technical questions surrounding the election and refusing to sign a consent agreement allows the employer to postpone the election for as long as is required to prepare an effective counterunion campaign and address any outstanding problems that may have contributed to the union problem. The importance of delay as an employer tactic and the extent to which it has become common is evidenced by the fact that whereas in 1962, 46.1 percent of all elections conducted by the NLRB were consent agreement elections, by 1978 this number had dropped to 7.3 percent.[19]

A word of caution is in order. There are limits beyond which the employer should not go in the use of delaying tactics. It is one thing to postpone an election by legal maneuver until the company has had an opportunity to prepare its campaign and take care of any short-run and correctable problems that exist. It is another to delay indefinitely for the sake of delay. The employees have a right to express themselves in regard to union representation through an election. The objective should be to convince them to vote with the company and against the union, not to deny them that right. Beyond a point, excessive delay will offend some employees who would have voted with the employer. It may also constitute evidence of the employer's bad faith and jeopardize the employer's good-faith doubt, support unfair-labor-practice charges or objections to a successful election, and, in conjunction with those unfair labor practices, a bargaining order. In an extreme case it may even result in the employer being ordered to pay the union's legal expenses.[20] Sooner or later the employer must fight it out with the union on the issues. Proper timing of that fight is an important element of the company campaign; however, beyond trying to gain time to plan and execute an effective campaign, correct any outstanding causes of employee complaint, and cause the union to suffer some attrition, the company should center its campaign on the issues.

ISSUES

The substance of any campaign is the issues: those charges and retorts directed at the employees in the hope that they will influence the vote. Since the union initiates the contest, it has the job of defining what the dispute is all about. In an election which can go either way, it is essential to the union that it identify and exploit the appropriate issues. Should it not do so, it will have little chance of winning. Similarly, in a close election, if the employer can effectively counter the union issues with offsetting information or draw attention away from them by introducing different company issues, the union may lose support. For example, if the union contends that the company pays substandard wages, the company may offset this by costing out the full compensation package and comparing it with that of a unionized plant or point out that the union's objective is to raise the employer's labor costs so as to protect unionized plants even if it means forcing the employer out of business.

The union seldom has trouble identifying a number of relevant issues, since its supporters readily provide the needed information. Its main danger is in listening to a nonrepresentative group of employees who may have concerns not shared by their co-workers, or in introducing outside issues that are of little interest to the employees. A seasoned organizer seldom makes either mistake.

How does the company identify the appropriate issues upon which to build its campaign? Most will be obvious or thrust upon management by the union. If the company is a low-wage employer or lacks a pension plan or other common benefit, this fact will surface during the campaign and will have to be answered. It should be expected that new issues will be introduced by the union. As a result of their contact with the union organizer, the employees may become convinced that working conditions or some other aspect of the employment relationship needs improvement. The fact that the employees accepted the conditions that predated the arrival of the union is unimportant. The newly discovered inequities are real and must be dealt with during the campaign.

The employer may become aware of existing problems and potential campaign issues through employee attitude surveys, supervisory observation, and exit interviews before the campaign begins. If problems cannot be corrected, the company should be ready to respond to the charges during the campaign.

The company may also create issues of its own during the campaign.

262

Some of them will be in the nature of offsetting the union's allegations. If the company is in a labor-intensive industry, subject to foreign competition, or unable to take advantage of the economies of scale of its unionized competitors, it may be necessary to explain the economic facts of life to the employees. Care must be taken to do this in a way that does not contain illegal threats or promises that could constitute unfair labor practice or other objectionable activity. The company may also discover that there are important issues of an antiunion nature that it can inject into the campaign with good effect. For instance, if it is found that the union's leaders receive surprisingly high salaries or are of questionable character, it may be appropriate to provide the employees with such information. If the union has a history of organizing new entrants to the industry which then tend to go out of business, or if it has not bothered to explain all the costs of unionization (dues, initiation fees, special assessments, and the possible loss of wages due to strikes), it may be appropriate to provide such information. Similarly, it may be appropriate to mention the infringement upon the employees' freedom and independence of action contained in a labor organization's right to discipline members who violate its rules. As usual, care must be taken and no statement made without advice of counsel. In general, though, the employer may provide information to the employees as long as it is accurate, relevant to the campaign, and not unduly inflammatory.

The company should choose its central campaign issues with care. Although union campaigns average 25 issues and company campaigns 30, the employees remember only about three from each side.[21] Assuming that employees recall those issues that are of importance to them and had an influence upon their voting behavior, this suggests that the campaign hinges upon a small number of issues that the company cannot ignore. This is echoed by the observation that campaigns usually boil down to one or two key issues.[22]

The assumption that the outcome of the campaign rests on a few key items should not be misinterpreted. Employees may be influenced by matters that they do not recall after the campaign or by the context of the campaign that contains information that may not be of specific importance. A few employees may be strongly influenced by fringe items in the campaign, such as the union's right to discipline its members or the political orientation of the labor movement, while others may be generally influenced by a number of minor matters that total up to a feeling that unions are not for them. Also, the company that bases its entire campaign from the beginning of a single issue or on only a few issues runs the risk of missing something that may surface as central during the course of the campaign.

It follows that the company should enter the campaign prepared to address a large number of questions that may arise or that it may find advantageous to introduce. Ideally, the campaign will distill to a few key items on which the company can effectively fight the union. If, on the other hand, the contest is less structured or if the company cannot better the union on the issues that surface, it will be to its advantage to take the offensive by introducing additional items of information. In fact, other than in those situations in which the union is inept enough to base its campaign on the wrong issues, the company should take command and introduce those issues upon which it would like to have the election decided. This raises the question of the general orientation of the company campaign.

ORIENTATION OF THE CAMPAIGN

One often recommended approach is for the company to run a campaign that gets the employees to vote against the union rather than for the company.[23] This has intuitive appeal. Some labor organizations or their leaders are vulnerable to a well-planned and well-researched attack on the basis of their finances or character. Others are so poorly run or have an ideological or social orientation so in conflict with the employees that it may be incumbent upon the employer to provide the employees with this information. However, care must be taken not to become overly specific in this regard. It is possible for an employer to become so good at running against a particular union, such as the Teamsters, that another union that does not share the same qualities starts to look good. The company campaign should be directed against unionization as well as against the particular union.

There are limits to the extent to which the employer can rely on an antiunion campaign. Kochan found that the most frequently offered reasons for favoring unionization were that a union would improve wages and benefits (12 percent) and represent workers' interests (6 percent). The most common reasons against unionization were that unions were not needed (20 percent), that the respondents preferred to handle their own problems (10 percent), and the negative image of unions (8 percent).[24] Getman, Goldberg, and Herman also found that job-related issues were dominant and most remembered in organizing campaigns.[25] This suggests that, with the exception of the negative image that unions have in the minds of some employees, the important issues are job-related. It is unlikely that an employer campaign based entirely on antiunion issues will offset legitimate complaints about wages, benefits, and conditions for long. Notice that the two most important reasons for voting against the union—"not needed" and "prefer to handle own problems"—imply that the employees are satisfied with their present pay and conditions and that the company is open and responsive enough to allow the employees to handle their problems individually. Such positive attitudes (and the organizational climate that fosters them) take time to develop. If they are not present at the beginning of the organizing drive, it will be difficult to create them overnight.

It should also not be assumed that because most nonunion employees report that they would not vote for a union, they are negative on unions. Between 60 and 70 percent of the American people approve of unions in general and in the right of workers to join them. Eighty percent believe that unions improve pay and job security and protect the employees from unfair treatment by the employer. Moreover, 73 percent of all union members are satisfied with their unions.[26]

Where does this leave us in regard to the orientation of the employer campaign? The intuitive appeal of running against the union notwithstanding, it appears that many American workers hold a generally high opinion of trade unions. Of course, this will vary with the location of the plant, the workers involved, the union involved, and the groundwork done by the employer over the years. Other things being equal, an antiunion campaign directed against the Teamsters in Arizona will have a better chance of success than a similar campaign directed at the United Automobile Workers in Michigan. The logical conclusion is that before a company chooses the orientation for its counterunion campaign, it should carefully evaluate its situation.

A second conclusion is that the employer should begin its preventive labor relations planning early. In light of the fact that most employees establish their voting position before the active campaign begins, it is essential that the employer's campaign be directed at encouraging and rekindling favorable attitudes toward the company and/or unfavorable attitudes toward unions. The orientation of the employer's campaign will to a great extent be a function of such preexisting attitudes. If the right attitudes are not present, there are important limits to what the employer can expect from the campaign. This, of course, reinforces the main theme of this book: preventive labor relations must start early to be effective.

SOURCES OF CAMPAIGN INFORMATION

It is important that the company have accurate information upon which to build its campaign. As part of its preventive labor relations program, management should make it a point to know as much as possible about the unions that are likely to mount an organizing drive against the company. Remember, the number of labor organizations with a particular interest in a given situation is usually small, and they can be identified from the *NLRB Election Report*.

Constitutions

There are a number of sources of information about unions that deserve mention. One is the union's constitution and by-laws.[27] The labor movement is tied together by thousands of constitutions, by-laws, and charters that establish the relationships between the various organizational entities and between them and their members. All labor organizations are constitutional democracies, and the interrelationships resemble those of the United States, the states, and the American people. Thus there are constitutions for the AFL–CIO and its various state and local subordinate bodies. Similarly, each national and international union has its constitution, as does each intermediate body and local union.

Management should obtain a copy of the constitution of any local union and its parent organization likely to mount an organizing drive against the company. When there is an important intermediate level in the union, such as the five conferences within the International Brotherhood of Teamsters, its constitution should be obtained as well. This may be difficult or take more time than expected. Some unions are reluctant to distribute constitutions, even to their own members. A disgruntled member armed with a copy of the union's constitution and an understanding of parliamentary procedure can really liven up a dull union meeting. Moreover, a study of the constitution often reveals a number of interesting facts that may be embarrassing to the organization and its leadership. Such information may prove useful to an employer in thwarting an organizing drive.

Many, if not all, labor organizations are less democratic than they appear at first glance or than they present themselves to their members and potential members. Numerous institutional and leadership devices have been developed over the years to protect the union, and especially its leadership, from internal and external attack. While an examination of the inner workings of trade unions is beyond the limits of our study, it is interesting to note some results. National and international union officials are almost never voted out of office. The three or four exceptions over the past 30 years prove the rule. And when a senior union official retires or dies, he is replaced by another reliable member of the executive committee or a long-service staff member who has proved his loyalty to the team. The process is similar at the intermediate level and in locals large enough to support a full-time professional leadership. Officials are usually elected at highly controlled conventions that never get out of hand or through equally well-controlled referenda. Similarly, dissatisfied local unions almost never succeed in withdrawing from their parent organizations, even though the members may overwhelmingly wish such a separation. Should this be attempted, the local is placed under "trusteeship," as allowed by the national union's constitution, which suspends local political control. Other matters, such as whether or not the members of a local may or must go on a strike or may or must accept an agreement negotiated on their behalf are also often under the effective control of the national leadership, notwithstanding appearances to the contrary. The rights and duties of the members, as well as the internal judicial system under which they may be judged and disciplined for infracting union rules, will also be found in the constitutions. It will usually be discovered that the union has considerable authority over its members, that the national organization has considerable control over the locals, and that the national leadership is firmly entrenched and virtually immune from membership dissatisfaction. When such information is viewed in the light of the compulsory union membership that usually follows unionization in the form of a negotiated union-shop provision (except in right-to-work states), it may provide the employer with a campaign issue that can be of considerable importance to those employees who value their independence.

Financial Reports

A second important source of information on labor organizations that may be helpful during a campaign is the reports that labor organizations file with the Department of Labor under the Labor-Management Reporting and Disclosure Act of 1959 (Landrum-Griffin) and under Executive Order 11491. Most unions must file Forms LM-1 (the Labor Organization Information Report), which contains organizational or constitutional information, and LM-2 (the Labor Organization Annual Report), which contains financial information. Organizations with receipts of less than $30,000 per year file a simplified Form LM-3 unless they are under trusteeship. The most interesting information for our purposes is contained in the LM-2.

A copy of the completed LM-2 may be obtained for a small charge by furnishing the union's name, local number, and location to the U.S. Department of Labor, LMSA, Unit of Disclosure, Room N5616, 200 Constitution Avenue, N.W., Washington, D.C. 20216. Information reported in the LM-2 includes the union's assets, liabilities, receipts, disbursements, contributions, loans payable, and a list of the names of the officers and staff with their individual salaries and allowances. While it is unlikely that improper financial activity will be detectable in the LM-2, an analysis may provide useful campaign information. For instance, the salaries and expenses of some officers may be surprisingly high. The number of paid officers and staff relative to the size or financial position of the local may also be of interest. Or a review of the last names of the officers and staff may suggest nepotism or a high degree of control by a particular ethnic group. Such information may be of interest to the employees; however, this should not be overdone, and advice of counsel should be obtained beforehand.

Labor Agreements

A third, and valuable, source of information about the organizing union is its contracts with other companies. Most companies are willing to provide a fellow employer with copies of labor agreements, since, unlike much compensation information, it is thought to be in the public domain. The importance of reviewing *several* of the union's contracts is that the organizer will often compare the target firm's compensation and conditions with his best contract while failing to mention those things in which the nonunion company is superior. He will also make his comparisons against his most recently negotiated agreements. This may be important if the company's wage levels had fallen behind before the organizing drive commenced and it is effectively prohibited from making improvements during the critical period. When the company compares its total pay and benefits package with those of selected unionized plants or an average of such plants, it may also find that it presents a better picture than that

268

offered by the union. If so, this information should be provided to the employees in an effective and timely manner.

Miscellaneous Sources

Additional sources of information on unions that deserve mention are the local press, government documents, and informal communication with other managers. As part of its ongoing preventive labor relations program, the company should build a file on each union of interest. Much of the information about unions that appears in the media is inherently negative. It deals with strikes, violence, internal dissension, and corruption. While this may be unfair to the many honest and dedicated union leaders in the United States, it does provide valuable campaign information on occasion. Government-generated information on major strikes may also be usable, as may less formal communication on strikes and plant closings. As usual, care must be exercised and advice of counsel sought before anything is said that might be construed as a threat or promise.

MONITORING THE CAMPAIGN

Once the organizing drive has begun, the company will want to monitor its progress. This will involve obtaining information on the union's efforts and, more important, how they are received. The company will also need feedback on the effectiveness of its own communications to the employees. Gathering information on what the union is doing and saying is usually easy. Its charges and positions are typically carried in leaflets or stated in public in such a way that the employer has no difficulty collecting and analyzing them. Information on what is said at union meetings and rallies is also easy to come by through *voluntary* reports from employee-attendees. The more difficult task is to evaluate how the employees respond to the communication received from the union and from the company.

Remember, attitude surveys and the direct questioning of employees during the critical period are, for all practical purposes, prohibited. It is also important that management not assume that the employees will respond to the union's and the employer's messages in the same way that managers would. The best feedback on the progress of the campaign is supervisory reporting. Most supervisors will have a good feel for the attitudes and responses of the employees in their charge. They will also overhear or be told things that will be of value to the campaign manager. Procedures should be established to facilitate the gathering of such information from supervisors throughout the campaign. This may include periodic meetings at which supervisors and managers discuss the subject. Additionally, the supervisors may be asked to evaluate the impact of an important piece of union or company information shortly after its release. If this is done individually with each supervisor, the campaign manager may be able to draw a composite or average from the various reports that provides timely and accurate feedback. It should be understood by all concerned that management is in need of accurate and objective information and not compliments.

A word of caution is in order. The supervisors must be instructed not to question the employees about anything connected with the union or the campaign. While they may listen or otherwise receive anything that an employee voluntarily offers, they may not seek it out without risking charges of illegal interrogation. This is not usually a serious constraint on the monitoring of a campaign. There is nothing unlawful about the employer being in possession of information on union matters if it is innocently and lawfully acquired.[28] Many employees regularly report information on union meetings, home visits, and union telephone calls.[29] Their response to the union communication and that of other employees can usually be inferred from such comments. Moreover, voluntarily offered information may be more reliable than anything that supervisors could obtain by asking. The response that a supervisor is likely to get to a direct question on a union-related subject is sure to be distorted in one direction or the other.

THE EMPLOYER CAMPAIGN AND THE LAW

It has been observed that employers sometimes intentionally commit an unfair labor practice so as to delay representational proceedings through litigation.[30] There may be situations in which this tactic is appropriate; however, in the overwhelming majority of cases the company's best course will be to run as clean a campaign as possible. In addition to avoiding having a successful election set aside or a bargaining order issued, this approach will be at least as effective as a campaign marred by unfair labor practices and other objectionable behavior. The company seldom has trouble postponing the election long enough to prepare its campaign and get its message across without breaking the law and thereby detracting from its image as a good and law-abiding employer. Second, it has been found that unfair practices are not effective in convincing union supporters that they should vote for the company or that unions lose more support during campaigns characterized by unlawful conduct than in clean ones.[31] On the other hand, should the employer engage in enough illegal activity to arouse fear in the minds of the employees, some will conclude that they need a union to protect them.[32] When this is viewed in light of our conclusion that the effective company campaign must awaken and strengthen existing pro-company or antiunion feelings, it follows that the employer should run as clean a campaign as possible. The usual difficulty is not one of deciding whether or not to commit unfair labor practices but of knowing what can and cannot be done. Before focusing on the specifics of the company campaign, it will be helpful to review four general legal points that have already been discussed in other contexts.

1. *The General Shoe doctrine.* The NLRB has long held that conduct by the winning party that makes an untrammeled free choice by the employees improbable warrants setting an election aside, *even if no unfair labor practices were committed.*[33] This so-called General Store doctrine is extremely important to preventive labor relations. It means that there are few firm rules as to what the employer may safely do or say during the critical period. Acts and statements that may in themselves be legal can contribute to a pattern of objectionable behavior when viewed against the employer's total conduct. Of course, anything that constitutes an unfair labor practice will almost always result in the setting aside of the election.[34] Beyond the range of obviously harmless and legal conduct, the best that can be done is to identify those things that are definitely illegal or unsafe and then observe that there is a large "gray area" within which the employer must exercise caution. Everything said or done must be evaluated beforehand for possible impact on the so-called "laboratory conditions" that the NLRB requires for representation elections.

2. *Limitations on Section 8(c).* Our second point is that the employer's Section 8(c) freedom-of-speech protection pertains only to unfair labor practices and not to representational matters.[35] Taken in conjunction with the General Shoe doctrine just discussed, this means that the employer must be especially careful in the selection of things to say and print.

3. *Wide definition of "employer."* Our third point is that the employer's position may be compromised by the words and deeds of supervision. It is not enough that "management" refrain from threats, prom-

ises, and illegal questioning; supervisors (or anyone else acting as an agent of the employer) must stay within the bounds of allowable behavior throughout the critical period. It is incumbent upon the employer to ensure that supervisors and anyone else in a position to compromise the company be aware of the seriousness and the requirements of the situation. It should also be understood that third parties (other employers, clergymen, public officials) not directly connected with the company can also jeopardize the employer's position with an inappropriate statement. The company's defense against this is to disassociate itself publicly from such a statement in an effective and timely manner.[36]

4. *Misrepresentation.* An election may be set aside if the winning party engages in substantial misrepresentation or other "campaign trickery," whether deliberate or not, when the other party does not have time to reply and when it is reasonable to conclude that the statement had an effect on the outcome of the election.[37] This does not mean that anything said by either party will result in a rerun of the election unless completely accurate. It is recognized that both sides will exaggerate their position in the heat of the campaign and assumed that the employees are knowledgeable enough to see through such exaggerations. However, there are limits, and the employer should not jeopardize an otherwise successful campaign with misrepresentation.

A particularly sensitive area in some campaigns involves racial appeals. In some parts of the country and among some employees, anti-union appeals based on the liberal position of the union on racial matters are especially effective. Unfortunately, some employers have not hesitated to use such material. The position of the NLRB is that camapign material designed to generate or inflame racial prejudice will warrant setting an election aside. This does not mean that a relevant campaign statement may not be used simply because it has racial overtones. The Board's standard is that if a party limits itself to a truthful statement on a racial matter and does not deliberately attempt to exacerbate racial prejudice, the election will not be set aside. However, the burden of proof rests with the party using the racial appeal.[38] As a practical matter, the employer should avoid the use of racial campaign material.

EMPLOYER CAMPAIGN TACTICS

Beyond the questions of timing, choice of issues, and general legal position, the employer's campaign is largely one of communication. The company communicates its position on the issues of the campaign for the purpose of influencing voting behavior. A number of the points made in our discussion of union campaign tactics apply to the employer as well. However, there are a number of things that are of particular interest to the company, either because of the nature of the employment relationship or because of its different legal position, which will be discussed under topical headings.

Employer Speeches

One of the most important employer communication vehicles is the speech to the assembled employees on working time, usually called a "captive-audience speech." The stand-up speech or "lecture" is usually the most effective way to deliver a large amount of information to a large number of people with some assurance that they will receive the message. The employer has an important advantage over the union in being able to assemble all the employees in one place at one time for such communication. Compare this with the difficulties faced by the union organizer in attempting to hold a meeting of the employees (discussed in Chapter 8). This, no doubt, explains the extensive use of captive-audience speeches in employer campaigns.

The employer speech should be used with care. If the company has never done such a thing before, the effect may be disappointing. The employees may not appreciate being talked "at," and some union supporters may view the occasion as an opportunity to ask embarrassing questions or later deride the company's message or the way in which it was delivered. It follows that management should give careful thought to the number of campaign speeches to use, their timing, content, format, and the choice of a speaker.

If employer speeches are used as part of a campaign, they should be used sparingly. A speech every week or two throughout a lengthy campaign may do more harm than good. A better approach is to have two speeches: one at the beginning of the active campaign and one at the end. In the former, the company should inform the employees of what is taking place, what their rights are, and what the company's position is in regard to unionization. It may also be appropriate to assure the employees that the company intends to stay within the letter and spirit of the law, and suggest certain questions that they may want to ask themselves about the costs and benefits of unionization. In the latter speech the company will be more interested in discussing the various issues that have arisen during the campaign. Finally, the employer may want to use the second speech to explain the election procedure and the fact that all votes are entirely confidential. Whether or not additional employer speeches should be used during an extended campaign to explain important developments, such as a bargaining unit determination or a major postponement, will be a matter of judgment. The decision will be based in part on the relative success of the first speech and on the need to explain the company's position to the employees before the union does.

The content and format of the speech should be given careful attention. The speaker should go into the room knowing exactly what to say and with a good idea of what questions, if any, to expect. In many situations, the employer speech is written by a labor-relations consultant or counsel. One authority has observed that the mettle of a labor consultant is tested by the quality of his captive-employee speeches.[39] At the very least, an employer speech should be reviewed by counsel before delivery and a tape or verbatim transcript made for legal reasons.[40]

Question-and-answer periods are often discouraged to prevent the meeting from getting out of control.[41] This too should be given some thought. Questions from the employee audience, especially at a meeting taking place early in the campaign, may provide the company with information on the concerns of the employees and on how they perceive the company and its efforts to remain nonunion. If this information is not available from other sources, a question-and-answer session may be worth the risk. Moreover, if the company's position on the issues is strong and the company spokesman is "good on his feet," this may be an opportunity to answer employee questions in a constructive manner. It may be more advisable to restrict questions during the second or final employer speech so as to prevent a union supporter from asking a question or raising a new issue to which the company has insufficient time to respond. If so, this can be done by scheduling the meeting for a specified period in a location that must be vacated at a certain time (the lunchroom from 11 AM to 12 noon) with a large number of items to be covered and with an important nonpartisan item last on the list (the mechanics of the voting procedure). Simply to prohibit questions or comments from the floor will leave the employees with a bad impression.

The choice of the speaker should also receive the attention it deserves. Obviously, he should be a manager with enough stature in the company to speak on its behalf in an authoritative and knowledgeable manner. However, in a large organization, the use of the chief executive officer or a corporate vice president should be avoided, because he will be viewed as an outsider and may remind the employees of the distance between them and the people who make the decisions that influence much of their working lives. In most cases, the top line manager on the property, or one close to him organizationally, who is both popular and articulate, will be a better choice. Under most circumstances, personnel or other staff management should not be used (unless the target unit happens to be the staff department), and under no circumstances should an attorney or consultant be used.

There are a number of legal requirements and restrictions applying to employer speeches that should be mentioned before we move on. One is that the general prohibition against threats, promises, and illegal interrogation must be carefully observed. While it may be permissible for management to make certain carefully phrased predictions regarding the outcome of the election if they are based on objective fact, conditions beyond the control of management, or decisions already made,[42] the matter is so complicated and equivocal that it does not allow safe generalization. The best advice is to have all copy reviewed by counsel. When the speaker departs from that copy, caution must be used. Statements to the effect that a union victory will inevitably be followed by strikes or that the resulting higher labor costs will result in the removal of the work to Mexico are not allowed.[43]

A second legal restriction on employer speeches involves their timing. The Peerless Plywood rule prohibits the employer from conducting a captive-audience speech within 24 hours of the election.[44] The reasoning behind this is that since the employer has no obligation to allow the union to address the employees on company time, management could use a last-minute speech to make statements or charges to which the union would be unable to respond before the ballots are cast. This is not an unreasonable rule, nor is it a serious restriction on the company campaign. An employer speech 25 hours prior to the voting is close enough to summarize the company's position on the issues and bring the campaign to an effective and dignified end. Furthermore, the Peerless Plywood rule does not apply to less formal conversations, the distribution of printed material, the inclusion of a pro-company message in the employee's pay envelope, or to employer speeches at which attendance is *voluntary*.[45] It applies only to the captive-audience speech on company time within 24 hours of the election.

Informal Discussions

Meetings and discussions between managers or supervisors and employees, either individually or in small groups, are one of the most effective employer campaign tactics.[46] They have a number of advantages

275

over the more formal employer speech discussed above. One is that they do not interrupt production or otherwise interfere with the company's operation as do captive-audience speeches. Second, they do not give the impression of talking "at" or "down to" the employees. Third, both the content of the discussion and the company representatives can be selected to fit the individual or group. If the group supporting unionization consists of a number of segments, such as women concerned with equal treatment or older workers concerned with matters of security or retirement income, management can arrange to have the relevant topics addressed by a knowledgeable and accepted company representative. Finally, the 24-hour Peerless Plywood restriction on captive-audience speeches does not apply.[47]

An important legal constraint should be noted. Meetings and discussions that take place in a location that is management in nature (locus of final authority) are considered to be coercive, regardless of content.[48] Calling employees into the plant manager's office, the personnel department, or any other location that is identified as management or supervisory to discuss unions or the impending election is not allowed. This restricts most informal discussion to the supervisory staff or to those managers who normally interact with the employees in the production areas, lunchrooms, and so on. In most (nonoffice) situations, senior managers do not stroll into the work area or the lunchroom for a chat. To do so during a union drive would probably create the wrong impression. It follows that if the supervisors are to convey the employer's position through individual or small-group discussion, they must be kept informed and be considered an integral part of the company campaign. Remember that a supervisor can commit unfair labor practices or otherwise engage in conduct that results in having a successful election set aside. This can be done just as easily in an informal discussion as in a formal employer speech. In fact, it may be easier for the company representatives to slip up under such conditions, since they will not have counsel to review their "copy," an agenda to keep them on track, or the pressure of the formal setting to remind them of the importance of their words.

Campaign Literature

The third employer instrument that we will examine is written communication. This will usually take the form of a letter or series of letters to the employee's home rather than the leaflet or throw sheet favored by the union. The company has an advantage over the union in the use of such letters. It has a complete and accurate list of the employees' home addresses early in the campaign. Thus it can assure that the letters are delivered to all employees. Should management decide to distribute the material at work (either in place of or in addition to a home mailing), it also has the advantage of knowing that the material will be delivered to each employee. This may be especially important for a written communication distributed just before the election. Remember, the 24-hour restriction on captive-audience speeches does not apply to written material.

It has been found that employees who receive letters and other employer literature recall a significantly larger number of employer issues after the election.[49] This suggests that such communication may have an impact on employee attitudes and voting behavior. Letters are an important part of an effective company campaign and should be treated accordingly.

The best campaign literature is designed specifically for the company and for the immediate campaign. Letters written and used in other situations may be helpful as a source of ideas and as examples of how to approach the problem. The person in charge of preventive labor relations should accumulate sets of company letters on an ongoing basis so that they are available for comparison when needed. However, they should not be copied verbatim, as they will lack the specificity and spontaneity of an original letter. Moreover, the union may be familiar with literature that has been used before and have prepared effective replies.[50] This is especially likely if the company uses the "canned" letters provided by some law and consulting firms.

As with union written material, employer literature should have eye appeal, present an idea in simple, vigorous language, and suggest a course of action. Similarly, it should be in good taste and avoid personal abuse.[51] In addition, employer letters should be personalized and written to the employee (and perhaps his family). That is, they should use "you" rather than "the employees" or "the workforce."[52] It is also a good idea to refer to "our company" and "our accomplishments" whenever appropriate.

Campaign letters should carry the signature of a popular manager. When a series of letters is used, a progression from formal to less formal format may be appropriate. For example, the first letter in the series should be signed with the full name and title of the manager (Joseph W. Blow, Personnel Manager). The second may drop the title, since everyone now knows who he is and the reminder of the authority or status difference serves no purpose. In the third, the typed name may be omitted and replaced with the signature "Joe Blow." The series may end with a more formal, but still friendly, letter from the CEO to impress upon the employees the seriousness with which the company takes the matter. Of course, the individual(s) over whose signature the letters appear, the degree of informality, and the content of the letters will be a function of the company involved, its management style, and the flavor of the organizing drive. A friendly informal letter from a hard-nosed manager in an authoritarian company will do more harm than good.

Whether or not cartoons and other expressions of humor should be employed is a difficult question that must be decided in the context of the company and the organizing drive in question. In some situations humor may be appropriate and effective. In others it may fall flat. It should be assumed that most of the employees, including those who are committed to the company, take the union drive seriously. In addition, many of the union promoters, and perhaps the outside union organizer himself, will be popular. Humor that ridicules such persons may backfire. In my opinion, humor should be used sparingly. Cartoons, in particular, should be left to the union. Not only is humor usually ineffective, but it often insults the intelligence of the reader.

One observer recommends that black print be avoided whenever possible.[53] This is an interesting observation. By extension, the company should pay attention not only to the color of ink used, but also the color and quality of paper and whether or not to use company letterhead. Again, the decision should rest with the specifics of the situation and the tone of the message being carried. If the company uses a series of letters to the employees, it will be helpful to print them on different-colored stock to emphasize their difference and avoid confusion. This will also facilitate referencing them in a subsequent speech, informal discussion, or written communication.

When several written communications are used, the company should approach them as a single project. It should decide upon the total message that it wants to convey to the employees through the written word and divide it into a sensible number of components to be distributed throughout the campaign. Further, the individual letters should complement the other elements of the counterunion effort. Ideally, each letter in the series should contain a single important item and lead into the one that follows and/or relate to speeches and informal discussions. If the active campaign lasts three to four weeks, three to five letters would seem appropriate (three or four from a popular local manager and one from the CEO), spaced at least several days apart. The content and the sequencing of the various pieces of the total message will depend on the situation; however, the company should save some of its best material for the end. It should never fall into the trap of responding directly to the union's charges. It is better to take command of the situation and discuss the issues of the campaign on the company's terms.

As usual, a word of caution is necessary. The prohibition against illegal threats and promises, of course, applies to written communication. Anything in writing is by definition strong evidence. All written communication should be reviewed by counsel before being distributed. In fact, counsel should be involved in the drafting of such letters as well.

Granting Benefits

The employer's best course of action when confronted with an organizing drive often is to correct those problems that are its cause. Not only will this mollify some of the employees and remove those issues from the campaign, but it allows the company to take the initiative.[54] If the company learns of the union's presence before a petition has been filed, it is free to make such changes and should take advantage of the opportunity. However, once the petition has been filed and the critical period begun, there are restrictions on what the employer may do in the way of making changes.

The Supreme Court has held that the well-timed improvement in benefits while an election is pending suggests the fist in a velvet glove.[55] The granting of an improvement is a reminder to the employees that the company is the source of such benefits and that they can be taken away as well as given. Thus the granting of benefits during the critical period in response to the union drive constitutes illegal interference and may result in the setting aside of an employer-won election.

On the other hand, if the improvement is motivated by valid business reasons and especially if the decision was made before the union entered the picture, the employer may grant the benefit. In fact, if the improvement had been scheduled and announced before the union drive, the employer must go ahead with it as planned, since withholding it would also be considered interference. The general rule is that the company must conduct itself in regard to the granting of benefits during the critical period as though the union were not present.[56]

It should be noted that this restriction pertains only to economic benefits. There are no effective constraints on improving the quality of supervision, becoming more responsive to employee problems, and becoming a more considerate employer in those quiet but important ways that do not lend themselves to outside scrutiny. Such "propaganda of the deed" should be used whenever appropriate.

Other Employer Campaign Tactics

There are a number of minor employer tactics that deserve brief mention for the sake of clarifying their legal status. One is the home visit. It will be remembered that this is available to the union and, under the right circumstances, can be effective. However, if managers or supervisors engage in home visitations during the critical period, it will probably result in the setting aside of the election, regardless of the content of the conversation.[57] It is important that management and supervisory personnel be informed of this restriction and that they refrain from doing home-visit missionary work on their own. It will also be remembered that employee-members of a "vote no" committee are not covered by this restriction, provided the employer has not created or encouraged the committee.

Second, pro-company employees may distribute and display "vote no" buttons, decals, badges, T-shirts, matchbooks, bumper stickers, and the like. Again, the employer may not encourage them to do so.[58] Nor may the company supply the insignia or be involved in its design, distribution, or purchase in any way.

Third, the employer may not give the employees money or other gifts as an inducement to vote for the company. However, management may promote a "get-out-the-vote" contest by providing chances for a TV set or other prize to those who vote.[59] It is also permissible for management to provide a small sum for lunch money or transportation to the polls for off-shift workers under certain circumstances, as long as such inducements are made available to all voters.[60]

Finally, under some circumstances it may be necessary or desirable to pay attention to the public-relations aspects of the campaign. This may be thrust upon the company by the union's decision to use the media as part of its campaign along the lines discussed in Chapter 8, or it may be adopted as the most effective way of counteracting organizational or informational picketing. Needless to say, care should be taken to ensure that the company's public pronouncements are well within the limits of the law.

CONCLUSION

It should not be thought that the various employer tactics are mutually exclusive. They should be used in combination in a way that they will complement each other. It is impossible to say in the abstract just what the optimum number of employer speeches, informal discussions, and printed communications is. However, in a given campaign such an optimum exists. A balanced company campaign using all or most of the communication devices available will be more effective than one based on a single tactic. For an example, one need only look at product advertising. No advertising department would expend its entire budget on, say, newspaper ads. Similarly, no counterunion campaign should be based only on letters to the employees or any other single instrument. Rather, a combination should be adopted that maximizes the overall impact of the campaign.

NOTES

1. Richard J. Anthony, "When There's a Union at the Gate," *Personnel,* November 1976, p. 52.

2. Julius G. Getman, Stephen B. Goldberg, and Jeanne B. Herman, *Union Representation Elections: Law and Reality,* New York: Russell Sage Foundation, 1976, pp. 27, 29, 62, 143.

3. Thomas A. Kochan, "How American Workers View Labor Unions," *Monthly Labor Review,* April 1979, p. 25.

4. Getman, Goldberg, and Herman, op. cit., pp. 96–97, 143.

5. Ibid., pp. 128–129, 144.

6. Ibid., pp. 108, 135–136, 145–146.

7. J. W. Lawson II, *How to Meet the Challenge of the Union Organizer,* Chicago: The Dartnell Corporation, 1973, p. 115.

8. M. Scott Meyers, *Managing Without Unions,* Reading, Mass.: Addison-Wesley, 1976, p. 127.

9. Lawson, op. cit., p. 126.

10. Ibid., p. 117.

11. Ibid., pp. 128, 141; Robert Lewis, "The Law and Strategy of Dealing with Union Organizing Campaigns," *Labor Law Journal,* January 1974, p. 42.

12. I. Herbert Rothenberg and Steven B. Silverman, *Labor Unions—How to Avert Them, Beat Them, Out-Negotiate Them, Live with Them, Unload Them,* Elkins Park, Pa.: Management Relations, Inc., 1973, p. 227.

13. Richard Prosten, "The Longest Season: Union Organizing in the Last Decade, a/k/a, How Come One Team Has to Play with Its Shoelaces Tied Together?" *Proceedings of the Thirty-First Annual Meeting of the Industrial Re-*

lations Research Association, August 29–31, 1978, p. 243. This reference is
based on the first six months of delay.

14. Getman, Goldberg, and Herman, op. cit., pp. 100–101.

15. Phillis Payne, "Consultants Who Coach the Violators," *American Federationist,* September 1977, p. 27.

16. Lewis, op. cit., p. 47.

17. Office of the General Counsel, National Labor Relations Board, *An Outline of Law and Procedure in Representation Cases,* Washington, D.C.: U.S. Government Printing Office, 1974, p. 280. Hereinafter, NLRB, *An Outline of Law and Procedure.*

18. Payne, op. cit., p. 27. Of course, Payne does not recommend the use of such tactics but criticizes their use by employers.

19. Prosten, op. cit., p. 244; 43 NLRB Ann. Rep. 259, Table 10 (1978).

20. 37 NLRB Ann. Rep. 137, 1972. At about the time these words were written, the NLRB ordered J. P. Stevens & Co., Inc., to reimburse with interest the Amalgamated Clothing and Textile Workers Union its costs in organizing 1,000 employees in a North Carolina plant and the union and the NLRB for their litigation expenses. NLRB News Release dated August 23, 1979.

21. Getman, Goldberg, and Herman, op. cit., p. 74.

22. Thomas M. Rohan, "Would a Union Look Good to Your Workers?" *Industrial World,* January 26, 1976, p. 40.

23. Lewis, op. cit., p. 47; Frederick J. Naffziger, "When Management Faces a Union Organizing Campaign," *Management Review,* August 1974, p. 25.

24. Kochan, op. cit., p. 28.

25. Getman, Goldberg, and Herman, op. cit., pp. 76, 82.

26. Kochan, op. cit., pp. 24, 30.

27. By-laws are extensions of the provisions of the union constitution. They often apply only to the local union and may be bound to the union constitution or separately. Both the by-laws and the union constitution usually take the form of a small book.

28. NLRB, *An Outline of Law and Procedure,* p. 310.

29. Myers, op. cit., p. 127.

30. Ibid., p. 129.

31. Getman, Goldberg, and Herman, op. cit., pp. 115, 141.

32. Ibid., p. 30.

33. General Shoe Corporation, 77 NLRB 124 (1948); NLRB, *An Outline of Law and Procedure,* pp. 319–320.

34. NLRB, *An Outline of Law and Procedure,* p. 310; Getman, Goldberg, and Herman, op. cit., p. 3.

35. NLRB, *An Outline of Law and Procedure,* p. 320. Hereinafter, NLRB, op. cit.

36. Ibid., pp. 339, 344.

37. Ibid., pp. 323–24. There may be some confusion on this point. The Board adopted this standard in 1962 in Hollywood Ceramics Co., 140 NLRB 221. In April of 1977 it substantially abandoned the practice in Shopping Kart Food Market, 228 NLRB No. 190; 42 NLRB Ann. Rep. 25, 55–57 (1977). Then in De-

cember 1978 it returned to the Hollywood Ceramic doctrine in General Knit of California, Inc., NLRB News Release, December 11, 1978. In 1979 it ruled that General Knit would *not* be retroactive to cases decided under Shopping Kart, BNA, *Labor Relations Reporter,* April 23, 1979, p. 5. Thus, at this writing, misrepresentation may result in the setting aside of an election.

38. NLRB, op. cit., pp. 320, 328ff.
39. Payne, op. cit., p. 28.
40. Rothenberg and Silverman, op. cit., p. 229.
41. Payne, op. cit., p. 29.
42. NLRB, op. cit., pp. 295–296.
43. Ibid., p. 298.
44. Peerless Plywood Company, 107 NLRB 427 (1954); NLRB, op. cit., p. 336.
45. NLRB, op. cit., p. 337.
46. Lawson, op. cit., p. 122; Lewis, op. cit., p. 46; Getman, Goldberg, and Herman, op. cit., p. 93.
47. BNA, *Labor Relations Reporter,* October 9, 1978, p. 2.
48. NLRB, op. cit., pp. 321–322.
49. Getman, Goldberg, and Herman, op. cit., p. 89.
50. Lawson, op. cit., p. 121.
51. Eastern Conference of Teamsters, *Manual for Union Organizers* (revised 1970), Bethesda, Md.: Eastern Conference of Teamsters, 1974, p. 22.
52. Payne, op. cit., p. 28.
53. Lawson, op. cit., p. 123.
54. Ibid., p. 108.
55. NLRB v. Exchange Parts Co., 375 US 405, 409 (1964).
56. NLRB, op. cit., pp. 314–315.
57. Ibid., p. 322.
58. Lawson, op. cit., p. 158.
59. NLRB, op. cit., p. 365.
60. Ibid.; Lawson, op. cit., p. 165.

12

THE REPRESENTATION ELECTION

The employer campaign usually ends with the representation election. Important exceptions occur when it is necessary to rerun the election because of unfair or objectionable conduct on the part of the winning party or when a runoff election is necessary because none of the choices on the ballot received a majority of the votes. For our present purposes, however, the election may be thought of as the termination of the employer campaign and as a distinct stage (with a number of separate problems and opportunities) in the process of remaining nonunion.

This chapter will examine the election procedure from the pre-election conference through certification by the NLRB. Of course, this is not necessarily the end of the process. In many situations, the losing party files objections to the election, which may result in litigation and possible invalidation and rerun. The employer should approach the election with this in mind. If management perceives its chances of winning as high, it must be careful not to engage in activity that may support union objections which could result in the setting aside of its victory. This is largely a continuation of the policy of not committing unfair labor practices or other objectionable activity throughout the campaign, with the important qualification that there are special requirements that pertain to the election. If it looks as though the company will lose the election, it should be particularly interested in observing and documenting union (and, perhaps, Board agent) activity that will support employer objections which may give the employer a second chance. Again, this should be a continuation of the company's posture throughout the campaign. If it looks as if the election could go either way—which almost by definition means that the vote will be close—the company should avail itself of the right to challenge questionable voters whenever appropriate and take advantage of any other legal opportunities. In fact, the company should employ all these approaches; they are by no means mutually exclusive.

It is assumed that the company will have had counsel and/or staff expertise available by the beginning of the active campaign. If not, it would be well advised to get help before the pre-election conference.

THE PRE-ELECTION CONFERENCE AND HEARING

An election cannot take place without communication among the parties and the NLRB. There are a number of important questions to be answered before the voting can begin. Thus some sort of pre-election meeting is necessary. Chronologically, the pre-election conference may overlap considerably with the campaign; functionally, it relates more closely to the election.

The representation election process usually begins with the union filing a petition with the NLRB. The union may or may not have previously demanded recognition from the employer. It will be recalled that such a demand and refusal from the employer is not required for the NLRB to find that a question of representation exists.[1] The next step is for the regional office of the National Labor Relations Board to arrange a conference among the parties and the Board agent(s) handling the case.

If the parties agree to a consent election—either consent agreement or stipulation—a formal hearing will not be necessary.[2] The important questions surrounding the election, such as the scope and composition of the bargaining unit, will have been determined by agreement among the parties. The mechanics of running the election can usually be worked out in a less formal conference. If there are no serious disagreements, the election will be scheduled for two or three weeks after the conference. If agreement is not possible, the matter will move to a hearing.

The pre-election hearing is a formal proceeding presided over by a hearing officer from the regional office of the NLRB, with the parties present and usually represented by counsel. Other labor organizations may be permitted to intervene in the proceeding. Evidence is received in the form of stipulations and sworn testimony, with cross-examination allowed. The hearing officer's responsibility is to conduct the hearing in an impartial manner and develop a full and complete record. Upon the completion of the hearing, the hearing officer submits a report to the regional director or, if the case has been transferred to the Board, to the NLRB in Washington. The parties may submit post-hearing briefs to the regional director within seven days of the close of the hearing. This time limit may be extended by up to 14 days at the discretion of the hearing officer. Upon review of the transcript and the hearing officer's report, the regional director (or the Board) may dismiss the petition, remand the matter for additional hearing, or direct an election.

As can be seen from Table 12-1, the great majority of representation cases are disposed of by agreement by the parties before a decision is rendered. In fact, only 17 percent of the cases are determined by a formal decision by the regional director or the Board. This is important in light of the employer's need to influence the bargaining unit determination, as discussed in Chapter 3. Table 12-2 provides additional detail of more interest to preventive labor relations.

TABLE 12-1. DISPOSITION OF REPRESENTATION (RC) CASES BY THE NLRB, FISCAL YEAR 1978.

Stage of Disposition	Number of Cases	Percent
Total RC Cases	9,926	100.0
Before notice of hearing	2,934	29.6
After notice, before close of hearing	5,240	52.7
After hearing, before decision	105	1.1
After Regional Director's decision	1,598	16.1
After Board decision	49	0.5

Note: Excludes employer (RM), decertification (RD), and deauthorization (UD) petitions and elections.
Source: 43 NLRB Annual Report 258, Table 9 (1978).

TABLE 12-2. METHOD AND STAGE OF DISPOSITION OF RC REPRESENTATION CASES BY THE NLRB, FISCAL YEAR 1978.

	Number of Cases	Percent of Total Cases	Percent of Elections
Total of all RC cases:	9,926	100.0	
Certification Issued	7,177	72.3	100.0
Consent Agreement Elections	524	5.3	7.3
Before notice of hearing	233	2.3	
After notice, before hearing closed	286	2.9	
After hearing closed, before decision	5	0.1	
Stipulated Elections	5,349	53.8	74.5
Before notice of hearing	1,648	16.5	
After notice, before hearing closed	3,662	36.9	
After hearing closed, before decision	39	0.4	
Expedited Elections	22	0.2	
RD-Directed Elections	1,246	12.6	17.4
Board-Directed Elections	36	0.4	
By Withdrawal—Total:	2,228	22.5	
Before notice of hearing	891	9.0	
After notice, before hearing closed	1,175	11.8	
After hearing closed, before decision	26	0.3	
After RD decision and direction	131	1.3	
After Board decision and direction	5	0.1	
By Dismissal—Total:	521	5.2	
Before notice of hearing	161	1.6	
After notice, before hearing closed	97	1.0	
After hearing closed, before decision	34	0.3	
By RD decision	221	2.2	
By Board decision	8	0.1	

Note: Excludes employer (RM), decertification (RD), and deauthorization (UD) petitions and elections.
Source: 43 NLRB, Annual Report 259, Table 10 (1978).

Note first that of the 9,926 representation (RC only) cases processed by the NLRB in 1978, only 7,177 resulted in certification. That is, only 72.3 percent went to an election and resulted in a "certification of representation" when the union won or a "certification of results" when the union lost. In the remaining cases either the union withdrew its petition at some point in the proceeding or the petition was dismissed. Additional detail as to the stage in the procedure at which the petition was withdrawn or dismissed is provided in the table.

Second, 74.5 percent of elections that took place were stipulated elections. Remember that consent agreement elections are completed considerably earlier, on the average, than stipulated elections. When the directed elections are added to the stipulated elections, it shows that 92.4 percent of all elections involve the potential for considerable litigation and/or administrative delay. Given the extent to which delay operates to the advantage of the employer, this is an important feature of the union representation process.

Third, it is interesting that 22.5 percent of the petitions were withdrawn during the administrative procedure. Of the 2,228 petitions withdrawn, 40 percent were withdrawn before the notice of hearing was issued and another 57.2 percent before the close of the hearing. Thus it appears that the company's willingness to go to a formal hearing or its handling of the matter in the hearing results in the union voluntarily backing away from the election in a large number of cases. When the 5.2 percent of the cases that were dismissed is added to this, it demonstrates the importance of the formal hearing to the employer as an instrument in preventive labor relations.

Finally, please note that a relatively small number of elections are actually directed by the regional director (17.4 percent of the elections, 12.6 percent of the cases). The number of cases resulting in a Board-directed election is very small. Moreover, the number of cases withdrawn or dismissed after either a regional director's decision or a Board decision is also small. The large majority of cases are resolved prior to the final determination by the regional director or the Board. This suggests that the hearing period between the notice of hearing and the issuance of a decision or direction lends itself to voluntarily negotiated election arrangements by the parties or to convincing the union that it is better off withdrawing than engaging in a future election. The point is that the hearing and the period leading up to it are an important stage in the employer's effort to remain nonunion. The fact that a hearing has been scheduled should not be viewed as indicating the employer has lost control. A great deal of influence over the arrangements for the election remains in the hands of the company, and this influence should be used accordingly. The hearing officer or other Board agents handling the matter prefer to get voluntary agreement by the parties and may perform a mediating role.

The union will in most cases be interested in an early election so as to forestall the loss of any more support than necessary and may be willing to trade some administrative advantage for time. This places the employer in a strong bargaining position during the hearing and the period leading up to it.

If the election is directed, the technical matters not agreed upon by the parties will usually be determined by the regional director. A request for review of the regional director's decision may be made to the NLRB in Washington. If such a request for review is filed, the regional director may proceed with a notice of election but, in the absence of a waiver from the parties, may not conduct the election.

Regardless of whether the questions surrounding the election are resolved by negotiation between the parties or by a directive from the regional director or the Board, they will have to be answered before the election can be held. Some of them may be important to the outcome of the election.

Date and Time of the Election

As discussed earlier, the employer can usually postpone the election for a period long enough to prepare and conduct an effective campaign. Delay may also be effective in wearing down the union's majority. What is of interest at this juncture, however, is the more tactical decision as to the day and hour of the election.

The election may not take place prior to 10 days after the regional director receives from the employer the so-called Excelsior list of the names and addresses of the employees eligible to vote. In practice, it is usually scheduled for some 20 days after the close of the conference.[3] Of course, the exact day and time are negotiable.

While there is no ready-made prescription for the best day and time to conduct a representation election (except perhaps "never"), a number of commonsense suggestions will be offered. They are intended more as "food for thought" than as recommendation.

First, the employer may want a date for the election that allows the inclusion of company campaign material in the employees' pay envelopes. This may be an effective way to get the final word into the debate in a manner that guarantees that all voters will receive it at the time intended. Apart from that, pay day may catch the employees in a better mood than a few days before or after.

Second, if the employees in the bargaining unit have an especially busy period each month or quarter (billing or closing the books in some office situations, registration on a university campus, preholiday shopping or important sales in retail), it may be best to avoid this period for an election. Not only would the election add to the disruption of the company's operation, but the harried employees may also be more inclined to vote union under such conditions.

Third, the employer should pay attention to local or national labor news. If, for example, a large and visible local employer is likely to have a strike within the next few weeks, the employer may want to have the election a day or two after the beginning of the strike. On the other hand, if a newsworthy negotiated settlement is about to be announced that will make the compensation or other employment-related benefits at the target firm appear relatively poor, the employer may prefer to have the election take place before the news is released. The employees will be sensitized to other labor news, especially local labor news, during the campaign and will be aware of what is happening, with or without the aid of the union or the company. The employer may be able to capitalize on helpful developments and avoid the impact of negative news by attaining the appropriate election date. Of course, this requires that management be aware of what is taking place.

Fourth, if the employer's operation is seasonal or cyclical, some thought should be given to the impact that the usual expansion and contraction of the workforce will have on the vote. Will the newly hired or recently laid-off employees vote? How will they vote? The NLRB prefers to hold the election at or near the seasonal peak whenever possible.[4] But in most situations the NLRB does not actually set the date; the parties do. Moreover, unless the seasonal adjustments are preordained by harvest (food processing), holiday seasons (retail), or snow (ski resorts), the employer may have control over when employment is expanded or contracted.

Finally, other things being equal, employees are probably more satisfied with their employment on Friday than on Monday, and at 10 AM or at the beginning of the shift (unless it begins early in the morning) than at 4 PM or at the end of the shift. Also, if the employer has engaged in some last-minute campaigning, such as a letter mailed to the home or pay-envelope material, it may be better to have the employees vote early in the day, before the union supporters have an opportunity to counter the message or exert peer pressure.

It is unlikely that the day and time of the election will have an important effect on its outcome unless it hinges on a very small number of votes. However, many elections are close, and it serves no purpose not to take advantage of such marginal factors. It costs the company nothing to agree to a date and time that is most favorable (or least unfavorable) to its cause. Wouldn't it be awful to lose an election by one or two votes after not having given some thought to such detail?

Location

Where the voting is to take place is seldom at issue. It is almost always on the employer's premises. This is usually the most convenient location for all concerned, and it would be unlikely that an off-premises election would operate to the employer's advantage. Union supporters are, almost by definition, more determined or dedicated than company supporters and those who remain uncommitted. An election conducted on "neutral" ground would probably reduce the size of the vote in the wrong quarters. An election conducted at the union hall would have the same effect, with the added possibility of giving the union a "home-court advantage." Consequently, in the absence of a strong reason to the contrary, representation elections are, and should be, conducted on company property.

The Ballot

The ballots are provided by the National Labor Relations Board, and at no time are they handled by anyone other than the voter and the Board agent. The choice or choices and the wording of the ballot will accord with the consent agreement or the direction of election. In a one-union election this will be clear-cut: the choice will be between the union and "no union." It is not possible to have the choice stated as between the union and "the company." In a multiple-union election there may be some controversy over how some unions are listed or their order on the ballot. This will be a matter to be resolved among the unions; provided the ballot is clear, it is doubtful that the employer could exert enough influence to have an impact on the outcome of the election anyway.

Another complication may emerge when some of the voters in the proposed unit are professional employees. In that case a "self-determination" election will be conducted to determine whether to lump the professionals in with the production or other bargaining unit personnel. This matter was discussed in Chapter 3. Once the decision is made that a self-determination election is appropriate, it is doubtful that the employer will have much influence on the details of the ballot.

Under unusual circumstances, balloting may be conducted by mail (merchant seamen), or part of the election will be conducted that way. That is, ballots will be mailed to the employees eligible to vote but unable to come to the polling place. Ballots are not mailed to employees who are ill, on vacation, or on military duty. And in the absence of agreement of the parties, ballots are not mailed to employees on temporary layoff. Rather, they are sent a notice of the election and allowed to come in to cast their vote.[5]

Eligibility to Vote

One of the important election-related decisions involves who will be allowed to vote. The answer to this question may determine the outcome of the election. The most important aspect of this matter involves the scope and composition of the bargaining unit, which has been discussed at length. Here it need only be noted that the actual bargaining unit will be spelled out in the consent agreement by the parties or in the direction of election by the regional director or the Board. Within the limits of the bargaining unit agreed upon or assigned, there may arise a number of questions with importance for the outcome of the election.

The general rule is that those persons in the unit who were employed during the payroll period immediately preceding the consent agreement or direction of election (referred to as the eligibility period) and are employed on the date of the election are eligible to vote. Employees who are ill, on vacation, on military duty, and on temporary layoff are also deemed to be eligible. The potential for disagreement in regard to employees on layoff or on military duty is obvious. The general guideline is whether or not such employees have a reasonable expectation of employment in the future.[6]

Strikers are an interesting and often important category. Employees engaged in an economic strike may vote in an election held within 12 months of the beginning of the strike, provided they are still on strike at the time of the election. They are presumed to be economic (as opposed to unfair-labor-practice) strikers and on strike in the absence of affirmative proof to the contrary. The replacements for those strikers are also eligible to vote if they were hired as *permanent* employees, unless they were hired after the eligibility period to replace employees who went on strike *prior* to the direction of an election.[7] This is a simplification of a complex matter that lies beyond our present interest. Suffice it to say, the employer experiencing a strike in conjunction with an organizing drive should seek advice of counsel and give some thought to the use of delay, the appropriate election date, and the hiring of replacements. Since it may be presumed that all such strikers will vote for the union and all replacements for the company, this is an important matter.

If the strike is in response to the employer's unfair labor practices, the striking employees will eventually be reinstated and are generally considered voters. Employees who have been discharged and who have filed charges alleging the discharge was unlawful are allowed to vote, subject to challenge.[8]

EMPLOYER RESPONSIBILITIES: LISTS AND POSTING

The employer has two responsibilities directly associated with the election that deserve discussion. One is to provide certain lists to the NLRB; the other, to post a Notice of Election.

The Excelsior List

Since 1966 employers have been required to provide the regional director with a list of the names and addresses of all employees eligible to vote in a representation election. This so-called Excelsior list must normally be provided within seven days of the direction of an election or the approval of a stipulation or consent agreement by the regional director.[9] However, if the payroll period used to determine eligibility to vote falls after the direction or agreement, the list must be submitted within seven days of the close of the period.

The Excelsior list *must* be provided, in contrast to the initial list of the employees in the proposed bargaining unit mentioned earlier. Failure to furnish it will warrant setting aside the election if the union files proper objections. The NLRB gives a copy of the list to the union or unions involved in the election, and the list is used to determine who may vote and who should be challenged at the pole. Of course, it may also be used for a mail or home-visit program by the union.

It follows that under some circumstances—such as when the union has been unable to develop its own mailing list and the number of employees involved is large—the employer should not help the union mount an effective mail or home-visit campaign. This can best be done by not providing the list of names and addresses any earlier than necessary and by having the election scheduled as soon after the submission of the list as practicable. When possible, the company should postpone the signing of the consent agreement or stipulation until fairly late in the campaign and then agree to an eligibility period that is close to the election. Of course, other considerations will be involved; but when the election is close enough to be influenced by a last-ditch mail or home-visit campaign and the union has been constrained from using such tactics because of a lack of home addresses, the company should not give the union any more help than necessary.

Posting

It will be remembered that the National Labor Relations Board "suggests" that the employer post a *Notice to Employees* (Form NLRB-666) in its initial written communication after the filing of a petition. The Notice to Employees states that a petition has been received and that an election *may* be held. It outlines the employees' rights, gives examples of conduct (mainly employer conduct) that will not be allowed, and assures the reader that the employees' rights will be protected. The employer may decline to post this notice; it is not mandatory. This should not be confused with the *Notice of Election* (Form NLRB-707), which, in addition to a statement of the employees' rights, contains a sample ballot with the names of the parties inserted, a description of the bargaining unit, and the date, time, and location of the election.[10] The Notice of Election is larger than the Notice to Employees—too large to reproduce—and is available in several languages.

The Notice of Election *must* be posted by the employer, normally three working days before the voting. Failure to do so may result in having the election set aside. The employer has no discretion in this matter. Moreover, the notice must be posted in an apppropriate place and may not be covered, altered, or defaced in any way (such as by checking the "no union" choice, tempting though it may be). The NLRB takes its Notices of Elections very seriously, and the employer should do so as well.

OBSERVERS AND CHALLENGES

The representation election is conducted by the Board agent, not by the parties. However, the parties usually have an equal predesignated number of "observers" at the poll(s). This is not required in the Act, and in a directed election they are allowed as a privilege rather than as a right. In consent elections, the parties have a right to have observers, provided the parties agree to their presence in the consent agreement or stipulation.[11]

Observers are usually drawn from the employees of the company who are not members of the election unit and are not supervisors or associated with a "vote no" committee. Their purpose is twofold. First, they witness the conduct of the other party and the Board agent during the voting to ensure that the election is fair and that the other side does not benefit from an irregularity. They also witness the vote count to ensure that only valid ballots marked only with an "X" or "$\sqrt{}$" are counted. If all goes well, the observers are asked to sign a certification of the conduct of the election.

The second important function of the observers is to challenge for cause anyone who should not vote or whose eligibility to vote is questionable. The Board agent is required to challenge anyone whose name does not appear on the eligibility list. The observers' role is to challenge those voters of whom it may be argued that they do not properly belong in the bargaining unit. For instance, there may be a question regarding whether a particular employee is a supervisor or whether the work of a group of employees lies within the bargaining unit. Challenges must be made at the time the individual appears to vote but before the ballot is cast. The Board does not permit post-election challenges. Given the secrecy of the election, once a ballot is cast there would be no way to determine how the challenged employee voted. It is therefore important that the management observers go into the election prepared and knowledgeable about who they are to challenge and for what reason. The eligibility list should be reviewed before the election and those voters who may be challengeable identified. This is where sound judgment as to how particular employees are likely to vote becomes invaluable. Management may not wish to challenge a questionable member of the voting group if it is known that that person will vote "right." Board policy prohibits keeping a list of voters at the poll other than the official voting list in the possession of the Board agent.[12] Thus, if the list of management challenges is long, the observers should be provided with something other than an annotated eligibility list.

Challenged ballots are set aside and not counted with the others. If their number is too small to affect the outcome of the election, they are left out of the tally and, for all practical purposes, are ignored. If, on the other hand, they are "determinative," the NLRB will investigate them and may hold a nonadversary hearing.[13] In practice, challenges are often resolved voluntarily among the parties.

In 1978, the NLRB ruled upon challenges in 404 of the 7,311 representation (RC only) elections reported.[14] The Board does not report the presumably much larger number of nondeterminative challenges upon which it does not rule. Nor does it report the details of the resolution of those that it does process.

CONDUCT AT THE POLL

The conduct of all involved in the running of a representation election is strictly controlled in the interest of achieving a fair and unmarred vote. Electioneering within 50 feet of the poll is generally forbidden. However, the Board allows itself broad discretion in the running of elections, and the specifics of the nonelectioneering area and similar matters are up to the Board agent present and, ultimately, the regional director.[15] Just what is considered to be electioneering may be debated. However, sustained conversation with employees waiting to vote has been held to be electioneering, independent of its content. Supervisors and others associated with management should therefore be instructed not to engage employees waiting to vote in conversation, even if the content is unconnected with union or election matters.

An election can be set aside because of inappropriate conduct on the part of the representatives of the winning party. Thus the employer should avoid everything that might invalidate a successful election, and its observers should be instructed to witness and document unlawful activity on the part of the union(s). Elections can also be set aside because of improper conduct on the part of the Board agent. For example, elections have been invalidated because not all eligible employees got a chance to vote because the poll opened late, because the security of the ballots was compromised, or because the Board agent was seen drinking beer with the union representatives.[16] Although NLRB field examiners are capable and conscientious, the employer should make it a point to help the Board agent avoid making mistakes that may jeopardize a successful election. It may also be appropriate to document any irregularities that occur that may support employer objections should the union win.

OBJECTIONS

It is fairly common for the losing party to file objections to the conduct of the election once the ballots have been counted. If sustained, the objections may have the result of invalidating the election and requiring that it be rerun. Objections may be filed only by the parties to the election (employer or union) and only within five working days of the tally of the vote. The objection must be worded in specific, as opposed to conclusionary, terms and accompanied by sufficient evidence and statements of witnesses to support a *prima facie* case. Once an investigation has commenced, the regional director, not what is written in the objections or the wishes of the parties, determines its scope.[17] In general, the regional director decides whether or not to conduct a hearing. However, it has recently been established that if the alleged misconduct is serious enough to warrant setting aside the election, a hearing must be held.[18]

If the election was conducted pursuant to an agreement-for-consent election, the regional director issues a "report" upon completion of the investigation. In a stipulation-for-certification election, a regional director's report containing a recommendation to the Board or a "notice of hearing" that transfers the case to the NLRB in Washington is issued. If the regional director issues a report in a stipulated election, the parties have ten days in which to file "exceptions" to the report with the Board. In a directed election, the regional director's ruling on objections is contained in a "supplemental decision."[19]

Regardless of the instrument and the procedure involved, if the union wins the election and the employer files supportable objections, the duty to bargain with the union is suspended until the matter is resolved. If the employer is willing to fight it all the way and incur the legal costs, this may take as long as two years.[20] Such post-election delay can be an important tactic in coping with the union after the election. Needless to say, such stalling is a source of considerable, and often justified, complaint by the unions.[21]

In 1978, objections were filed in 954 of the 7,311 (RC) representation elections reported, or 13.0 percent. Employers filed in 414 (43.6 percent), unions in 516 (54.1 percent), and both parties—presumably in multiple-union elections or as countercharges—in 22 (2.3 percent) of the cases. Since objections were withdrawn in 187 of the elections, the NLRB ruled on only 767 of the cases. Of these, 618 (80.5 percent) were overrruled and 149 (19.4 percent) sustained.[22] It appears that a relatively small number of the objections are upheld and consequently result in a rerun of the election. However, this does not detract from their importance as an instrument of post-election delay nor from their importance in those cases in which one of the parties won through objectionable behavior serious enough to influence the outcome of the vote.

RERUN ELECTIONS

If the union wins the election and the employer successfully files objections, the first election will be invalidated and a rerun election ordered. This gives the company a second chance. Similarly, if the company wins and the union's objections are sustained, the election will be rerun. The restriction in Section 9(c)(3) against conducting a second election within 12 months of the first does not apply in such cases.

The rerun election is essentially the same as the initial election, with two exceptions. First, the Notice of Election explains to the employees that the election is being rerun because of misconduct on the part of one of the parties.[23] Second, the eligibility period of the repeat election is usually the payroll period immediately preceding the issuance of the new Notice of Election.[24] If the period between the elections is fairly long, some of the former voters will have been replaced with new hires. This suggests that the company should be particularly concerned with where it takes its turnover and with its selection decisions in the interim. It should also take advantage of the time to correct or eliminate the causes of employee complaint and union interest. Advice of counsel should be sought before making any changes, because the critical period continues until the election is conclusive.

In 1978, there were 120 (RC) elections rerun out of the 7,311 reported, or 1.6 percent. In 33 of the 120 reruns, the outcome of the original election was reversed, with the union winning 42 (35 percent) and the employer 78 (65 percent).[25] Whether such numbers are substantial or not is a matter of perspective. To the 42 employers who won the initial election only to lose the rerun, they are substantial indeed. Moreover, the possibility of having a successful election rerun operates as a check on the campaign activity and statements of both sides.

RUNOFF ELECTIONS

Runoff elections must not be confused with rerun elections. They are quite different. When there are two or more unions involved in the election, in addition to the "no union" choice, it is possible for none of the alternatives to receive a majority of the valid votes cast. Under such circumstances, the NLRB conducts a runoff election between the two leading choices to determine the winner.[26] The runoff may be between the top union and "no union," or it may be between the two unions receiving the largest number of votes. The difference to the employer is important.

The runoff will occur soon after the initial election if there are no objections from the losing party or parties. Just how the company should approach the new campaign will depend on the specifics of the situation and the time available. Given the small number of such runoff elections, there is little information available for generalization. Since the NLRB-generated data are largely based on "conclusive" elections, runoffs are subsumed within general representation election figures. However, one thought that may be offered is that, if "no union" is one of the choices, the company may find it appropriate to redirect its campaign from an attack on unions in general (which may have been appropriate in a multiple-union election) to one against the particular union remaining. Some of the employees will no doubt remain loyal to their former choice and may be induced to vote "no union" to avoid becoming a member of the other labor organization. Under such conditions, an antiunion campaign may be appropriate. The employer should suggest that a victory by the remaining union may end the chances of the other union(s) ever gaining bargaining rights in the unit. This approach may be especially effective if the competition between the unions during the organizing drive was bitter and if the vote was close. It may even result in the unsuccessful union campaiging for a "no union" vote in the runoff election. A labor organization operating under such conditions is free to say and do things that management may not and, for all practical purposes, becomes a "vote no" committee for the duration of the runoff election campaign.

If "no union" is no longer on the ballot, there is little that the company can do openly. Helping a preferred union would be illegal. Section 8(a)(2) of the National Labor Relations Act makes it an unfair labor practice for the employer to assist a union. Moreover, open support from the company would probably operate as a "kiss of death" to the preferred organization. The employees would logically conclude that the company is supporting the weaker of the two unions and vote for the one perceived to be the stronger. Therefore, any support of the preferred choice or action against the unwanted union will have to be subtle.

The technicalities of the runoff are similar to those of the initial election. Of course, the ballot is different, as it will contain only two choices; but everything else has already been determined and will continue to apply, including the voter eligibility period. The exception to this occurs when there has been a substantial increase in the workforce. If so, then a new and current payroll period will be used for the runoff election.[27] If the number of employees in the bargaining unit happens to increase between the initial and the runoff elections, management will naturally recruit and select with care. As usual, caution is urged and counsel should be sought.

CERTIFICATION

The final procedural step in most elections is certification. In consent agreement elections, the regional director issues a "certification of representative" to a union receiving a majority of the valid votes cast (not a majority of the potential voters in the bargaining unit). If "no union" wins, the regional director issues a "certification of results." The same thing occurs when the election is conducted under a stipulation for certification, provided no objections or determinative challenges are filed. Where they are, the certification of representative or results is issued by the Board. If the election was directed, the certification comes from the regional director if no objections or determinative challenges have been filed. When objections or determinative challenges are involved, the certification may come either from the regional director or the Board, depending on the location of the investigation and hearing procedures.[28]

Once a certification of representative has been issued, the employer has a legal duty to recognize and bargain with the union as the exclusive representative of the employees in the unit. Correspondingly, the union has a duty to represent those employees. If the union loses and a certification of results is issued, another election may not be held in the same bargaining unit for 12 months.

BARGAINING ORDERS

Most of us are used to thinking of the election as the end of the representation process and assume that the union either wins or loses on the basis of the vote. This is often not the case. There are other ways in which a union can win, and the election may not be the end to the conflict.

It has long been established that a company may decline to grant recognition on demand, provided it does not have independent knowledge of the union's majority status and it has not committed serious unfair labor practices.[29] The early decisions in this area centered on whether the employer acted in good or bad faith under the so-called Joy Silk doctrine.[30] Then in 1968 the Supreme Court, in Gissel Packing Co.,[31] shifted the Board's attention toward the impact of the employer's illegal conduct on the effectiveness of the election process. Subsequently, issuing "bargaining orders" was viewed as the appropriate remedy for employer misconduct. For our purposes, the importance of the Gissel decision is that it permits the Board to order an employer to bargain with a union that has lost an election when the employer's misconduct has made it improbable that a fair election can be held. The fact that the union may have lost its majority status by the time the order is issued is irrelevant.[32]

A great deal of litigation has emerged from the bargaining-order question and will, no doubt, continue to unfold in the years ahead. One question is whether or not a demand for recognition must have been made and refused before a bargaining order may be issued. At this time the answer appears to be in the negative.[33] Another development of considerable interest involved the issuance of a bargaining order on the basis of a combination of 14 ballots cast for the union and six authorization cards signed by employees who did not vote or whose ballots were challenged. This occurred in a case in which the union had lost the election and had never demonstrated a majority by any means.[34] Various other technical questions have emerged, such as whether or not the bargaining order should be retroactive to the date of the unfair activity and whether the Board may simply adopt the reasoning of the regional director in issuing its order. None is particularly important from our present perspective. The basic question of whether or not the Board should order the employer to bargain with a union that has lost the election and does not represent a majority of the employees in the unit is not under review, nor is it likely to be in the near future. The impression that emerges is that everyone agrees that the election is the preferred way to determine a union's majority status but that the bargaining order is so powerful and effective a remedy that it will continue to be used whenever the NLRB finds substantial campaign misconduct on the part of the employer.

I have been unable to discover any published data on the number of Gissel-type bargaining orders issued. The subject is confused by the fact that bargaining orders have long been used as remedies in cases in which the employer withdraws recognition from an established union for one reason or another. The impression drawn from the substantial amount of litigation on this matter is that the number of Gissel-type bargaining orders employed by the Board is large and growing. For what it is worth, the author recalls hearing somewhere that there are between 60 and 80 of them issued each year.

This is an important development for preventive labor relations. Not only must nonunion companies worry about losing union elections or having them invalidated and rerun, they must also be concerned with winning in the wrong way. Everything involved in the active campaign has become more risky; the critical period has become more critical. The chances of ending up with an obligation to bargain with a labor organization due to a careless remark about shutting down the plant or an untimely or insufficiently documented discharge of a union adherent have grown. This tends to enhance the importance of the material covered in the earlier chapters of this book. It has become more important than ever that the company intent upon remaining nonunion take the actions necessary to avoid and deter unions and at an early date adopt employee-relations practices that make them unnecessary.

NOTES

1. Office of the General Counsel, National Labor Relations Board, *An Outline of Law and Procedure in Representation Cases,* Washington, D.C.: U.S. Government Printing Office, 1974, p. 59. Hereinafter, NLRB, op. cit.
2. Ibid., p. 33.
3. Ibid., p. 275; Robert Lewis, "The Law and Strategy of Dealing with Union Organizing Campaigns," *Labor Law Journal,* January 1974, p. 46.
4. NLRB, op. cit., p. 228.
5. Ibid., p. 277.
6. Ibid., pp. 282–284.
7. Ibid., pp. 284–287.
8. Ibid., p. 288.
9. Ibid., pp. 332–336; Excelsior Underwear, Inc., 156 NLRB 1236 (1966).
10. NLRB, op. cit., p. 276.
11. Ibid., pp. 277 and 355.
12. Ibid., p. 367.
13. Ibid., p. 278; 43 NLRB Annual Report 228 (1978).
14. 43 NLRB Annual Report 262, Table 11B (1978).
15. NLRB, op. cit., pp. 363–364.
16. Ibid., pp. 346–351 and 356.
17. Bureau of National Affairs, *Labor Relations Reporter, Summary of Developments,* February 27, 1978, p. 2. Hereinafter, BNA, *Labor Relations Reporter.*
18. Ibid., March 27, 1978, p. 3.
19. NLRB, op. cit., pp. 278–279.

20. Julius G. Getman, Stephen B. Goldberg, and Jeanne B. Herman, *Union Representation Elections: Law and Reality,* New York: Russell Sage Foundation, 1976, p. 162.

21. Phillis Payne, "Consultants Who Coach the Violators," *American Federationist,* September 1977, p. 29.

22. 43 NLRB Annual Report 262–263, Tables 11B, 11C, and 11D (1978).

23. NLRB, op. cit., p. 367.

24. Ibid., pp. 287–288.

25. 43 NLRB Annual Report 264, Table 11E (1978).

26. NLRB op. cit., p. 278.

27. Ibid., p. 287.

28. Ibid., p. 281.

29. Linden Lumber Div., Summer & Co. v. NLRB, 419 U.S. 301.

30. Joy Silk Mills, 85 NLRB 1263 (1949); NLRB Annual Report 63 (1971).

31. 395 U.S. 575 (1969).

32. 36 NLRB Annual Report 93 (1971).

33. BNA, *Labor Relations Reporter,* May 22, 1978, vol. 98, no. 7 citing Hedstrom Co., 98 LRRM 1105; 41 NLRB Annual Report 24, 138 (1976); 42 NLRB Annual Report 95 (1977).

34. Pinter Bros., 227 NLRB No. 123; 42 NLRB Annual Report 94 (1977).

13

AFTER THE ELECTION

The certification of representative or certification of results marks the end of the election and the company's active counterunion campaign. It does not represent an end to the company's labor problem or industrial-relations function.

If the company has won the election, it has a breathing spell of about a year. Section 9(c)(3) of the National Labor Relations Act prohibits holding a second Board election within the same unit within 12 months of the first election. This does not preclude holding an election in a larger unit. Moreover, the Board will process a petition for an election filed within 60 days of the expiration of the one-year period, thus commencing a new critical period. Petitions filed earlier than that are dismissed.[1] Therefore, a company that wins an election is guaranteed a period of only 10 months to evaluate its performance and make any called-for changes before possibly entering another critical period and active campaign. It is important that this time be put to good use.

If the company loses the election, it has an important decision to make: Should it accept the situation and learn to live with the union, or should it continue the fight? This decision is too important to be made lightly or left to counsel or staff. It should be made by top management and made as objectively and carefully as the original decision to fight or not to fight unionization. The result of the decision will be the adoption of an objective either to tame the union or to "kill" it. What the company does in the months immediately following certification of the union will be critical to the attainment of that objective. The alternatives are mutually exclusive: the company cannot do a little of both. The decision must be made, and it must be made early.

LEARNING TO LIVE WITH THE UNION

Once a union has been certified, there is a "continuing and irrebuttable presumption" that it is the majority representative of the employees in the unit for a period of at least one year.[2] If during that year a labor agreement is consummated, the protection extends for the life of the contract, since the NLRB will not entertain a petition for decertification (to be discussed) other than during a 30-day period falling between 90 and 60 days before the expiration of a valid collective-bargaining agreement. This is the "contract-bar rule," and it applies to labor agreements of up to three years' duration.

The employer's decision to accept the union or to continue the fight will hinge, in part, on the outcome of the election and on the reasons for that outcome. If voter turnout was high, the union won by a substantial majority, and its victory cannot be explained away by an inappropriate bargaining unit decision, a lack of preparedness or mistake on the part of management, or some other correctable condition, the company would usually be well advised to get to work on developing a successful relationship with the union. The details of this subject lie beyond the limits of this book. Suffice it to say that once the "smoke has cleared," management should direct its attention at giving the union *leadership* what it needs to survive and prosper so that it may become "responsible." It will be necessary to grant adequate concessions and, perhaps, take a strike to allow the union to fulfill some of its campaign promises and to allow its leaders to establish themselves as competent and militant unionists. If management is dealing with local or inexperienced union leaders, it will have to educate them on the facts of business life. If the national or international level is in control, the union representative may do most of the educating. It will also be necessary to give the union leadership the organizational security it needs. In non-right-to-work states this will usually include a union-shop provision requiring employees to join the union 30 days after starting work. It may also include a checkoff provision whereby the company deducts union dues and fees from the employees' pay and forwards the money to the union. These two items are of considerable administrative value to union leadership and, principles aside, cost the company little. It may also be necessary to negotiate a three-year agreement to give the union the full benefit of the contract-bar rule, discussed earlier. This is more serious. The company should never enter into a "three-year book" unless it has fully decided to make peace with the union and knows what it is doing.

A newly organized company should not attempt to negotiate its first agreement without competent staff familiar with collecting bargaining *and* the company's operations and problems at the table. Negotiating the first contract is quite different from renegotiating subsequent agreements.[3] In the first negotiation, the company may not know what it wants and needs. Yet it will end up agreeing to a document that will shape the whole future relationship with the union and with its employees. If mistakes are made, they will take years to straighten out. A particular problem to be aware of is that the union negotiator may "sell" management language—or even a whole contract—from another company or industry that does not fit the employer's needs. In fairness, most able and honorable union officials and staffers will not do this and may even help the employer stay out of trouble. The danger lies in dealing with inexperienced union leadership that does not understand the process or have command of the technical information needed to negotiate a successful and workable agreement. Another possible problem—to which there is no comfortable solution—may occur when the employer has been organized by a union determined to create or maintain an areawide or industrywide standard at all costs.

The company negotiating for the first time must think through and "cost out" every proposal before agreeing. Little things—such as call-in procedures, seniority districts, progression or promotion ladders, and time limits on the processing of grievances—that may seem unimportant in comparison to a threatened strike or the main items on the table can end up costing more money and causing more trouble than might be imagined. Remember, the company is not only agreeing to the words adopted; it is also agreeing to the interpretation of those words by a generation of arbitrators (assuming a grievance procedure terminating in final and binding arbitration is adopted).

CONTINUING THE FIGHT

If the recently unionized company decides not to accept the union as a permanent feature, things are much different. The objective then becomes one of getting rid of the union or, more accurately, doing nothing to impede the employees' efforts to get rid of the union.

The Section 9(c)(3) restriction on having another election within the same unit for a period of one year applies. Similarly, if the parties enter into a labor agreement, the protection is extended for the life of the agreement. If the employer engages in "surface bargaining" or in some other way fails to satisfy its statutory responsibility to bargain in good faith, the certification period may be extended by the NLRB.[4]

If the company's objective is to divest itself of the union, it should initially do almost the opposite of what it would do to tame the union. Again, space does not allow full treatment of the subject, but, in short, management should do nothing to make the union or its leadership "look good" to the employee-members. Nothing should be conceded that is not absolutely necessary. If the union is not in a position to strike the company with effectiveness, this may be very little indeed. Most important, the company should not grant a union shop if it can be avoided. If it is necessary to enter into a labor agreement, its duration should be limited to one year. If possible, the company should not conclude an agreement with the union.

Of course, refusing to bargain or engaging in surface bargaining is illegal and will have to be done with tact and skill. The company cannot refuse to sit down, and it cannot be patently unreasonable in its position. It can, however, bargain hard and refuse to agree to anything that either makes the union look good or helps secure its organizational position unless necessary. This usually boils down to whether or not the union is in a position to strike and whether the company has the ability and willingness to take a strike. The cost of a strike on the company is by no means fixed or preordained. There are many things that management can do to lessen the impact of a work stoppage, including inventory buildup, partial operation, alternate production, and much more. The employer who has lost or anticipates losing a representation election would do well to explore the subject of strike planning.[5] In many situations, the ability to weather a strike is central to remaining nonunion in the long run. If the union cannot effectively strike the employer, it has no way of extracting those concessions needed to make itself look good to the membership and those employees who have not yet joined or been forced to join. It also has no way to force the employer to grant those institutional arrangements that will protect it from the disappointed employees. Notice the interaction between the factors involved.

It should not be thought that the certification of a union is always followed by the negotiation of a labor agreement and a permanent collective-bargaining relationship. When a union gains certification, there is a 20 percent chance that it will never attain a contract and an additional 13 percent chance that, even if a contract is negotiated, the collective-bargaining relationship will be temporary.[6] Table 13-1 provides details on the experience of unions that gained certification in 1970. It is obvious that many employers who acquire a union succeed in disposing of it in one way or another. In some cases the plant closes or moves. In others the union loses its support and withdraws. Such developments often involve breaking the law, and consequently, few details are made public. In other situations, the employees decertify the union. Remember our recommendation to do nothing that will make the union or its leadership look good or add to its organizational security; this will contribute to either voluntary withdrawal by the union or its decertification.

Decertification

As the term implies, decertification is the opposite of certification. It is a formal procedure in which the NLRB conducts an election to allow the *employees* to get rid of an unwanted union. From our perspective, decertification is a logical extension of preventive labor relations: if a company loses a representation election or in some other way acquires a union, a decertification election may be viewed as the next step in the long-run program of remaining nonunion.

There is an important difference between decertifying a recently acquired union and getting rid of one that has represented the employees for several years. In the former case the matter is essentially an extension of the employer's counterunion campaign. Relations with the labor organization are already hostile and the alternatives continue to be "union" or "no union." Assuming it made sense to resist unionization in the first place, the company usually has a lot to gain and nothing to lose if it *law-*

TABLE 13-1. EXPERIENCE IN UNITS IN WHICH UNIONS WON NLRB-CONDUCTED ELECTIONS IN CASES CLOSED N 1970.

Reason	No Contract Negotiated				Initial Contract Negotiated but Not under Contract in Mid-1975				Totals			
	Units		Employees		Units		Employees		Units		Employees	
	No.	%	No.	%	No.	%	No.	%	No.	%	No.	%
Plant sold, closed, or moved	63	28.1	2,374	22.2	105	48.6	6,363	55.0	168	38.2	8,737	39.2
Union lost majority, abandoned unit, or had charter revoked	130	58.0	6,784	63.4	71	32.9	2,969	25.7	201	45.7	9,753	43.8
Union decertified	31	13.8	1,549	14.5	36	16.7	2,161	18.7	67	15.2	3,710	16.7
Construction project completed	—	—	—	—	4	1.9	81	0.7	4	1.0	81	0.4
Total	224	100.0	10,707	100.0	216	100.0	11,574	100.0	440	100.0	22,281	100.0

Note: Columns do not sum because of rounding.

Source: Richard Prosten, Research Director, Industrial Union Department, AFL–CIO, "Special Analysis of 1970 Election Victories." Cover letter to IUD Executive Committee and Executive Board dated June 23, 1976.

fully encourages the decertification move. In contrast, if the union has had recognition for several years, it is a more serious matter. If the employees are unhappy enough with the union to throw it out, there must be a reason, and management should ask few questions before putting its weight behind the move. Are the employees unhappy with unionism or with the particular union? If the disenchantment is general and employees have come to realize that they can deal directly with management without the help and expense of an intermediary, the company should support the move or at least not impede it. If, on the other hand, the employees feel that the present union has not been aggressive enough in its representational functions, the choice may be between the present union and another which is certain to be more difficult to deal with. Management would seldom favor such a change and may find it appropriate to support the incumbent union. Of course, this must be done with tact and must not involve actions that could be construed as unlawful assistance.

If management encourages a decertification drive against an established union with which it has had relatively successful relations, it will be viewed as a breach of trust by the leaders of the union involved *and* by the leadership of other labor organizations with which the company does business. After all, one of the reasons the union is in trouble with its members is that it has been "responsible" and not caused as much trouble for the employer as it might have. If the decertification drive fails, it is certain that relations with the recertified union will be difficult for a long time to come. If it succeeds, relations with other unions with which the company does business may suffer.

The company should not jump on the "bandwagon" of a decertification drive against an established union unless it has a very good chance of winning. This can usually be ascertained from the degree of support accompanying the petition for decertification. A 30 percent showing of interest is not enough. The average percentage of petition signers in successful decertification elections was found to be 74.7, while that in unsuccessful elections averages 47.5.[7] Of course, if the company has recently been organized and has no other established collective-bargaining relationships, none of this matters.

The most important thing that a company can do to encourage a decertification of a newly established union is to decline to make the union or its leaders look good and refuse to grant organizational security. Beyond that, the role of the employer in a decertification drive is limited by law. It is the employees who decertify the union, not the employer. The company may not initiate, inspire, or actively encourage any move to dump a union without jeopardizing the outcome of the election. While the employer's Section 8(c) free-speech protection remains in force, it does not preclude the setting aside of a successful decertification because of employer interference.

On the other hand, there is nothing in the law that prevents the employer from providing the employees with lawful information on their rights and the procedure for decertifying a union should they inquire.[8] In practice, employers often get involved in providing such information either directly or through consultants. It has been reported that some consultants have been highly effective in this area.[9] Indeed, it is complained by union supporters that a whole new breed of specialized "de-cert" consultants has emerged in recent years.[10] Obviously, there are many fine lines in regard to decertification that must be left to more specialized hands.

The mechanics of initiating a decertification election are similar to those for a representation election. The petition must be filed by an employee who must not be a supervisor or confidential employee. The person(s) filing the petition must demonstrate a 30 percent showing of interest, and the bargaining unit must be coextensive with that certified by the NLRB or recognized by the employer.[11] Beyond that, the rules governing the campaign and the election are similar to those of other elections and do not call for separate discussion.

Table 13-2 reports various data on decertification petitions and elections. It shows that the number of petitions filed in recent years has grown considerably, as has the number of decertification elections. A slight majority of the petitions are dismissed or withdrawn for one reason or another (insufficient showing of interest, inappropriate bargaining unit, responsive action on the part of the incumbent union and/or employer, a realization that the petition has no chance of success, and the like). Most interesting is the fact that of those elections held, over 70 percent result in decertification. However, when this is compared to the percentage of eligible voters in units decertified, the number drops to about 50 percent. This supports our earlier contention that the smaller the bargaining unit, the easier it is to organize and the easier it is to decertify. Table 13-3 casts this in sharper focus. It reveals that the average bargaining unit size in successful decertification elections is 35.0 employees, as compared to 87.2 in those that were unsuccessful. Once again the power of the size of the bargaining unit is demonstrated. However, it is difficult to see how

TABLE 13-2. DECERTIFICATION (RD) PETITIONS AND ELECTIONS, 1970–1978.

Year	RD Petitions Filed	Total RD Elections	Percent of Petitions Resulting in Elections	Number Resulting in Decertification
1970	766	301	39.3	210
1971	942	401	42.6	279
1972	1,080	451	41.8	317
1973	1,144	453	39.6	315
1974	1,177	490	41.6	338
1975	1,166	516	44.3	379
1976	1,457	611	41.9	445
1977	1,793	849	47.4	645
1978	1,754	807	46.0	594

Year	Percent Resulting in Decertification	Number Eligible to Vote	Number in Units Decertified	Percent of Eligible Voters in Units Decertified
1970	67.7	20,344	8,558	42.1
1971	69.6	20,726	10,773	52.0
1972	70.3	20,790	10,028	48.2
1973	69.5	20,007	10,094	50.5
1974	69.0	24,697	11,470	46.4
1975	73.4	23,817	13,849	58.1
1976	72.8	28,426	15,303	53.8
1977	76.0	41,850	22,398	53.5
1978	73.6	39,555	19,888	50.3

Source: Derived from 35 through 43 NLRB Annual Reports (1970 through 1978), Tables 5 and 13; pagination varies.

the nonunion employer can put this to use. The larger bargaining unit is almost always more effective for keeping the union out, while the smaller one makes it easier to get rid of it once it is in. The NLRB almost always requires that a decertification election take place in the same unit as was originally certified. Management's only consolation is that if it is unionized on the basis of one or more small bargaining units, it will have a better chance of having the union decertified at a later date. Meanwhile, the company should maintain the small unit as a separate unit for collective-bargaining purposes. That is, two or more small units should not be combined for collective-bargaining purposes, and the number of employees in

TABLE 13-3. BARGAINING UNIT SIZE IN DECERTIFICATION ELECTIONS, 1970–1978.

Year	Average Unit Size		
	All Decertification Elections	Successful Decertification Elections	Unsuccessful Decertification Elections
1970	67.6	40.1	128.5
1971	51.7	38.6	81.6
1972	46.1	31.6	80.3
1973	44.2	32.0	71.8
1974	50.4	33.9	87.0
1975	46.2	36.5	72.8
1976	46.5	34.4	79.1
1977	49.3	34.7	91.3
1978	49.0	33.5	92.4
Average	50.1	35.0	87.2

Source: Derived from 35 through 43 NLRB Annual Reports (1970 through 1978), Tables 5 and 13; pagination varies.

the organized unit should not be increased (unless the additional employees are known to be "safe").

Employer Petitions

Closely related to decertification is the RM petition, whereby the employer may seek an election to test the union's majority status. There are two main occasions in which RM petitions are appropriate. One is where an organizing union presents an employer with a demand for recognition or starts noninformational picketing. The other, which is of more immediate interest, is where a union has been certified or recognized and the company questions its continued majority position. Unfortunately, the published data do not distinguish between the two. But since the vast majority are either consent agreement, stipulated, or expedited elections, it may be assumed that relatively few involve an employer using the procedure to get rid of a certified or recognized union which has lost its majority. There are two—not mutually exclusive—reasons for this.

First, NLRB procedures make it difficult to initiate an RM election once the union has been certified or recognized. For the company to get the NLRB to test the union's majority with an election, it must demonstrate with "objective considerations" that the union has lost its majority.[12] A 30 percent showing of interest is not required, nor is it allowed.

In fact, the employer is prohibited from questioning the employees as to their continued support of the union. While there is nothing to prevent the employees from *voluntarily* offering such information or the employer from receiving and acting upon it,[13] this restriction presents problems. In practice, it is difficult to get rid of a union through this procedure unless it "walks away" from the contract. It is usually easier to allow the employees to decertify the union through the procedures discussed earlier.

The second reason why we hear little of RM elections in nonorganizing contexts is that there is often no compelling reason for the employer to take action. If the union has abandoned the unit or acted in some other way that would support the RM petition, what purpose does it serve to throw it out? There is no or little cost to the company associated with having a relationship with an inactive union. Why stir up employee interest in unionization by pointing out that they do not have effective representation? The old adage about "sleeping dogs" fits well. Moreover, should another union come along, management may be able to claim that the company already has a union. If both organizations are affiliated with the AFL–CIO, this may cause problems for the organizing union, since AFL–CIO affiliates are pledged not to "raid" the "established collective-bargaining relationships" of their fellow affiliates. While this will not present the new union with an insurmountable problem, it will take time to straighten out—time that the employer may put to good use.

Deauthorizations

The Taft-Hartley Act, passed in 1947, contained a requirement that the NLRB conduct referenda to determine whether employees wished to authorize their unions to negotiate union-shop provisions. After a few years of overwhelming majorities in favor of maintaining the union security arrangements, Congress wisely repealed the authorization election requirement but left the parallel deauthorization procedure now contained in Section 9(e) of the Act.

Deauthorization of union security arrangements is of less importance to preventive labor relations than decertification. For one thing, a newly organized employer should resist granting a union shop, thereby avoiding the whole matter. For another, if the employees are willing to deauthorize (for the right reasons), they are willing to decertify. If not, then the deauthorization drive is probably intended to put pressure on the union leadership for internal reasons that seldom operate to the advantage of the employer.

It is usually more difficult to deauthorize than to decertify a union.

Deauthorization requires that a majority of the eligible employees *in the unit* vote for deauthorization, whereas decertification (or certification) requires only a majority of those voting. Those employees who do not cast their ballot are effectively counted as having voted for continued authorization. In recent years, about 78 percent of those eligible to vote in deauthorization polls have done so (Table 13-6). Thus unions enter the contest with a 22 percent advantage and need the approval of only 28 percent of the employees on the average to retain authorization.

Tables 13-4 and 13-5 report various data on deauthorization polls.

TABLE 13-4. DEAUTHORIZATION (UD) PETITIONS AND ELECTIONS, 1970–1978.

Year	UD Petitions Filed	Total UD Elections	Percent of Petitions Resulting in Elections	Number of Petitions Resulting in Deauthorization
1970	158	87	55.1	54
1971	168	97	57.7	57
1972	172	97	56.4	56
1973	213	103	48.4	56
1974	203	118	58.1	69
1975	209	110	52.6	61
1976	235	111	47.2	62
1977	305	142	46.6	81
1978	298	140	47.0	89

Year	Percent Resulting in Deauthorization	Number of Employees Eligible to Vote	Number of Employees in Units Deauthorized	Percent of Eligible Voters in Units Deauthorized
1970	62.1	8,652	5,842	67.5
1971	58.8	6,518	2,430	37.3
1972	57.7	6,158	2,799	45.5
1973	54.4	4,641	1,791	38.6
1974	58.5	9,345	6,261	67.0
1975	55.5	7,616	3,227	42.4
1976	55.9	5,269	1,631	31.0
1977	57.0	9,125	3,036	33.3
1978	63.6	9,060	3,087	34.1

Source: Derived from 35 through 43 NLRB Annual Reports (1970 through 1978), Tables 5 and 12; pagination varies.

TABLE 13-5. BARGAINING UNIT SIZE IN
DEAUTHORIZATION (UD) POLLS,
1970–1978.

| | Average Unit Size | | |
Year	All Deauthorization Polls	Successful Deauthorization Polls	Unsuccessful Deauthorization Polls
1970	99.4	108.2	85.2
1971	67.2	42.6	102.2
1972	63.5	50.0	81.9
1973	45.1	32.0	60.6
1974	79.2	90.7	62.9
1975	69.2	52.9	89.6
1976	47.5	26.3	74.2
1977	64.3	37.5	99.8
1978	64.7	34.7	117.1

Source: Derived from 35 through 43 NLRB Annual Reports
(1970 through 1978), Table 12; pagination varies.

They show that the number of petitions filed and the number of polls conducted are small, but when a poll is conducted, there is a better than even chance that the union will lose its authorization. Note again the impact of bargaining unit size on the success rate in Table 13-5. The inertia of the larger unit applies to all employee elections. Table 13-6 shows data on the number of eligible voters who actually voted and the number and percentage who voted for deauthorization. It reveals that a fair number of authorizations are retained by a minority of the employees in the unit and that if the determination were based on a majority of those voting, as in other representational matters, the percentage of successful deauthorizations would be significantly higher.

Apart from the stiffer requirement to win, the mechanics of the deauthorization procedure are similar to those of decertification. A 30 percent showing of interest is required, and a second poll may not be held within 12 months of the first.[14] However, the contract-bar rule does not apply to deauthorization polls.

In my opinion, it is unwise for an employer to become involved in a deauthorization drive. They are often motivated by internal union matters, such as an attempt by the local to get better service from the international. If the company comes out in favor of deauthorization in such a fight, it will look as though it is supporting the dissidents. This will make the international union more difficult to deal with in the future. More important, if the union reacts to the deauthorization drive by becoming more responsive to the members, it may eliminate the possibility of a successful decertification in the future. On the other hand, if the company takes a position *against* the proposed deauthorization, it will appear to the employees that the union is "in bed with" the company. Of course, management would not want to project this image, whether it is true or not. Thus deauthorization drives often present management with a no-win situation.

This reasoning is not universally accepted. One authority recommends the use of the deauthorization procedure to create antagonism between the union and its members so that when the contract expires, the employees are more inclined to decertify.[15] This may be sound advice when the objective is to dislodge an entrenched union and the company is locked into an agreement that bars decertification for some time to come. However, the question should be asked whether it would not be better to let the em-

TABLE 13-6. VOTING EXPERIENCE IN DEAUTHORIZATION (UD) POLLS, 1970–1978.

Year	Total Eligible to Vote	Valid Votes Cast	Valid Votes Cast as a Percentage of Total Eligible to Vote	Number Cast for Deauthorization	Percent of Total Eligible to Vote Cast for Deauthorization
1970	8,652	6,371	73.6	4,353	50.3
1971	6,518	5,335	81.9	2,308	35.4
1972	6,158	4,536	73.7	1,602	35.3
1973	4,641	3,787	81.6	1,537	40.6
1974	9,345	6,797	72.7	4,698	50.3
1975	7,616	6,035	79.2	2,519	33.1
1976	5,269	4,288	81.4	1,443	27.4
1977	9,125	7,095	77.8	3,551	38.9
1978	9,060	7,116	78.5	2,451	27.1
Average			77.8		37.6

Source: Derived from 35 through 43 NLRB Annual Reports (1970 through 1978), Table 12; pagination varies.

ployees' dissatisfaction with the union build up until they are ready to decertify at the end of the contract when the union has less time to respond. Having a union without compulsory union membership may be to the advantage of those employees who prefer not to pay union dues. However, principle aside, it offers little to the company. In fact, it may make the union more difficult to do business with, since its leadership will be subject to more pressure from dissatisfied members who can withdraw at will. It will be the more militant, pro-union and anticompany employees who remain in the organization. Indeed, many of the employees who would be most inclined to vote against the union in a decertification election may be quite content to have a union on the property, provided they are not forced to join and pay dues. In my opinion, the employer should not encourage deauthorization drives. It is much better to have the union decertified by the employee-members at a later date.

NOTES

1.   Office of the General Counsel, National Labor Relations Board, *An Outline of Law and Procedure in Representation Cases,* Washington, D.C.: U.S. Government Printing Office, 1974, pp. 110–111. Hereinafter, NLRB, op. cit.

2.   I. Herbert Rothenberg and Steven B. Silverman, *Labor Unions—How to Avert Them, Beat Them, Out-Negotiate Them, Live with Them, Unload Them,* Elkins Park, Pa.: Management Relations, Inc., 1973, p. 402.

3.   Ibid., p. 284.

4.   NLRB, op. cit., p. 113.

5.   See John G. Kilgour, "How to Respond to an Impending Strike," *Personnel Journal,* February 1979, pp. 98–101.

6.   Richard Prosten, "The Longest Season: Union Organizing in the Last Decade, a/k/a, How Come One Team Has to Play with Its Shoelaces Tied Together?" Industrial Relations Research Association, *Proceedings of the Thirty-First Annual Meeting,* August 29–31, 1978, p. 244.

7.   William E. Fulmer, "When Employees Want to Oust Their Unions," *Harvard Business Review,* March/April 1978, p. 170.

8.   Rothenberg and Silverman, op. cit., p. 406.

9.   Fulmer, op. cit., p. 167.

10.   Phillis Payne, "Consultants Who Coach the Violators," *American Federationist,* September 1977, p. 29.

11.   NLRB, op. cit., p. 65.

12.   Ibid., p. 64.

13.   Rothenberg and Silverman, op. cit., pp. 404–405.

14.   Ibid., p. 400.

15.   Edwin Ricker as reported in Payne, op. cit., p. 29.

14

CONCLUSION

We have come a long way. The author has learned a great deal in the writing; he hopes the reader has done so as well. Most of what has been covered is common sense or logical deduction from readily available information and data. If this book has made a contribution, it is in the examination of such material from the perspective of the nonunion firm and in the integration of the several personnel and industrial-relations functions within that examination. No doubt, many readers share with the author the feeling "I knew that, but I didn't know that I knew it" about much of the material in this book.

My intention was to write an objective study of the more technical aspects of preventive labor relations, with a minimum of editorial and philosophical comment. Hopefully, this has been done. At this point, however, it seems appropriate to offer a number of observations and prophecies about the future of industrial relations management in the United States.

REMAINING NONUNION IN THE 1980s

Barring substantial changes in the labor law of the United States, there is no reason for a well-run company operating in the 1980s to find itself with an unwanted union. There are so many things that can be done to prevent this outcome that in all but the most unusual circumstances it is almost negligent for a company to allow unionization to happen. Plants may be located in such a way as to minimize the serious attentions of labor organizations. The work organization can be structured and rules adopted to impede the introduction and easy flow of union information. A bargaining unit strategy can be adopted that makes it difficult or impossible for a union to organize the plant. Employees can be selected in such a way as to minimize the chances of acquiring union supporters and potential union supporters. The entire personnel and compensation function can serve to minimize those sources of discontent that are the seeds of union interest among employees. When done properly and in combination, such measures will all but eliminate the chances of a serious organizing drive getting under way.

Should a union drive get started, the well-run company will know about it well in advance of formal action on the part of the union and should have ample time to correct the problems that are its cause. Indeed, the company should have information on employee dissatisfaction before it translates into union interest, and should engage in the necessary corrective action and communication without the added incentive of the organizing drive. Beyond that, an understanding of how unions organize and of the large number of defenses and legal opportunities available to thwart such organizing efforts should serve to minimize a union's chances of ever getting to an election. An effective employer campaign, designed to take advantage of the many features of the company's long-standing preventive labor relations program, should reduce to almost zero the union's chances of winning the election. Finally, there are things that the knowledgeable employer can do even after a union is certified to ensure that the union victory is short-lived.

When one surveys all the things a nonunion employer can do to stay that way, it must be concluded that the odds are heavily in favor of management. Indeed, one is left with the feeling that in all but the most unusual circumstances, the employer would almost have to try to get itself organized to end up with a union.

Please note for one last time that almost all the things that should be done to remain nonunion require an early start. Little can be done if the employer waits until the organizing drive is well under way before giving serious thought to the subject.

PREVENTIVE LABOR RELATIONS MANAGEMENT

As this book attests, there exist a substantial body of information and a large number of techniques that pertain to remaining nonunion. They are timely, relevant, and of great importance to the overwhelming majority of business organizations in the United States. This suggests the possibility of a new management specialty. It is at least conceivable that preventive labor relations will be broken out of the personnel management area, as have been general labor relations, compensation, safety, and the like. It is even possible that we will someday see preventive labor relations management taught as a specialized subject in business schools and pursued as a specialized career in the larger business organizations. In the near future, however, this is unlikely.

The elements of preventive labor relations are too integrated with the other aspects of the employment relationship to allow for specialization in any but the largest corporations. Even then, to do the work right, the manager would have to have a good grounding in the other important areas of personnel administration in the widest sense of the term. For example, the preventive labor relations dimensions of wage and salary administration would be meaningless in the absence of an understanding of the technical aspects of compensation administration in general. Thus it is more likely that within the limits of the time horizon of this book—the 1980s—preventive labor relations will remain incorporated in the general personnel function. This in no way detracts from the importance of the subject matter.

The personnel professional working in or entering the field during the 1980s should become knowledgeable about the various preventive labor relations aspects of personnel administration. Undoubtedly, many readers are in the process of doing just that. As will be devloped, the 1980s will be a period in which private-sector work organizations in the United States become more determined and more open about remaining nonunion than has been the case in the past. There are now a fairly large number of job listings in personnel which carry an implicit or explicit requirement that the successful applicant have an understanding of how to perform the work in a way that contributes to the company's preventive labor relations objectives. It is certain that this will continue in the years ahead, and it is a safe assumption that the demand will create its own supply. We will see the personnel management job market take on more of a union-prevention complexion in the 1980s. Practioners and those just entering the field would be well advised to prepare for it.

A final word of caution is in order. It has been stressed in this book that employee interest in union representation and the process of union organizing is rational. Indeed, it is this rationality that allows an effective employer response. The employer response and, by extension, the managers involved in that response, should be just as rational. In addition to being technically proficient and familiar with the law surrounding the subject, the effective preventive labor relations manager will be as objective and as highly principled as effective managers in other functional areas. In fact, given the nature of much of the activity in the preventive labor relations area, it is even more important that a sense of ethics and honor be maintained. This will not detract from the effectiveness of the manager involved; it will add to it. It should not be necessary to break the law or engage in underhanded tactics to remain nonunion. In fact, such practices may threaten an otherwise effective program.

THE STATE OF THE UNIONS

The labor movement in the United States is in trouble. As has been demonstrated, union membership has declined, union victories in representation elections have hit an all-time low and will continue to decline, and union losses in decertification elections are up. Union leadership appears uninspired and uninspiring and in poor shape to meet the challenges of the 1980s. What gains have been made have been in the public sector and are a result not of the organizing and negotiating efforts of the unions but of recent changes in federal and state law that allow and encourage collective bargaining for the first time. When these easy gains have been completed, the full force of the decline of the American labor movement will become apparent.

None of this is to suggest that unions will disappear from the American scene. There are numerous situations in which they perform useful and necessary functions. There have always been and will always be employers who approach the employment relationship with an attitude that requires that the employees band together to get fair treatment. There are others where the nature of the work or some other factor makes it impossible not to have some form of employee organization and representation. There are also many situations in which the union organizes what would otherwise be a chaotic labor market through a hiring hall and/or provides some other useful economic service to the employers. And, of course, there is the whole political dimension of the labor movement. As discussed, organized labor supports and operates an extensive political fundraising and lobbying apparatus. Even though labor's economic strength may decline in absolute terms, and is certain to decline in relative terms, its political influence will continue. In fact, it may even increase as the public sector—with its more direct relationship to political decision making—continues to become unionized and as the United States continues its disturbing drift toward an administered economy.

This, of course, is fortunate. An industrialized democracy without an effective labor movement is probably an impossibility. The Constitution of the United States was written in preindustrial times and, therefore, contains no explicit reference to labor organizations. Were it to be written today, it would almost have to contain provisions protecting the workers' right to organize. In fact, it would be hard to improve on the language of Section 7 of the National Labor Relations Act as it is now written.

Unions may be necessary in an industrialized democracy, but they are not necessary in any given employment relationship unless the employees deem them to be necessary.[1] And what appears to be happening in the United States is that an increasing number of employees—with or without the encouragement of their employers—have decided that they do not need union representation. Moreover, many American employers who accepted unionism either wholeheartedly or as a necessary evil have within the last few years changed their minds. Many others who escaped unionization in the past more from luck that from any direct action on their part have become serious and more skilled at remaining nonunion. When these forces are taken together, they almost assure a continued decline of organized labor in the private sector.

A NEW ERA IN INDUSTRIAL RELATIONS

The industrial-relations history of the United States comprises a number of distinct periods. Restricting our survey to recent times, it appears that the year 1919 ushered in an era of hostility toward unions that erased the gains of World War I and the Wilsonian progressive years. The next 15 years were characterized by employer attacks on organized labor and general abuse of employees and their organizations. The New Deal response to such abuse—and to the economic problems of the times—was the National Labor Relations Act of 1935 and other related laws that gave organized labor the tools to change the industrial landscape of the United States. The next 15 or 20 years continued to be dominated by industrial conflict, but the contestants were more evenly matched. In some cases the unions won; in some they lost. However, by about 1950, and certainly by 1955, a spirit of acceptance and even cooperation had been created in those industries in which unions had been successful. In the vast nonunion part of the economy, an armed truce existed in which the union organizer was met with some (but not too much) resistance. Whether or not a company became unionized was up to the will of the employees and chance. This accommodation lasted from about 1955 until about 1975. Future historians may date the period with the retirement of George Meany in 1979 or with the failure of passage of the Labor Law Reform Act of 1978. However, there is evidence of a hardening of management attitude toward unions before these events that reflects a general feeling that the investment in labor peace has not paid off.[2] Labor has been unable to protect its contract companies from low-wage competition—or, more accurately, low-labor-cost competition—because it could not organize the whole market.[3] The other side of this observation is that many of the companies that have grown and prospered during the past 20 years have done so without the costs and constraints of unionization and appreciate the value of nonunion operation. In addition to being determined to remain nonunion, many of these companies have become very good at it and now stand ready to teach others how it is done.

The main thrust of the new attitude toward unions comes not from the old-fashioned union haters but from the objective manager who has decided that remaining nonunion is in the best interest of the company.[4] This is of enormous signficance to organized labor, for it is this type of manager and this type of decision that can take a union apart.

There is no question that the management of most American corporations is very good at what it does. When the considerable management skills that have been developed in the United States are directed at the project of remaining nonunion, there is little doubt that they will be effective. This is an important observation. Until recently, the preventive labor relations program of most companies consisted in reacting to crises perceived to be short-run in nature. This has allowed unions certain organiz-

324

ing advantages. When the more objective, longer-range, and integrative management decision making employed in other areas of business activity is applied to preventive labor relations, the balance will be weighted heavily in favor of remaining nonunion. As companies incorporate preventive labor relations considerations into plant location, plant design, acquisition decisions, and the numerous other topics covered in this book, it will become more difficult than ever for unions to gain a victory in a large, well-run company. And as the experience spreads by example and by the intercompany mobility of personnel professionals, the techniques will become commonplace throughout the economy.

Of one thing we can be certain: the new era will not last forever. However, it is unlikely that it will be reversed in the 1980s. Throughout the professional lives of most readers, preventive labor relations will be a topic of increasing importance.

NOTES

1. Myron Roomkin and Hervy A. Juris, "Unions in the Traditional Sectors: The Mid-Life Passage of the Labor Movement," Industrial Relations Research Association, *Proceedings of the Thirty-First Annual Meeting,* August 29–31, 1978, p. 221.
2. A. H. Raskin, "Management Comes Out Swinging," ibid., p. 228.
3. Peter J. Pestillo, "Learning to Live Without the Union," ibid., p. 234.
4. Ibid.

Index

INDEX

INDEX